MOUNT

Harry N. Abrams, Inc.,
Publishers, New York

The Conquest of Denali
McKinley

Photographs by Bradford Washburn

Text by Bradford Washburn
and David Roberts

Preface by Ansel Adams

DEDICATION

To Dad and Mother, who opened my eyes to the wonders of mountains
with love and faith and encouragement;
to Barbara, first woman to stand on McKinley's two summits,
and my constant companion in our exploration of this glorious wilderness;
and to Carl and Dorothy Fuller, for their extraordinary generosity.
BRADFORD WASHBURN

Page 1: June—daybreak at Wonder Lake
Pages 2–3: February—northward from the Tokositna wilderness
Page 5: First freeze—a tiny forest pond in the Teklanika Valley

Editor: Robert Morton
Designers: Doris Leath and Maria Miller

Library of Congress Cataloging-in-Publication Data

Washburn, Bradford, 1910–
Mount McKinley : the Conquest of Denali / text by
Bradford Washburn and David Roberts ; photographs by Bradford
Washburn and others ; preface by Ansel Adams.
p. cm.
ISBN 0–8109–3611–9
1. Mountaineering—Alaska—McKinley, Mount—History.   2. McKinley,
Mount (Alaska)—Description and travel.   3. McKinley, Mount
(Alaska)—Pictorial works.   I. Roberts, David, 1943–
II. Title
GV199.42.A42M3275   1991
796.5′22′097983—dc20   90-30565

CONTENTS

McKinley's twin summits rise above the foothills and across russet tundra—from mile 10.2 on the Denali Highway

Exquisite flowers flourish in every nook and cranny in the lowland.

Alaskan cotton near Broad Pass

Bluebells at Wonder Lake

Foxtail grass by a Denali roadside

Nugget Pond marsh at Camp Denali

Mount Fellows seen from near Park Headquarters

A loon defends its nest at Wonder Lake

Golden eagle nest (Gus Wolfe)

Toklat grizzly

Bull caribou in the fall (Steven C. Kaufman)

Long-tailed jaeger (Michael Wotton) *Below:* Lesser yellowlegs (Heinrich Gohl) Willow ptarmigan (Steve Maslowski)

Parka squirrel (Ed Cooper) Dall sheep on a foothill crag (Jim Thompson)

Mount Brooks and Mount Silverthrone in early morning.

Overleaf: Tokositna River gravel bars buried deep in fresh snow. *Inset:* A frantic moose drowns midsummer mosquitoes (Bill Ruth).

Second overleaf: West Buttress at twilight, from 29,000 feet

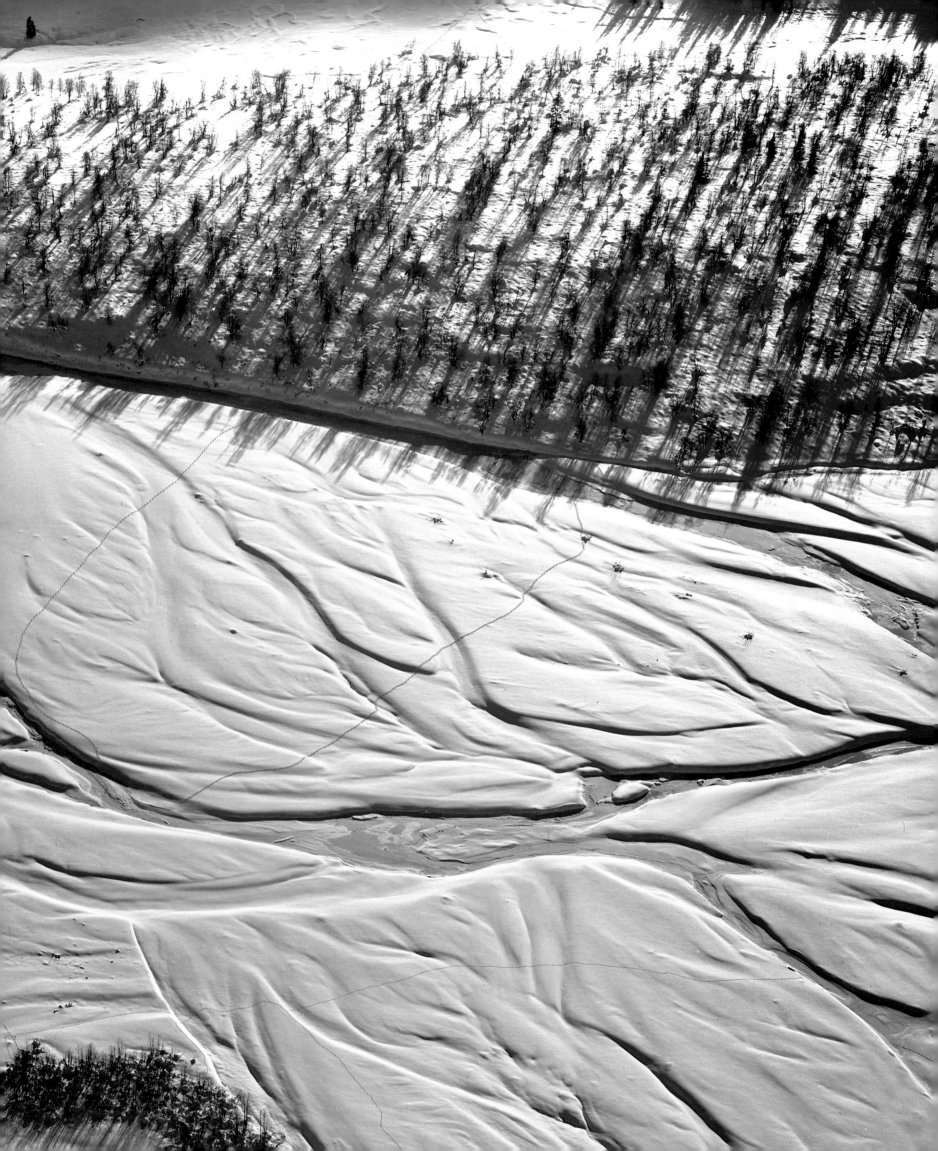

PREFACE

by Ansel Adams

YOU RECOGNIZE THE EXPLORER in Bradford Washburn at first sight. There is something about the eyes, the set of the chin (not fierce, just determined), the consistent energy of mind and spirit. Physically, Brad is not a giant, neither is he conspicuously hardy. He does not immediately remind one of the vast bulk of McKinley, but he has in fact conquered this extraordinary mountain three times—once with his wife, Barbara, who thus became the first woman to reach the summits of both McKinley's peaks.

Not only Mount McKinley has commanded his eye and heart. The Grand Canyon (of which he has completed a monumental map, as he has of McKinley), the great peaks of the western Yukon, and, most recently, the Himalaya, have come under his inquiring attention and the well-directed eye of his camera. Without exaggeration, I fully expect to hear someday that Brad has visited the moon, climbed Copernicus, and photographed the lunar Apennines from a private, orbiting module.

In planning, funding, and developing Boston's Museum of Science during the last forty years, Brad has made a tremendous contribution to public education. He is an imaginative planner and administrator, and his museum is considered one of the finest teaching museums in the world. It stands as clear proof that America is capable of highest achievement in applied technology—under the direction of those of real intelligence.

Brad Washburn's dedication to Mount McKinley, as well as to his museum, has been his prime focus for nearly half a century. His involvement with McKinley has represented not merely "conquest" of the heights but scientific and aesthetic curiosity, and most clearly his desire to share the McKinley experience through his revealing ground and aerial photographs of the great mountain of the North.

A climb to the summit of a noble peak is a heroic and exciting undertaking, but most photographic views along the way are usually only a panoramic index of local geography. Brad's aerial photographs of McKinley, however, are far more. It is astounding to realize what tremendous physical risks he took to get these shots—many, for instance, were taken from unpressurized airplanes or helicopters, often at temperatures far below zero, with the door removed and Brad tethered to the opposite side of the cabin.

Even so, the photographs look almost inevitable, perfectly composed. These are not simply documents of McKinley's wilderness; we sense in each one the presence of an individual, highly intelligent eye. The photographs are the result of the explorer's consistent energy of mind and spirit—and so they truly *mean* something. Add to this the fact that Brad's aerial photographs of the McKinley landscape are the very first of their kind and still the finest ever made of the great natural landmark.

Brad's first encounter with McKinley was when he photographed it from the air as leader of the *National Geographic* flights of 1936. Since then he has hiked to it, helicoptered around it, snowshoed, floundered, and hacked his way to its summit, and confronted every detail of its approaches, summer and winter, on foot and on horseback. This book is not merely a mountaineer's album. It is a loving, lifelong study of Mount McKinley, from the birds, flowers, and animals of its forested lowlands to the last snow-corniced ridge that guards its summit.

Brad's latest photographic tool has been the Learjet, the use of which was inspired by a stunning glimpse he had of McKinley as he flew past it on the way from Point Barrow to Anchorage some twenty years ago. His old friend, the peerless scientist Edwin Land, fascinated by the idea of high-quality oblique photography from a jet aircraft at high altitude, teamed up with Lear to provide Brad with a special emergency exit assembly with a three-quarter-inch optical glass photo-window. Experts of the Itek Corporation then honed his Fujinon lens to razor-sharp focus. Finally, his Harvard friend and optical wizard Jim Baker designed an ingenious viewfinder that eliminated the complex parallax.

The speedy magic carpet has now yielded hundreds of marvelous photographs.

Bradford Washburn is one of the very few people who have combined spectacular experience in the wilderness with equally spectacular achievements in the world of civilization. One never knows what next to expect from this roving genius of mind and mountains, but whatever it is, we know it will be excellent and effective.

Carmel, California
February 23, 1983

Editor's note: Ansel Adams wrote this Preface shortly before his death, when this book was first planned. Publication was postponed, however, because of the illness of Bradford Washburn's wife. The Preface appears now with the gratitude of the authors and publisher.

Left: Brad Washburn with his Fairchild K-6 camera before a Bellanca Skyrocket airplane in 1938. (Walter Clark)

Overleaf: A summer thunderstorm overwhelms McKinley—Ansel Adams' favorite photograph by Washburn.

FOREWORD

by Bradford Washburn

MY LIFELONG LOVE of geography and mountains can be traced to two sources: Miss Florence Leatherbee's wonderful fifth-grade geography lessons at Buckingham School and the horrible hay fever attacks that I encountered every summer as a youngster. Every child in Miss Leatherbee's class grew up with an intense interest in the world—a keen desire to learn by seeing, touching, *experiencing.*

In 1921, my family decided to vacation at Squam Lake in New Hampshire. There I had an exciting experience: friends led me to the top of 1,200-foot. Rattlesnake, then to 2,000-foot. Mount Morgan and finally to 6,288-foot Mount Washington. Two wonderful things emerged from that never-to-be-forgotten summer: I discovered a world where there was no hay fever, and I reveled in the fun of hiking on mountain trails and sharing the thrills of discovery with close friends.

My love affair with Mount McKinley can also be traced to a single moment. In January 1936, Dr. Gilbert Grosvenor, then president of the National Geographic Society, asked if I knew of any unusually interesting bit of geographical exploration that could be pulled off at "not-too-great expense." This unexpected challenge posed no problem. I had already read the thrilling stories of the exploration and conquest of Mount McKinley by Belmore Browne and Hudson Stuck. I had also learned to fly and had seven years of experience in aerial photography among the big peaks of the Alps and the Alaska Coast Range. I proposed a microexpedition to make the first large format photographic flights over and around Mount McKinley—to be done at a cost not to exceed $1,000.

Teaming up with the *National Geographic* and Pan American Airways, we made the flights in July 1936; and we sent back to Dr. Grosvenor some two hundred 8 × 10″ photographs and a check for $37—the unspent balance of his $1,000 grant.

In the half century since that memorable summer, I have climbed McKinley three times and spent many, many months on and above its slopes—on snowshoes and crampons, in tents, igloos, airplanes, and helicopters. Together with my wife, Barbara, and scores of lifelong friends, I've come to hold this great peak and its beautiful but rugged approaches in deep affection—and, at the same time, in profound respect.

We were lucky to climb it when we did. I was the eleventh man on top; Barbara the first woman. We lived and climbed on the mountain as if it belonged to us. As of today, more than six thousand people from all over the world have reached McKinley's summit. Almost exactly a thousand tried the climb this past summer. But McKinley itself hasn't changed. Just to be in its presence is still as exciting to me as it was the first time I saw it.

This book has been nearly a lifetime in the making. Its contents are a response to the questions and suggestions of hundreds of people from everywhere who want to know more about McKinley, whether they've climbed it (or hope to) or have merely been tourists who marveled at it from afar. Our purpose is to share with others as much as possible of the exciting history of McKinley's exploration and conquest.

For my partner in the text, I chose David Roberts because he is, at the same time, a gifted writer and a brilliant climber—one, in fact, who was a member of the team that made the first ascent squarely up the middle of McKinley's staggering North Face.

We hope that these pages will stir up vivid memories among those who have already hiked or climbed in this glorious wilderness. Possibly it will tempt others to make new ascents or to travel to Denali Park. To view McKinley at dawn or sunset from Wonder Lake or in the Tokositna is among the most thrilling sights on earth. As Robert Tatum said about the first ascent: the experience from the summit is like "looking out the windows of Heaven."

Belmont, Massachusetts
October 1, 1990

INTRODUCTION

by David Roberts

MY FIRST VIEW OF MOUNT MCKINLEY came shortly before midnight on June 18, 1963. Seven of us, college kids barely turned twenty, had driven out to Wonder Lake to begin the thirty-five-mile hike to the base of the mountain's North Face—the Wickersham Wall, which at that time had never been climbed. We hoped to make its first ascent, even though we knew that its 14,000-foot rise in a single sweep of ice, snow, and rock made it one of the largest mountain walls anywhere in the world. Only one of our team of seven had set foot in Alaska before—and he alone had weathered the rigors of a major mountain expedition anywhere.

We would never have had the temerity to attempt this gargantuan challenge had it not been for the hearty encouragement of Bradford Washburn. By 1963 Mount McKinley in a certain sense belonged to Brad Washburn. He had been the first man to climb it twice, then three times; he had brilliantly pioneered its West Buttress Route, soon fated to become the *voie normale*; his wife, Barbara, had been the first woman to climb it, and, for fifteen years, the only woman to reach the top; and for twenty-seven years he had lovingly and obsessively photographed the mountain from every conceivable angle, both on the ground and from the air. Later, overwhelmed by the responsibility of planning and building Boston's Museum of Science and having passed the age at which he felt comfortable sitting out McKinley's fiendish blizzards, he had begun to nudge the younger generation toward the more difficult new routes waiting to be climbed on the mountain. He repeatedly said that their success gave him enormous vicarious pleasure.

It was one thing, however, to stare at Washburn's magnificent photos of Wickersham Wall in the security of his comfortable home in Cambridge; quite another to be standing here at the end of the narrow ninety-mile dirt road leading to Wonder Lake, strapping the last pots and pans onto our inhuman pack-loads, before we started off across the tussocky tundra toward the real Wickersham Wall, all 14,000 feet of it.

In the dusky light of a June midnight, however, McKinley was nowhere to be seen: heavy clouds obscured it. The tourists who make the daily summer pilgrimage out to Wonder Lake to see North America's loftiest eminence had come back disappointed for two weeks straight. Our own mood hovered between exhilaration and depression. It was unsettling to think of hiking toward this invisible challenge, knowing it rose somewhere out there under the fog, looming inevitably in our destiny. The night was dank and chilly; the sweet, somehow sorrowful scent of the budding willows lay on the air. Two miles ahead, we would have to wade the frigid waist-deep McKinley River, never (we had been told) an easy proposition.

We were almost ready to go. We locked up our Volkswagen bus and taped the key to the underside of the chassis, wondering if the vehicle would start thirty-five or forty days hence. Suddenly Rick straightened up; he was staring due south. "Look," he said, pointing. There was a small rift in the clouds, and through it we saw what at first looked like another cloud. But it had clean sharp lines scoring its dull white surface, a sharp upper edge tinged with twilight. It *had* to be McKinley. There was nothing else like that over there. Even thirty miles away, it looked immense. We stopped fussing with our packs and stared in silent amazement. Gradually the clouds thinned, and we could see the summit. After two weeks of storm the mountain was at last clearing. Merely to look at it seemed an act of reverence.

Then Don cried, "Oh, my God." Twenty-seven years later, I still feel a chill as I recall that moment. He was looking a bit farther to the right. We had been Lilliputians discovering Gulliver's foot. The summit we had seen was only one of McKinley's snow-capped satellites. There, where Don gaped, was McKinley itself—three times as high as Gulliver's foothill. It was impossible that a mountain that far away could take up so much of the sky; but there it was.

We started screaming out loud, in sheer giddy astonishment—and praise, and fear. We had agreed to try climbing *that* thing! We were stunned and thrilled and no little scared. The only response our dizzied spirits could make to the sight of McKinley was to drive our bodies into motion. We grabbed our massive packs and yanked them from the ground onto our backs, then set off toward the river, still whooping as we headed southward into the thick, damp spruce forest.

In my twenty-eight years of climbing since that midnight at Wonder Lake, I have never had another view of any mountain that affected me half so powerfully. One day a month later, after we had indeed climbed Wickersham Wall and tamed some of its terrors, I flashed back abruptly on that first glimpse through the thinning twilight clouds. In my mind's eye I saw McKinley again as we had first seen it, and in that moment the mountain seemed as profoundly unknowable as it had been to us seven scared kids on June 18.

McKinley is the highest mountain in North America; yet at 20,320 feet it is low by Himalayan and Andean standards. It is indeed a huge geographical feature, although not quite so huge as the relatively obscure and slightly lower Mount Logan in Canada's Yukon Territory. McKinley is far from the most demanding mountain in Alaska to climb: compared with any of the summits in a range such as the puny Cathedral Spires, seventy miles to the southwest, most of the ways to reach its summit are technically trivial.

McKinley is so well known by now that veteran mountaineers are tempted to dismiss it as an uninteresting challenge. Virtually all of its difficult routes that are not suicidally dangerous have been ascended. It has been climbed solo, in winter, and in a single day, scores of women have now reached its summit—one recently on a single leg—and some parties have even camped on top. It has not quite become, in the classic Alpine guidebook phrase, "an easy day for a lady", but in 1990 alone 998 different climbers attempted the mountain and 573 reached its peak.

Yet McKinley is always a serious proposition. Some of the world's best mountaineers have been defeated by it, even on its easiest routes. When a storm is raging on its final ramparts, mere survival is a battle for even the best-equipped teams. Peter Habeler, the great Austrian climber who was, with Reinhold Messner, the first man to climb Everest without oxygen, said after his 1980 effort on McKinley's "easy" West Buttress: "It's colder than all the peaks I have attempted in the Himalaya." More than fifty climbers, some of them experts, have died on the mountain, and of that number, the bodies of thirty-one still rest beneath its snows.

In its own massive way, McKinley is a beautiful mountain—but not classically so, as is the Matterhorn or the Grand Teton or K-2. The aesthetic case for McKinley can never be made more thoroughly or definitively than in Bradford Washburn's photographs that shape the backbone of this book. From a literary perspective, however, the most interesting thing about McKinley is its human history. No other mountain in the world—not even Everest—has attracted a more varied or fascinating collection of visitors, seen more outlandish projects launched, or borne witness to more improbable tragedies. The text that follows is aimed at proving this point, by means of a slightly rambling survey through the hundred years during which men—and more than a few women—have focused their attention on the mountain that the natives called Denali.

Editor's note:

A relief map designed for this book showing the McKinley Range
and the routes of early exploration appears on pages 186–87.

RECONNAISSANCE

by David Roberts

DENALI WAS THE NAME GIVEN the mountain by the natives of Alaska's interior. The coastal Indians called it Traleika. The early Russian traders knew it as Bolshaia Gora. The translation of all are virtually the same: the high one, the great one, the huge peak. During the late 1960s and early 1970s, there was a widespread feeling that Mount McKinley's name should be changed "back" to Denali, and considerable print was devoted to the sentiment that the original name would do justice to the profound reverence for the land exhibited by the native Alaskans.

The fact of the matter is, however, that the natives of south central Alaska were singularly uninterested in mountains. They named very few of them, and in this respect they make the greatest possible contrast with the Eskimos living beyond the Brooks Range in northern Alaska, who ornamented every pass and pinnacle with vivid labels. Moreover, as the incomparable explorer-geologist Alfred H. Brooks pointed out, "the Alaskan Indian has no fixed nomenclature for the larger geographic features. A river will have half a dozen names depending on the direction from which it is approached. The cartographers who cover Alaskan maps with unpronounceable names, imagining that they are based on local usage, are often misled." For, as Brooks noted, "the Alaskan native seldom goes beyond the limit of smooth walking and has a superstitious horror of even approaching glacial ice."

The name McKinley was the 1896 inspiration of a young Princeton-graduate prospector named William A. Dickey, who, searching for gold, had made a summer-long exploration of the Susitna and Chulitna rivers on the southern side of the Alaska Range. The first news that his highly Republican party received on its emergence from months in the wilderness was of William McKinley's nomination for the presidency. Then and there, rafting down the Susitna, they named their great peak McKinley. Shortly after his return to the east, Dickey wrote a now famous letter to the editor of the *New York Sun* (January 24, 1897) recounting the story of his explorations in the wilderness just south of McKinley, during which he had roughly surveyed its height with remarkable accuracy at 20,000 feet.

Thus the continent's highest peak was named for a man who never visited Alaska and had even less interest in mountains than had the natives of the Tanana. Because the name stuck, Dickey was widely thought to have been the first white man to have seen the mountain. It had, however, most certainly been sighted by Captain George Vancouver during his thorough exploration and charting of Cook Inlet in the late spring of 1794, and doubtless by Captain Cook and the Russians somewhat before that. In fact, it had already been called "Densmore's Mountain" for a number of years by the early explorers of the Tanana, and it could not possibly have been ignored by the prospectors who had swarmed to Cook Inlet after gold was found there in 1895. As Brooks sardonically commented about Dickey and Mount McKinley in 1903, "All honor to him for calling attention to it, but let us not make the absurd blunder of crediting him with its discovery."

It had long been supposed that the highest point in Alaska was graceful Mount Saint Elias in the coast-hugging Saint Elias Range. The mountain's sighting by Vitus Bering on July 17, 1741 marked the Russian discovery of Alaska. At slightly over 18,000 feet, Saint Elias is 2,300 feet lower than McKinley, but its lordly prominence only thirty miles from the Gulf of Alaska made it a focal point for early explorers. The first great mountaineering expedition to Alaska, and one of the most brilliant in its history, was executed by the brother of the king of Italy, Prince Luigi Amadeo di Savoia, duke of the Abruzzi. In 1897, his party hiked in from the ocean and smoothly climbed Saint Elias, mastering its easiest route on the first try. With four crack Alpine guides, ten porters, and five fellow climbers, including the world-famous mountain photographer Vittorio Sella, Abruzzi traveled in grand style. For the comfort of the gentlemen-climbers, five iron bedsteads were carried to an altitude of 10,000 feet—and on the night before the final climb, the duke slept cozily in his royal bed at 12,000-foot Russell Col even though the party was to arise at midnight for its attack on the summit.

Only two years after Dickey announced that McKinley was North America's highest peak, the United States Geological Survey sent two major forays northward to explore the wilderness that surrounded it. The northern approach was in charge of George Eldridge, who led an able party up the Susitna and Chulitna, "dragging their canoes against the swift current" and thence across Broad Pass to the Nenana River—to investigate the practical passes between the Susitna and Tanana rivers, to determine the location of a railroad or wagon route from Cook Inlet to the Tanana. Robert Muldrow was the topographer of this expedition, on which he made the first professional instrumental determination of the position and altitude of Mount McKinley (lat. 13°05′N, long. 151°00′W; altitude: 20,464 feet). Eldridge astutely remarked that a feature of this approach route "that should not be overlooked is its picturesqueness. It would be at the very foot of Mount McKinley and would pass through one of the grandest ranges on the North American continent." The memory of both Eldridge and Muldrow has been honored by naming after them two of the Alaska Range's greatest glaciers.

That same summer, the second USGS party, led by Josiah E. Spurr, succeeded in making the first crossing of the range, by boating and trekking up the Yentna and Skwentna rivers, and threading their way through an unnamed defile, later called Simpson's Pass, just northeast of what we now know as Rainy Pass. Thence they reached the Kuskokwim River, descended it to Bristol Bay and *recrossed* the range to Cook Inlet via Katmai Pass. This achievement is still regarded as one of the most daring and extraordinary feats in all Alaskan history.

As the turn of the century neared, efforts intensified to find a practical route northward from the coast to Alaska's interior. All attempts started from the tiny village of Tyonek, on the opposite side of Cook Inlet from presentday Anchorage, whose founding, as a railroad construction camp, was still fourteen years away. Fairbanks was now emerging as the chief supply depot for the interior explorations that were soon to lead to the great gold strikes in the Tanana and Yukon valleys. Spurr's expedition, though dramatic, yielded nothing of value to this search, and Eldridge's Broad Pass route began to make the most sense. But the U.S. government decided to make one or two more tries before settling on the best course for the new road or railroad.

At the same time as these serious explorations were under way, boosters like Dickey continued to plump for McKinley as Alaska's highest mountain, and adventurers started to scheme its ascent. The peak, however, lay in the midst of a mosquito-ridden fastness of tundra, rivers, and glaciers that had still been only slightly penetrated by white men—despite the fact that McKinley stood prominent and unmistakable for all to see, on the northern horizon only 150 miles north of Cook Inlet.

Against this background of probing and planning, the U.S. Army joined in the action. In 1899 they dispatched a young lieutenant named Joseph S. Herron, who made the first major breakthrough in this exploratory puzzle by crossing the great crescent of the range again, and, for the first time, exploring the northwestern approaches to McKinley.

Herron's official report may easily be the most laconic document in all Alaskan history: in fewer than nine pages his narrative covers five and a half months of what must have been an adventure rivaling Lewis and Clark's. With two native guides, five white colleagues, and a pack train of fifteen horses, Herron traveled by steam launch up the Susitna to its junction with the Yentna River, thence up the Kichatna River to its limit of navigation. From that point on, he discovered the tribulations of trying to apply horse-packing techniques developed in the Rocky Mountains to the boggy, bushy muskeg forest of south-central Alaska. Concise as Herron's writing was, it was often vivid in its simple detail:

The country, as will be seen, being wild and overgrown, exacted from us extraordinary labor at every step, and from this time on until winter the daily routine was as follows: A reconnaissance for the best route for the day's march; a search for fords, crossings, detours around or passages through ravines, swamps, and other obstacles; the construction of a pack train trail by chopping out timber and brush in dense forests, blazing in open forests and corduroying in soft mud and tundras; fording or swimming the pack train over the rivers encountered and the building of spar bridges for the horses, where mud-bottom creeks interposed, which were too shallow to swim, yet too deep to corduroy, too soft-bottomed to ford, and too wide to jump; investigation for wood, water, grass, and, if possible, a breezy locality for camp, wind, as an additional requisite, minimizing the mosquitoes, gnats, horseflies, and mooseflies; packing the horses in the morning. . . . driving, racing, dragging, or otherwise hustling them into and along the trail, and adjusting or repacking shifted packs during the day, and unpacking, washing backs and oiling ears, eyes, and other favorite mosquito resorts at night.

Burdened by such a routine, Herron covered an airline distance of only two miles during his first day on the trail. Nevertheless, he forced his way across the range just south of the extraordinary granitic Cathedral Spires, today considered among the finest mountaineering challenges in Alaska (their ascent would not be first attempted until 1965). His two native guides had pleaded vociferously with Herron to turn back, and on July 28 they deserted him in the middle of the night, before he had even reached the backbone of the mountains. However, he plugged on bravely, crossing the range via Simpson's Pass, then swinging to the right and traversing along the entire northern side of the mountains—even though for two weeks a sprained ankle prevented his walking.

When the party ran out of feed for the horses, Herron turned them loose and proceeded on foot. With September came the first snows. The men managed to build rafts and careen down an unnamed river before capsizing and losing some of their food and supplies. In desperate circumstances, at last on September 19 Herron found an Indian—"or rather," as he wrote, "the Indian found us. It is needless to say that we gave him a welcome, sincere if not verbose, our mutual vocabulary consisting of three words, 'yes,' 'no,' and 'good,' and the Indian seemed to think them synonymous at times." It took Herron eight days to persuade the native to guide the party to his village, but the successful negotiations saved the explorers' lives.

For two months Herron and his companions lived in the village of "Telida." A few maddeningly brief sentences described this involuntary layover, during which he "learned all that the Indians knew." When there was enough snow on the ground for good snowshoeing, Herron and his party set out to the north with a group of native guides. They ran out of food but finally reached Fort Gibbon on the Yukon River on December 11 after a wilderness trek of more than a thousand miles.

During the last leg of this remarkable journey, the party passed by Lake Minchumina, some sixty miles northwest of McKinley. They gave the name Mount Foraker to the great peak just to the southwest of McKinley, after the Republican senator from Ohio (a man at least as irrelevant to Alaska as McKinley), whose career ended in ignominy after he was driven from office for accepting bribes from Standard Oil. From the point of view of future exploration, however, Herron's journey was seminal. The Alaska Range had now been crossed for a second time seventy-eight miles southwest of Mount McKinley, proving that an overland traverse from Cook Inlet to the gold country of the interior was feasible—though outrageously circuitous.

In 1902 Alfred H. Brooks, who was one of a unique breed of great U.S. Geological Survey explorers to specialize in Alaska, led a brilliant eight-hundred-mile overland expedition that made the first close approach to McKinley. Brooks' party, slightly larger than Herron's, consisted of seven men and twenty horses carrying 3,500 pounds of gear and food. Significantly, Brooks chose not to rely at all on native guides. On Cook Inlet he had parleyed with an old chief about the country to the north, communicating in sign language aided with a smattering of Russian; at the conclusion of their talk, the chief "gravely shook his head as if to say that I was attempting the impossible."

Like Herron, Brooks used a boat to give his party a head start up the Susitna, the Yentna, and the lower reaches of the Kichatna. To facilitate crossings, he often towed his horses behind the boat, a practice he recognized to be dangerous but workable. In the boggy forest south of the Alaska Range, Brooks, like Herron, found it was often the most he could manage to cover two or three miles a day. Beyond all other trials, he was vexed by the relentless mosquitoes. "Five years of Alaskan travel," he wrote,

"have convinced me that there is no hardship so difficult to bear as this insect pest. . . . Men capable of enduring heat and cold, hunger and fatigue without murmuring, will become almost savage under the torture." Their horses, too, suffered and, maddened by mosquitoes, would charge blindly into the underbrush.

His canny geographical sense took Brooks through the Alaska Range at a gap he prophetically called Rainy Pass. The route was a vast improvement over the twisting itineraries of Spurr and Herron twelve miles farther to the northeast and would later become the path of the famous Iditarod Trail from Anchorage to Nome. As soon as he emerged on the other side of the range, Brooks began contouring toward the northeast across the relatively bare tundra that flanks the foothills north of the great peaks, keeping much closer to the mountains than had Herron three years before. It was becoming evident that the climate north of the Alaska Range was far drier and less stormy than that to the south and made for infinitely easier travel.

At the height of summer, Brooks approached McKinley. His narrative indicates that he never hoped to attempt the mountain's summit, but he had a great desire simply to set foot on its magnificent slopes. On August 3–4, 120 miles and three rugged weeks after crossing Rainy Pass, the little party camped on the banks of Slippery Creek, 2,600 feet above the sea and almost exactly sixteen miles north of the summit of McKinley. The fifth of August was a beautiful day and Brooks made a solo hike due southward, up onto a spur of the mountain as far as snowline, to obtain some clue to its geologic structure. But the satisfaction of standing on its slopes, nine miles from the summit, which had never before been approached by white man, could not but be tinged with regret that there was neither time nor means for reaching a higher altitude.

I had now consumed all of the time that could be spared to explore this mountain, which had been reached at the expense of so much preparation and hard toil, but at least I must leave a record to mark our highest point. On a prominent cliff, near the face of the glacier which had turned me back, I built a cairn in which I buried a cartridge shell from my pistol, containing a brief account of the journey, together with a roster of the party.

On July 8, 1954, this spot was rediscovered by another USGS party, which carried Brooks' map and a photograph that precisely located the position of his Slippery Creek camp. The cairn was carefully dismantled to reveal the cartridge. That spot is about 6,300 feet high and almost exactly three miles northeast of the 10,600-foot mountain now known as Peters Dome. The cartridge and note are now among the most treasured relics at the Denali National Park Museum.

From McKinley, Brooks' party continued northeast, more or less following the present route of the Denali Highway, finally reaching the Nenana River, which they followed down to its junction with the Tanana. Near the end of the trip, the men had to shoot some of their starving horses, but their own survival was never in question. The expedition had lasted 105 days, or a little more than half as long as Herron's comparable trek; but Brooks had been neither trapped by winter nor forced to count on natives for his survival. This exploit is still considered one of the greatest epics in the history of Alaskan exploration, with Brooks and his topographer, D. L. Raeburn, mapping as well as moving their whole outfit forward, often as many as a dozen miles in a single day. The map the two men produced was the bible for those who trekked or climbed in this wilderness for nearly half a century.

It was now evident that any real attempt to climb McKinley was going to be seriously hamstrung by the immense labor it took simply to get to the bottom of the mountain. Herron's and Brooks' pack routes were not conducive to the hauling of bedsteads to base camp. But there was an obvious shortcut. Travel was clearly easier on the north side of the Alaska Range, and McKinley had less elaborate defenses there in the form of thick forests, soggy swamps, rugged foothills, and lengthy glaciers. Why bother with a southern approach at all, with its necessity for swinging far to the west to cross the range at or near Rainy Pass? At the turn of the century, the only advantage of starting from Cook Inlet lay in the comparative ease of outfitting a major expedition there. After Felix Pedro's 1902 gold strike, however, Fairbanks began to boom, and it became a plausible base for far-ranging expeditions.

These considerations were not lost on Federal Judge James Wickersham when he moved his court from Eagle on the Yukon to Fairbanks early in 1903. That May, when he was able to take a few weeks' holiday from his judicial duties, this extraordinary man rounded up four able-bodied Fairbanks friends and took off to make the first bona fide attempt to climb Mount McKinley. Wickersham's modus operandi was not unlike Brooks' and Herron's, but the geographic reverse. The little party hitchhiked on a mail steamer that took them down the Tanana to its tributary, the Kantishna. The obliging captain made a one-day detour to take the explorers as far up the Kantishna as he could push in his tiny craft. When they disembarked, Wickersham's party still stood a full hundred miles from McKinley, but they could see it clearly to the south, across the level plain of the lowlands.

Wickersham's account of their journey makes it sound like a lark. His scenic passages amount to a prolonged encomium to the "beautiful virgin country" where "birds sing in the birch and spruce forests along the river banks" and "innumerable waterfowl—ducks, geese, and swan—are in the sky." Indeed the judge was so transported as to claim that the landscape seemed less arctic than like "a scene in the lower valley of the Mississippi."

Instead of a pack train of fifteen or twenty horses, Wickersham's party was accompanied only by two mules, which the nonplused natives called "White Man's Moose." These Athabascans found the party's ambitions equally baffling. "What for you go top—gold?" they asked. When informed that the white men wanted to see the summit for its own sake, the local wise man made a retort that was greeted with gales of "rude laughter." His interpreter translated the sagacious verdict: "He says you are a fool."

The party was traveling much lighter than Herron's or Brooks'. The mules carried the food, which consisted of flour, bacon, beans, dried fruit—the typical diet of the interior explorers of the day—and, for the beasts themselves, oats and hay. They carried no fresh meat, but shot caribou and dried it on the spot to supplement their provisions. Only a month after leaving Fairbanks the party stood beneath the gigantic north face of McKinley—the wall that Brad Washburn later named in honor of Wickersham.

The judge's party made their last mule camp near the terminus of what Brooks had called Peters Glacier, the somewhat hidden gateway to the base of McKinley's vast northern wall. In jovial fashion, they filled their knapsacks with three or four days' worth of chocolate, bread, and caribou jerky and, armed with ropes and alpenstocks (predecessors of the modern ice axe), marched up the smooth rock-strewn center of the glacier. As they walked, what may have been the most fearsome avalanches humans had yet seen anywhere on earth thundered down the precipices to the left. Then the men began to work their way up a side glacier (Jeffery Glacier today) that ramped its way, first steeply, then gently, across the bottom of McKinley's mighty face. Here the going became a bit more treacherous. The party roped up and threaded their way around great crevasses and over fragile snow bridges.

Finally, on the crest of a knife-edged spur at an altitude of only 8,100 feet, the bold first attempt to climb Mount McKinley came to an end. The massive instability of the whole north face of the mountain had become only too evident: as Wickersham delicately put it, "We recognize that we are inviting destruction by staying here." It is characteristic of the judge's sanguine disposition, however, that even as he described the seracs and ice blocks toppling around him, he wrote with lyrical bonhomie.

At the end of this exploit, the judge made a wise and rarely quoted comment. As they headed homeward from the base camp, he remarked that "the glacier rising from the northeast angle [now known as Muldrow Glacier] is clearly the one that the Munkho-tena Indians referred to as leading to the summit. . . . It seems to afford the road we have been looking for." Because of the warm summer days, the danger of avalanches, and dwindling food, however, Wickersham's party decided "to defer any further attempt to climb Denali's walls till another season." That northeast glacier, recommended by the natives, was indeed the route by which McKinley's summit would first be reached ten years later.

It would be another fifty-eight years before Wickersham Wall was again attempted. When it was, by the same route the judge had pioneered, the party reached 12,000 feet only to have its camp avalanched out beneath them as they lay in their tents. The climbers were lucky to escape with their lives. The wall was not climbed successfully until two separate expeditions did it by two different routes in the summer of 1963.

Precisely who went first and where and when in McKinley's lowland labyrinth of rivers, creeks, passes, alders, bogs, and mosquitoes will never be known, as many of the pioneers were natives and prospectors who kept no records. There were no maps when they did it, and now that there are excellent maps, all the actors in this extraordinary drama are dead. But it was the most exciting era in Alaskan history.

Wickersham Wall towers 14,000 feet above shadowed Peters Glacier.

Overleaf: This scene is exactly what Captain George Vancouver described in April 1794 when he visited Cook Inlet on his voyage of exploration: "Distant, stupendous mountains covered with snow, and apparently detached from each other." In this infrared picture, half of McKinley's height is hidden by 140 miles of earth curvature.

Second overleaf: Mount McKinley, looking southwestward from 12,000 feet over the headwaters of the Teklanika River on a cloudless, windless autumn day.

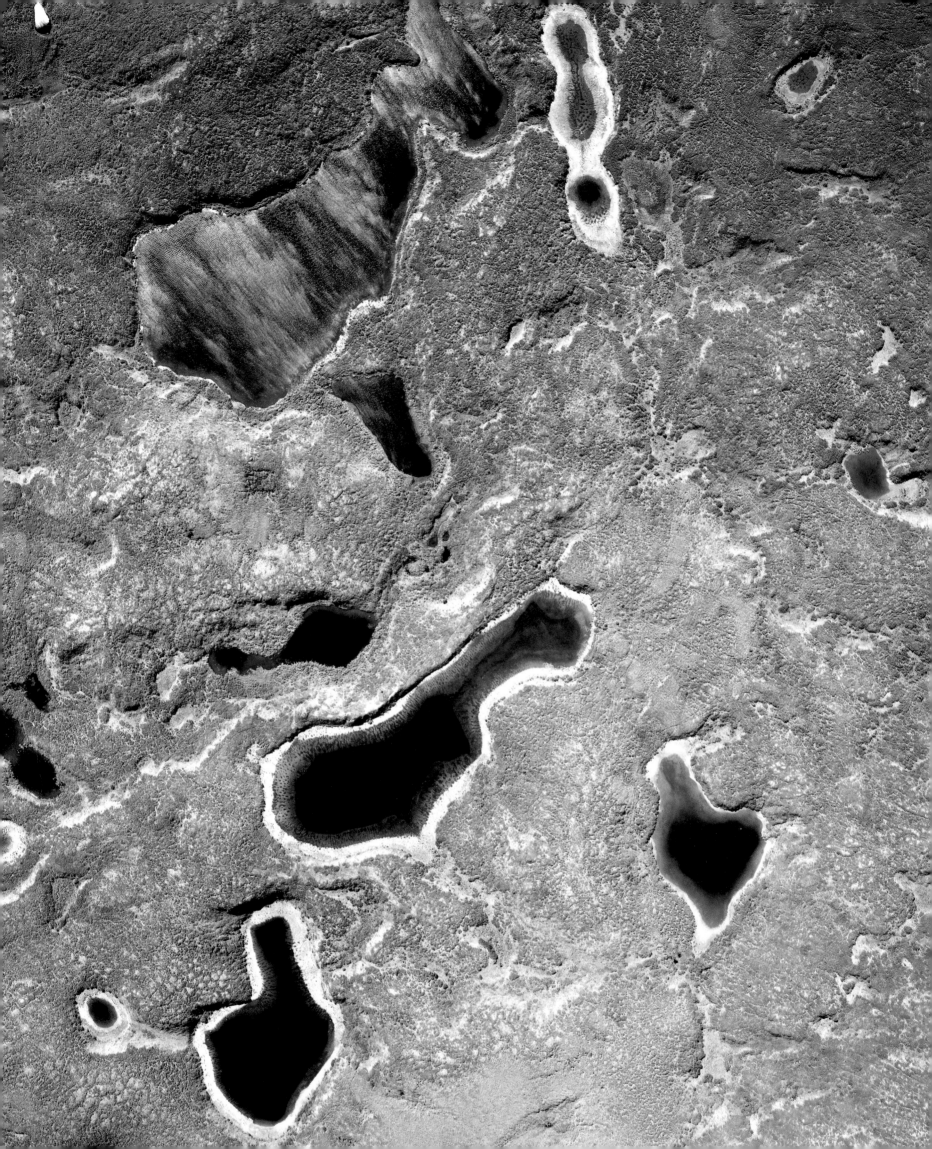

Left: Hundreds of ponds dot the tundra that stretches southward from the McKinley River to the foothills of the Alaska Range. (Aeromap/U.S.)

Above: The heavily forested plain stretches 25 miles southward from the end of Ruth Glacier to Talkeetna, not only dotted with many lakes and ponds, but bisected by the lazy Tokositna River. Here, near where it approaches the Chulitna River, the Tokositna flows through a bewildering array of meanders.

Overleaf: Mount Hunter and Mount McKinley, in early March, looking northward up the Tokositna Valley. This spot was a favorite campsite of Alaskan artist Sydney Laurence.

Second overleaf: Early morning clouds streak the sky above Mount McKinley—a reliable portent of foul weather to come by evening. In this infra-red telephoto picture taken from mile 81.9 on the Denali Highway, the scale is deceiving: the peak is 27 miles away and rises 18,000 feet above the level gravel bars of the McKinley River in the foreground; the trees that flank the river are nearly 40 feet tall.

Above: Charlie Ott, who took this picture of a migration of the Denali caribou herd, spent much of his life near Mount McKinley studying and photographing its wildlife.

Right: Muddy River constantly changes its course through a maze of gravel bars, flowing northward for only a dozen miles from Peters Glacier to the McKinley River, and carrying frigid meltwater from all the glaciers that pour down Wickersham Wall.

CHAPTER TWO

THE EXTRAORDINARY DR. COOK

by David Roberts and Bradford Washburn

MOUNT MCKINLEY HAS ATTRACTED egomaniacs of all stripes—bumbling amateurs greedy for fame, loners of possibly suicidal bent, climbers of international ability—but the most extraordinary of all was Dr. Frederick A. Cook of Brooklyn, New York. No more enigmatic character emerges from the many years of human enterprise on North America's highest mountain, or, for that matter, anywhere else in the long and eventful annals of exploration on this continent.

Cook ended his days in tragic solitude, rejected by the public after serving seven years in Leavenworth Federal prison for using the mails to defraud. Yet, as most experienced observers have pointed out, had he simply rested on his genuine achievements, he would be remembered today as a first-rate explorer. McKinley was the turning point in his life.

The focal dream of Dr. Cook's life was to be the first man at the North Pole. At the turn of the century, though he had participated effectively in an extraordinary series of major adventures, he was still largely unknown to the public. To attempt the Pole was a costly proposition, and he wisely decided that success in a highly dramatic yet much less costly exploit would win him the acclaim needed to secure major polar funding. So, in the spring of 1903 he organized an expedition to climb Mount McKinley.

And there he made his first serious mistake. Cook was not a mountaineer, neither did he have close mountaineering friends. Instead of assembling a powerful group of the best climbers of the day, he put together one of the most motley teams in the history of exploration: Robert Dunn, a young reporter and would-be adventurer on the staff of Lincoln Steffens' (New York) *Commercial Advertiser*; Ralph Shainwald, a young New York friend with a wealthy father; Walter Miller, a photographer; and, fortunately, Fred Printz of Darby, Montana, the veteran horsepacker who had been the most powerful member of Brooks' great Alaskan expedition the year before.

Cook, Dunn, and Shainwald crossed the United States by train and stopped briefly in Seattle. There they picked up Printz, Miller, fifteen untried Yakima packhorses, and headed for the north on the *Santa Ana*, a "quaint Alaskan coaster," on June 9, 1903—far too late in the year for the exploration and ascent of a huge, virgin Alaskan mountain. Late in June they docked at Tyonek, and on June 25 the first attempt to climb Mount McKinley from the coast was under way.

Printz, Dunn, and the pack train headed northwestward across the boggy lowlands, just as Brooks had the year before. But Dr. Cook and the rest of his little party chartered a tiny riverboat that took them on a long detour, up the Susitna, Yentna, and Skwentna rivers to an agreed-on meeting point nearly a hundred miles upstream. Miraculously, two weeks later the two groups met precisely where Printz told them he'd be waiting—in a cloud of the omnipresent mosquitoes on the banks of the Skwentna. A few days later the boat headed back to Tyonek, and the outfit headed up the ever steeper valley of the Kichatna River, still following precisely the Brooks route of the year before, through the same rain-soaked wilderness.

Cook, like his predecessors, never tired of writing florid descriptions of this country: "We learned to our heart's content that this enticing landscape, so beautiful to look upon, offered us the tortures of countless devils—mosquitoes, horseflies, gnats and marshes, thick underbrush, icy streams, and never-ceasing rains all combined to make life thoroughly miserable for us."

In an effort to trim their mileage a bit, the party avoided Rainy Pass and followed the shorter Spurr-Herron route across Simpson's Pass on July 27. Six days later they at last emerged from the mountains on the headwaters of the great Kuskokwim. Almost at the site of today's Farewell Airport, the doctor's party, like Brooks', now swung to the right, traversing northeastward along the dry tundra benches that form the northern side of the Alaska Range. Despite the fact that they had already been on the trail for five rugged weeks and had covered nearly two hundred miles, the little group was still a good hundred miles short of their goal.

It was not until August 24, sixty days from tidewater and exactly two months after Wickersham's departure from the mountain, that Dr. Cook reached the terminus of Peters Glacier, the gateway to McKinley's North Face. To their great surprise, the men came upon a set of chopped poles "arranged like a clothes-horse." At first they thought it the remains of an old native camp, but soon they had uncovered a discarded pair of overalls, a tin can, a film wrapper. "Whose camp is this?" wrote Robert Dunn in his diary. "What are white men doing here? Indians don't take pictures—nor do they discard a whole pair of overalls." Another team member declared the camp the work of railroad surveyors from the previous year. It was not until months later that the party learned that Judge Wickersham had beaten them to the base of McKinley.

From a snug camp in the timber near the glacier's snout, Cook and his companions advanced along the eastern edge of the valley to a huge, level gravel bar right at the base of McKinley. From here they worked their way up the center of Peters Glacier with minimal rations and equipment in hopes of making a swift and successful ascent. Unlike Wickersham, they did not attempt a direct ascent of the colossal North Face but penetrated up the glacier several miles farther than the judge's party had gone. After climbing the middle of a nasty cataract of ice, they became the first human beings ever to set foot in the magnificent 7,500-foot amphitheater of Peters Basin, right at the bottom of McKinley's precipitous Northwest Ridge. They had studied the mountain well, and this was clearly a possible route of ascent—but not for a group of this caliber, at the very edge of winter.

On August 29 the first climbing party started gingerly up the Northwest Buttress of McKinley. They were lucky. This steep 3,000-foot slope is usually solid ice, but they found it deeply veneered with snow. They ultimately wallowed and had to chop steps for hours (amazingly, the best axe-wielder was Fred Printz, the horsepacker). Cook later described their ordeal: "Slowly but steadily we advanced against a freezing wind charged with drift-snow, until the setting sun forced us to seek a camping place. We found nowhere a level place large enough for our tent, so we were compelled to dig away snow and cut down to the ice for a tent-flooring." This miserable camp was pitched at about 10,000 feet, "on not ten square feet of primeval level." Said Dunn, who usually had little use for Cook: "The Professor has been a real companion the last two days; intelligent and sympathetic. Probably he realizes that this is the final effort and is making a grand play to come up to scratch. At any rate, tonight I'm convinced that he's really trying for all he's worth to get up McKinley."

The next morning the veneer of snow was gone and they chopped hour after hour in solid ice, step after step, repeatedly changing the lead. Three thousand feet above Peters Basin, the trail came to an end. The slope lessened, then steepened above them into rugged granite crags—climbing that was obviously far beyond the competence of this intrepid little group. They were high enough now to look across the smooth snow brow of Kahiltna Pass to a streak of green—the lowlands south of the range, sixty miles away.

One last camp was dug in at close to 11,000 feet, with the tundra and its thousands of glittering lakes now far below them to the west. The next morning, reality hit them squarely as they looked upward. Farther progress on the northwest arête was impossible. There were successive cliffs for four thousand feet—and no way around them. Said Fred Printz after a brief final reconnaissance above the tent with Cook: "It aint that we can't

find a way that's possible, takin' chances. There aint *no* way!" And Dunn philosophized: "Something besides courage and determination is needed to climb a mountain like this. Forgive me if I call it intelligence." That ridge of McKinley was not climbed until May 27, 1954—fifty-one years later—by a brilliant team of mountaineers, and even they had their troubles getting up those "pink granite cliffs."

On September 1, Cook's little party was safely back in Peters Basin and a day later at base camp. Their thirteen horses, untethered to feed, had taken off, and Printz and Dunn had a wild struggle relocating any of them. Only six could be found, and the party settled for that, abandoning the rest to die in the wilderness. Now there was but one thought in all their minds: "How in Hell are we going to get back across this solid wall of mountains to Cook Inlet before we're overwhelmed by winter?"

The frantic march to the coast began on September 4. Curiously, the team headed northeastward instead of retracing their steps back to Cook Inlet. This strange decision seems to have been rooted in Cook's wish to continue to explore new ground—in a way, to atone for their failure to climb McKinley. It almost cost them their lives. On September 5 they passed the "flat gravel desert of Muldrow Glacier, named by Brooks, and the largest on the north face of the range." That evening, after making camp, they climbed a 5,000-foot hill that flanked the broad valley. From its summit the view of McKinley was magnificent. Wrote Dunn: "It rose like an unearthly castle of opalescent glass, wrapped in the streaked, cold clouds of a Turner sunset; its summit now seen from a different angle, a wilderness of peaks and gullies."

While they were on the hill, Cook described McKinley's twin peaks as the "tubercles of this giant tooth . . . separated by large glaciers whose frozen currents pour down very steep slopes" and remarked that "if it were not so difficult to get at this side of the mountain . . . here the upper slopes might offer a promising route." It was a prophetic observation, given the events of almost exactly three years later.

Three more days of trekking ever-farther eastward through the great valley that paralleled the range (now the route of the Denali Highway) brought them to the East Fork of the Toklat River. Sable Pass blocked the way ahead of them. Their salt and tea were gone; rations had been cut to the limit. Fred Printz, master of the wilderness trail, was deeply concerned that no low pass across the mountains might exist. Fresh snow now mantled even the low summits. The glaciers no longer melted in the daytime, the creeks were dwindling to rivulets, and the puddles froze at night. Their situation was critical. They *had* to find a pass.

The valley to the south of this miserable camp looked slightly more hopeful than all the dead ends they had encountered, so

they headed straight up it, horses and all, even though its floor turned out to be a glacier four miles long. Miraculously, this glacier was smooth enough for the horses to negotiate, and, even more miraculously, it led to the only pass in the Alaska Range between Simpson's Pass and the valley of the Sanctuary River—140 miles of rugged peaks—that could possibly be crossed by a pack train.

Somehow the party managed to cajole the horses over the 6,000-foot crest and down a very steep hillside to the valley of Bull River. Wrote Cook: "The most difficult task for the horses, among their long series of hard adventures, was the descent from this glacial pass. In less than two hours they came down three thousand feet at an angle sometimes too steep for the men! It was a route over sharp stones, ice, and frozen ground; but the animals, with their feet and legs cut and bruised—leaving bloody stains everywhere in their trail—followed us without being urged toward the green fields of the lower valley." When they reached the first grass, the horses stopped and would not move another inch, so the men pitched camp right there, at the end of a ghastly day. It was September 8. The range had been crossed.

The next day the group headed southward, first along grassy slopes, then into a box canyon, searching for the main course of the Chulitna. It was dreadful going, first in an icy river, then across it, then beside it. Dunn wrote in his journal: "Our clothes are falling to pieces, our boots are worn out; mine are a cast-off pair of [Ralph's]. . . not a blade of grass down here, and, stuck in this canyon, we can't get the beasts up these stage back-drop cliffs. Fred has just climbed them and reports swamps, lakes and confused tributaries ahead—making it impossible to travel up there—and no break in our gorge. We've no idea how far we are from the sea, what falls or rapids may be ahead, whether the water fills the canyon completely, as it may, and checkmate us."

On September 16, at last, the exhausted little team built two rafts and the next day abandoned their horses and started to run the river. They might have shot the horses: weakening in the foodless woods and canyon, the beasts would be killed by the wolves. But the men didn't have the nerve to murder the brave animals who had gotten them all the way here to survival. Two days later

the group passed Eldridge Glacier, then the Ruth Glacier (named then and there for Cook's stepdaughter). Just below it, they passed the Chulitna's confluence with the Tokositna, then rafted through the furious waters of the Chulitna canyon. The party soon stumbled upon some prospectors camped beside the river and reveled in sourdough, tobacco, bread, salt, and sugar again.

Next came the broad Susitna. Floating down it on a raft was "a delight compared with our troubles on the Chulitna. The beautiful autumn foliage, the clear winter air, the migrating birds and the absence of mosquitoes" made rafting down this river of mud a "fitting termination" for their trip. On September 26 the group reached Tyonek. They had not climbed McKinley, but they had made a trip that has never been repeated. At its end, Dr. Cook summarized Mount McKinley's defenses better than anyone else has before or since:

Mount McKinley offers a unique challenge to mountaineers, but its ascent will prove a prodigious task. It is the loftiest mountain in North America, the steepest mountain in the world, and the most arctic of all great mountains. Its slopes are weighted down with all the snow and ice that can possibly find a resting place, but unlike Mt. St. Elias, the glaciation is not such as to offer a route over continuous ice. The area of this mountain is far inland, in the heart of a most difficult and trackless country, making the transportation of men and supplies a very arduous task. The thick underbrush, the endless marches, and the myriads of vicious mosquitoes bring to the traveler the troubles of the tropics. The necessity for fording and swimming icy streams, the almost perpetual cold rains, the camps in high altitudes on glaciers in snows and violent storms bring to the traveler all of the discomforts of the arctic explorer. The very difficult slopes combined with high altitude effects add the troubles of the worst alpine climbs. The prospective conqueror of America's culminating peak will be amply rewarded, but he must be prepared to withstand the tortures of the torrids, the discomforts of the north pole seeker, combined with the hardships of the Matterhorn ascents multiplied many times.

Seen here over the gentle slopes of Thorofare Pass, McKinley rises 16,000 feet above the lush tundra of Stony Hill. This is the spot from which Charles Sheldon, Harry Karstens, and Dr. Cook all predicted that this side of the great peak would be most accessible for a first ascent.

CHAPTER THREE

CLOSING IN FROM THE SOUTH

by David Roberts and Bradford Washburn

ALTHOUGH DR. COOK HAD ACCOMPLISHED the well-nigh impossible by circumnavigating McKinley, his performance as a real leader in 1903 left much to be desired. His selection of personnel for this huge undertaking was haphazard, to say the least, and his oft-lyrical prose veils much of the grittier detail of what actually happened.

Robert Dunn excoriated Cook in his book called *The Shameless Diary of an Explorer*, but his attack is so brutal that, sadly, it too obscures much of the truth. From Dunn's account, Fred Printz, the horsepacker from Montana, clearly emerges as the only solid element in the motley little crew. Without his coolness and experience there would have been little chance of the party's even reaching Simpson's Pass. Only by carefully reading all of Cook's and Dunn's articles and books against a background of detailed firsthand knowledge of the country they traversed can one put together a reliable narrative of what took place on that trip.

The next expedition, in 1906, was at least at the start a very different matter from the one of three years before. Cook had whetted the interest of Herschel C. Parker, a well-to-do Columbia University professor of electrical engineering. Unlike the members of Cook's first party, Parker was an experienced alpinist, with Mont Blanc, the Matterhorn, and many of the big peaks of the Rockies already under his belt. He, in turn, managed to get Belmore Browne to join up—a competent, tough outdoorsman who was also a superb artist—and together they brought along Russell Porter as topographer. He too was able and well trained—and many years later would be one of the principal designers of the great Palomar telescope. To this strong nucleus Cook and Parker, who were co-leaders, added Walter Miller again as photographer and Fred Printz, once more assuming the duties of chief-of-the-horses. Printz then hired Edward Barrill, a blacksmith from Darby, Montana, as his assistant packer. Lastly, they secured the substantial financial backing of Henry Disston of the Disston Saw Company.

It is hard to understand why, given all that was then known about McKinley, it was once more decided to approach the mountain from the southwest. Eldridge and Muldrow had explored Broad Pass thoroughly. Hundreds of prospectors had worked in the Chulitna valley. And Brooks, Wickersham, and Cook had all clearly established the fact that it was a long, terrible approach via Rainy Pass. Possibly Cook and Printz still had such vivid

memories of the *end* of the 1903 trip that they never again wanted to enter the valley of the Chulitna.

At any rate the Cook-Parker Expedition of 1906, well financed by Disston and Professor Parker, hit the overland trail, starting again from Tyonek in early June 1906. Dissatisfied with the lengthy struggle through Simpson's or Rainy Pass, they made their first major tactical mistake by focusing all their strength on trying to find still another route through the range farther east, at the head of the Yentna, which might reduce the length of their trek by several miles. Cook had arranged to have built a shoal-draft motorboat, the *Bolshoy*, to speed up the river work, and, as before, the party split into two groups. Printz, Barrill, and the horses headed directly overland and the rest of the men detoured up the Susitna and the Yentna in the launch.

The boat party planned to travel upriver as far as the *Bolshoy* could go, then to press ahead on foot, hoping to find the new pass before the pack train overtook them. In less than a week the little boat had reached the limit of navigation, and a base camp was set up where the pack train could easily find it. Leaving Parker there, Cook, Browne, and Porter set out for the head of the Yentna. Browne described their trek: "Our real excitement came when the valley narrowed up. We found the river growing swifter day by day; the gravel was giving way to large boulders, and we were forced more often to the rugged mountainsides. By this time we had all had narrow escapes while crossing the streams. A man with a heavy pack is helpless when he loses his footing in bad water and is 'rolled.' He is lucky if he reaches the bank with no worse hurt than torn and bleeding hands and a bruised body."

Thirty miles above base camp the valley ended in a three-way fork. To the right was a big glacier flowing off the slopes of Mount Dall; to the left were other smaller glaciers leading westward into a barren mountain wilderness. Straight ahead was a narrow valley that led northwestward, exactly where the team wanted to go. Here they made a big mistake. The left fork led to the Dillinger River and the Kuskokwim lowlands, at that point only ten miles away, hidden around a corner. By going straight ahead they were forced into a hopelessly narrow defile, which soon forked again.

Their food was now running short, but they decided to press on anyway and climbed a steep hillside from which they could scout out what lay ahead. On June 14, they reached their limit on a mountainside looking northward. In Browne's words, "We camped by a mossy pool below a snowbank, and after climbing the hill above us, we could see the rounded sheep mountains of the Kuskokwim. It was a wonderful feeling to stand there and look out over the unknown mass of mountains. But even at that height the mosquitoes were troublesome, so, with my rifle lashed to the plane-table tripod, we pitched our little tent and rolled into our sleeping-bags."

The next day, food almost gone, the trio scrambled down the steep slopes to see if horses could possibly be led through this narrow gateway to the Promised Land. "We were weak from hunger and the mountain fell off in numerous precipices, and was covered with dense jungles of twisted alders and devil's-club. We traveled mostly on our hands and knees, our packs catching in the brush and our hands and bodies swollen from bruises and devil's-club thorns. . . . The canyon was a dreary spot: the roaring of the water was deafening and cold, damp winds swept down from the snowfields above." They finally gave up and retreated all the way to base camp, tired, bruised, famished, and discouraged. On June 25 the pack train joined them, equally battered, after another terrible journey across the bogs and thickets from Tyonek.

The boat headed off down the Yentna for civilization with its "Captain and mate." Now the incredible decision was made to attempt the crossing of that awful pass—somehow or other—with the horses. "The work of swimming loaded packhorses across glacier rivers is the most dangerous form of exercise that I have ever indulged in," wrote Browne. "The horses served as pack-animals and ferry boats! We were forced to swim the animals with their packs on, and we either sat on the packs, or held onto the ropes while we were in the water."

When the men settled in for the night, their "camps were picturesque in the extreme. They were usually situated on a bar of the glacier rivers. The camp-fires were built in the great piles of driftwood that the river brought down during the spring freshets. The men moved half-naked, like savages, in the crimson glow, while above the haze of the valley the Alaskan Range stood clear-cut against the evening sky."

Finally the expedition reached the forks where Cook, Browne, and Porter had been two weeks before. Dividing into two groups, the first with horses, the other without, they fought to find a way through to the lowlands, but failed. Browne's sorrowful account of that last fateful day concludes, "We climbed about one thousand feet and, on reaching a high shoulder, we could look down onto two passes that led to the Kuskokwim. . . . We lay for a few minutes looking sadly and yearningly toward that promised land . . . and then we slowly turned to the back trail, for while we were through the worst part of the range, we knew that horses could not follow us." The second retreat to base camp was a nightmare, as

A mule skinner rescues a bogged-down packhorse.

hot, snow-melting weather had swollen the streams to torrents. They barely made it on the evening of July 2.

They had played the wrong cards and they knew it. Two golden midsummer weeks had been lost—now they had to regroup and try the only conceivable line of attack that remained: a thorough reconnaissance of the vast wilderness of the Kahiltna, the Tokositna, and the Ruth, on McKinley's massive southern flanks.

A small team was immediately dispatched to cut a trail across the two miles of "jungle" that separated them from the East Fork of the Yentna, and the pack train followed that afternoon. It had all looked so easy as they had plotted the route from a nearby hill, but, according to Cook, a "soft green wilderness with a decorative parklike grouping of the spruce, the alders and the cottonwoods" speedily developed into another nightmare—"the whole jungle seemed afloat" with ice water and clouds of mosquitoes. Through a continual rainstorm they pushed on to a campsite near the top of 3,900-foot Mount Kliskon, which they had to climb on July 7 for Porter's surveying and to see where they were going. Then off through the jungle again to a tiny miners' settlement at Sunflower Creek, and, three miles farther, the waters of Lake Chelatna.

They were at last reaching country that wasn't afloat. Cook despaired that the water had followed them everywhere: "It spouts out of the sidehill, it shoots over the rocks, it oozes from everywhere. . . . We were forced to climb trees to get out of the water. . . . To climb Alaskan mountains we should be web-footed and duck-feathered and wing-finned like penguins!"

Beyond Chelatna things quickly improved. The party forded the rushing Kahiltna River, then, keeping close to the north side of the glacier, they hacked a trail upward along an old moraine to

Overleaf: The entire backbone of the McKinley Massif, seen looking northeastward from nearly 40,000 feet. The vast lowlands of Alaska's interior stretch northward to the horizon at left—and in the exact center of the foreground, outlined by dark shadows, is the narrow defile that thwarted the passage of Dr. Cook's 1906 expedition. In the right foreground are the headwaters of the west fork of the Yentna River. Mount McKinley is 75 miles to the northeast.

Dutch Creek and from there across the timberless uplands to a point from which, at last, they looked down on the headwaters of the Tokositna River. Here, atop a steep bluff, they got their first good look at the Tokositna Glacier and the rough wilderness of McKinley's southeast face, now barely thirty miles away.

From the bluff the party descended a thousand feet and camped on the edge of the wide gravel flats at the end of the glacier. On July 19, they climbed a 6,000-foot mountain just west of the Tokositna Glacier, from which they had a magnificent view of McKinley—and "for a few brief moments its death-dealing plunges of sheer granite cliffs were unveiled." Parker took one look and accurately appraised the situation: the mountain was unclimbable (by them) from the south or the east. It was a terrible shock after all the struggles that had brought them to that dramatic and lonely spot, but they all agreed, almost instantly. But rather than quit, Cook and Browne decided to set up a tiny camp and study the peak throughout the night to see if the changing shadows would reveal any weakness in the great mountain's defenses. That night was a turning point in McKinley's history as two good friends, who later became bitter adversaries, shared the same tent and appraised the problems of the climb that would face them both, separately, in the very near future.

Cook described their vigil: "The glory of color and contour was beyond the reach of the camera and beyond our powers of interpretation. We were only permitted to see bits of fascinating landscape through openings in the screen of vapor. . . . We drew the robes about us and peeped out every few moments. The clouds seemed to settle and freeze to the icy armor of the mountains. . . . The overwhelming bigness of the whole scheme . . . did not impress us until the first beams of light burned on the sky-scraped peaks and shot through gaps into the yawning cuts which separated the buttresses from each other. . . . The climb of Mount McKinley was now put down as a hopeless task."

And Browne wrote: "It was a wonderfully impressive experience. . . . We looked straight out through space at the wilderness giant. The night air had a chill, clean tang, and as the cold crept downward the sound of falling water ceased until the whole world seemed steeped in frigid silence. . . . As we watched, we talked in whispers, and we agreed that even a summer's campaign might be too short a time to allow a complete traverse of the southern base . . . From our point of view, southeast, the mountain looked absolutely unclimbable."

In the morning the pair descended to camp and decided to invest a few final days in "the general exploration of the eastern foothills." The party struggled up the boulder-strewn western edge of Tokositna Glacier (a native name, Tokositna means "the river that comes from the land where there are no trees"), then crossed its rough but uncrevassed mile of ice, "covered with crushed granite which ranged in size from coarse sand to blocks the size of a house." Thence they scrambled up to the crest of the broad grassy pass that separates the two great glaciers—Tokositna and Ruth—a peninsula of land only a mile and a half wide at this spot. While Porter surveyed from the ridge, Parker, Browne, and Cook descended to the Ruth and tried to get up onto it. From the ridge it had looked as though it would be easy walking, but once more they were thwarted. At the glacier's edge, they ran into a roaring, impassable torrent of ice water and, on the opposite side, a vertical wall of ice. Try as they would along a three-mile descent, they could not find a single spot where either the creek was passable or the wall scalable.

On July 25, their "enthusiasm gone," the party headed back along the arduous trail toward the Yentna and Cook Inlet, with the hope of reaching Tyonek in time for Cook, Browne, and Printz to guide their patron Henry Disston on a hunting trip.

In early September, however, back at the seashore, they learned that Disston could not join them, and an extraordinary series of events began. Professor Parker had to return to his teaching at Columbia. Printz and Miller went on a big-game-specimen collecting trip up the Kichatna, and Browne left on a similar trip up the Matanuska valley. Cook, Barrill, and a prospector called "Dokkin" (whom they had picked up on their retreat down the Yentna) took the *Bolshoy* up the Susitna: in Cook's words, "as a final task for our season's work I now determined to explore the river systems and glaciers to the east of Mount McKinley and to examine the northern arête for a route to the top of the mountain for a possible future ascent."

This plan seemed odd to observers at the time, and seems even more so today, in light of several important facts. First, in 1903 Cook's party had traversed every inch of the Chulitna and Susitna southward to Cook Inlet from Ruth Glacier, and they already knew it well. Moreover, only a few days before, they had stood on a pass that looked both up and down the Ruth Glacier's lower eighteen miles, so they knew exactly what problems it presented. Cook had also clearly stated "the hopelessness of further mountaineering from any point of attack which could be reached before the coming winter closed the gates to the upper world." And when Browne asked to be a member of this little exploring party, Cook told him that there would be no climbing, just checking to be sure that the river approach to the Ruth was "practicable."

Thus it is surprising that before heading upstream, Cook telegraphed to Henry Disston: "I AM PREPARING FOR A LAST, DESPERATE ATTACK ON MOUNT MCKINLEY!"

In a gathering storm, McKinley towers 17,000 feet above the rugged ramparts that flank the Tokositna Valley.

CHAPTER FOUR

THE FAKE PEAK

by Bradford Washburn

IN THE FIRST THREE WEEKS of September 1906, the most incredible scenario in all McKinley's climbing history unfolded.

Early in September, Dr. Cook, Ed Barrill, and John Dokkin (their prospector friend) headed up the Susitna. The *Bolshoy* was an amazing little craft: it took them only two days to cover the hundred miles from Tyonek to the Chulitna canyon. There, fortunately, because of the fall freeze-up in the mountains, the river was not at all violent, and they made good progress to the mouth of the Tokositna. Two miles upstream the trio reached Alder Creek, where they made their base camp at an elevation of almost exactly 1,000 feet. Dokkin decided to stay there for the winter, and Cook and Barrill prepared for their reconnaissance of Ruth Glacier, whose rock-strewn snout was now only a mile away. Cook later wrote that they did not plan "to climb to the top. The winter, with its heavy snowfall, its death-dealing avalanches, its storms and awful cold, was too far advanced in the upper world." They hoped only to "discover a route that would permit a future ascent and to explore the big glaciers starting from the northern slopes"—a ridiculous statement, as they were approaching the mountain from the southeast, and the extreme limit of vision from that valley is McKinley's eastern ridge.

At any rate, with forty-pound packs and no plans to relay supplies, the two climbers left the *Bolshoy* on the brisk, clear morning of September 8. Dokkin, intrigued by what they were doing, decided to accompany them for a while. At the start, they followed bear, moose, and caribou trails along the northern edge of the glacier. Then, a day later, they took to the ice, and Dokkin quit, quickly disillusioned by the amount of just plain work involved in mountain climbing. In another long day, they covered ten miles of bare ice with excellent walking and camped at 3,800 feet, on a "beautiful moss-carpeted point" that they thought to be about fifteen miles from Mount McKinley. This promontory is now called Glacier Point and is actually eighteen miles from the top.

Glacier Point is an idyllic spot, surrounded by magnificent granite peaks—the last dry land for a campsite all the way to the top of McKinley. That night Cook and Barrill slept "serenely happy," occasionally awakened by the "low-pitched rumbling noises" of distant avalanches. They got an early start on the morning of September 10, climbed through the big boulders of the moraine and out onto the vast expanse of ice that is now known as the Great Gorge. "The crevasses were still numerous; those visi-

ble were easily avoided, but those invisible were at times unintentionally located by breaking through snow bridges." It was bleak and cold, so they lunched in their tent, then pressed on in the afternoon, up the mile-wide expanse of ice, flanked on both sides by peaks that rose vertiginously for almost exactly a mile above them. The Great Gorge of Ruth Glacier is one of the most magnificent spots in all the mountains of the world.

At this point (page 202 in his book) Cook's narrative style abruptly changes from an interesting and accurate factual account to a new and flowery kind of prose, fashioned by the writer to lead the reader convincingly upward to the summit—in five action-packed days. The fanciful text, doubtless conjured up in Brooklyn, abounds in gross inaccuracies and exaggerations. Cook speaks of moraines, when the last ones were far back at Glacier Point; of the sun "settling into the great green expanse beyond the Yukon," when, in September, from their location it set squarely behind the lofty peaks of the Great Gorge. He describes going "from the west to the northern face" while he seems to be climbing McKinley's eastern ridge—and then talks of the ascent by the north ridge, which could not possibly be reached from the Great Gorge by any stretch of the imagination. In fact, Mount McKinley has no north ridge.

The final lyric pages that lead us to the summit are the most incredible of all, for they are illustrated with a beautiful picture, captioned "In the silent glory and snowy wonder of the upper world, 15,400 feet." The spot where this photograph was taken has been located with accuracy—in a small glacial basin 5,000 feet high, about three miles east of Glacier Point, and nearly twenty miles from McKinley's summit.

The sharply focused photograph of Ed Barrill holding the American flag on "the Heaven-scraped granite" of the top, September 16, 1906, proved to be the cause of Cook's eventual downfall. It has now been conclusively established that the picture was actually taken atop one of the tiny granite peaks seen near the right edge of Cook's "15,400-foot" picture. The true summit of McKinley is a small ridge of deep, wind-packed snow, and its approach from the north is a gently inclined snowslope, not a steep, rocky arête. Those who contend that the snow formations have changed over the years since Cook's picture was taken are forgetting that the summit today looks exactly as it did when Hudson Stuck climbed it in 1913, only seven years after Cook's expedition, and when the U.S. Army team made the third ascent in 1942.

Cook's description of the entire descent is handled as if he were running out of paper: "The descent was less difficult, but it took us four days to tumble down to our base camp. . . . The *Bolshoy* descended the river quickly and, taking the scattered parties from the Susitna Station on the next day, we pushed on to Tyonek, and to Kenai, and from there southward by the regular steamers."

Today, more than eighty years later, now that McKinley has been precisely mapped, climbed thousands of times, and photographed on the ground and from the air from every conceivable angle, and Cook's route and pictures scientifically researched, it is easy to see the explorer's duplicity. But such was not the case in 1906. Dr. Cook was one of the founders of the American Alpine Club and a member of the Explorers Club. He had served with competence under Admiral Peary in the arctic and with Roald Amundsen and the Belgians in the antarctic. He had performed a great feat by completely encircling McKinley in 1903. Statements by a man with this background simply were not questioned—at least not in public.

Belmore Browne and Herschel Parker, however, listened to Cook's story with astonishment and incredulity, for one simple reason: to climb McKinley in a thirteen-day round trip from Alder Creek was utterly impossible for two men, one of whom had had minimal climbing experience and the other none at all. But they kept their thoughts to themselves and their close friends, although their doubts were fueled by Barrill's classic remark to Browne as they walked the beach at Seldovia together on the way home: "I can tell you all about the big peaks just south of the mountain, but if you want to know about McKinley, go and ask Cook." And, writes Browne, "I now found myself in an embarrassing position. I knew that Dr. Cook had not climbed Mount McKinley. Barrill had told me so and, in addition, I knew it in the same way that any New Yorker would know that no man could walk from Brooklyn Bridge to Grant's Tomb in ten minutes" (a distance of eight miles).

The blood pressure of those who held these convictions steadily rose as Dr. Cook wrote and lectured on the conquest of McKinley. As he had hoped, the ascent won him the financial backing to make possible an attack on the North Pole, and, by the time that his McKinley book was published, in February 1908, he was already in the Canadian arctic far out of reach.

On September 1, 1909, Cook cabled the Danish government in Copenhagen from the Shetland Islands, announcing his attainment of the North Pole. On arrival in Copenhagen three days later he was greeted by the crown prince of Denmark and entertained by the king. But on September 6, Peary cabled from Labrador that he had reached the Pole, and on September 8 stated that Cook had never been anywhere near it. Of course, hell broke loose, and it has never quieted down to this day.

Overleaf: At center left, Ruth Glacier has carved its way through the Great Gorge. Dr. Cook's "Fake Peak" is indicated by a tiny circle in the center foreground.

Second overleaf: Looking directly up the Great Gorge of Ruth Glacier, this approach to McKinley is the most stunning of all. The glacier in the foreground is about a mile wide and the granite cliffs that flank it are a full vertical mile in height.

Above left: The broad crossroads of the Kahiltna Glacier lie between the rugged end of Mount Hunter's Western Ridge and the shadowed mass of Mount Foraker, across the valley at upper right—a dozen square miles of almost level, slowly moving ice and snow.

Above right: Ruth Glacier's lower gateway is effectively guarded by this array of crevasses where the confines of the Great Gorge end and ice, thousands of feet deep, spreads out across the lower Ruth Valley like a gigantic fan.

Overleaf: A giant lateral moraine forms a barrier between crevassed Ruth Glacier (left) and meandering gravel bars just below the Great Gorge.

Second overleaf: two close-up views of Ruth Glacier

Third overleaf: Huge crevasses, deep new snow, and howling winds created this pattern on the Kahiltna Glacier: each of these holes could swallow a freight car.

Fourth overleaf: Deep snow has been sculpted by hurricane-force winter winds that sweep through Silverthrone Col, eleven miles east of the summit of McKinley.

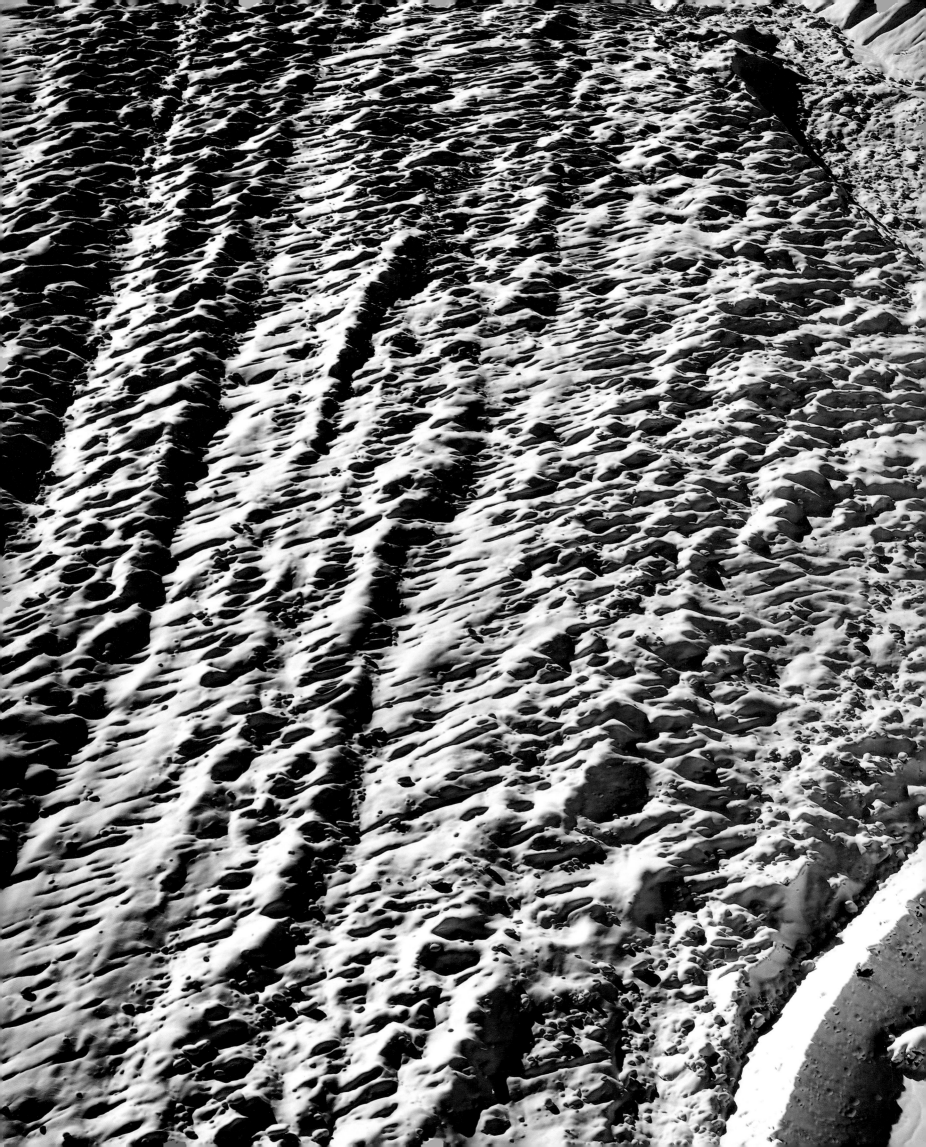

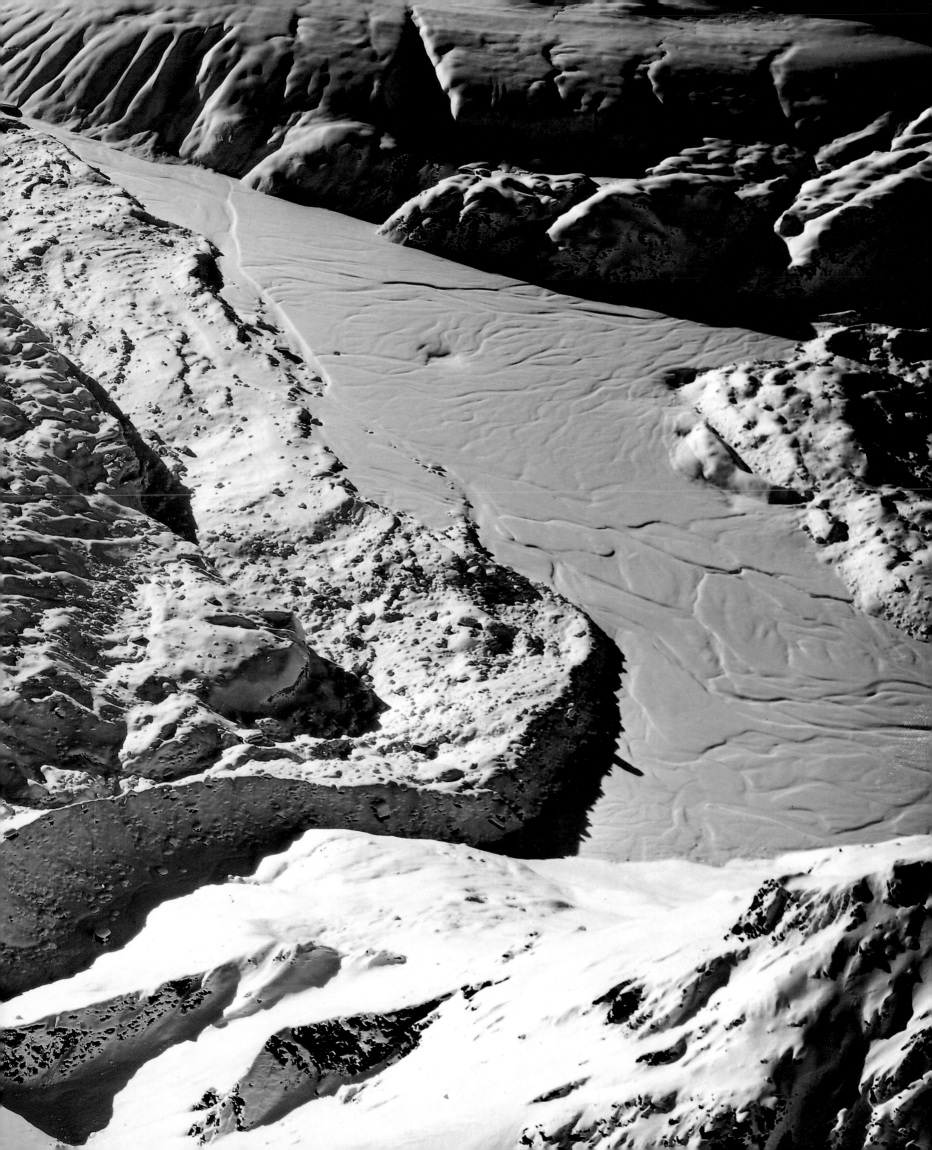

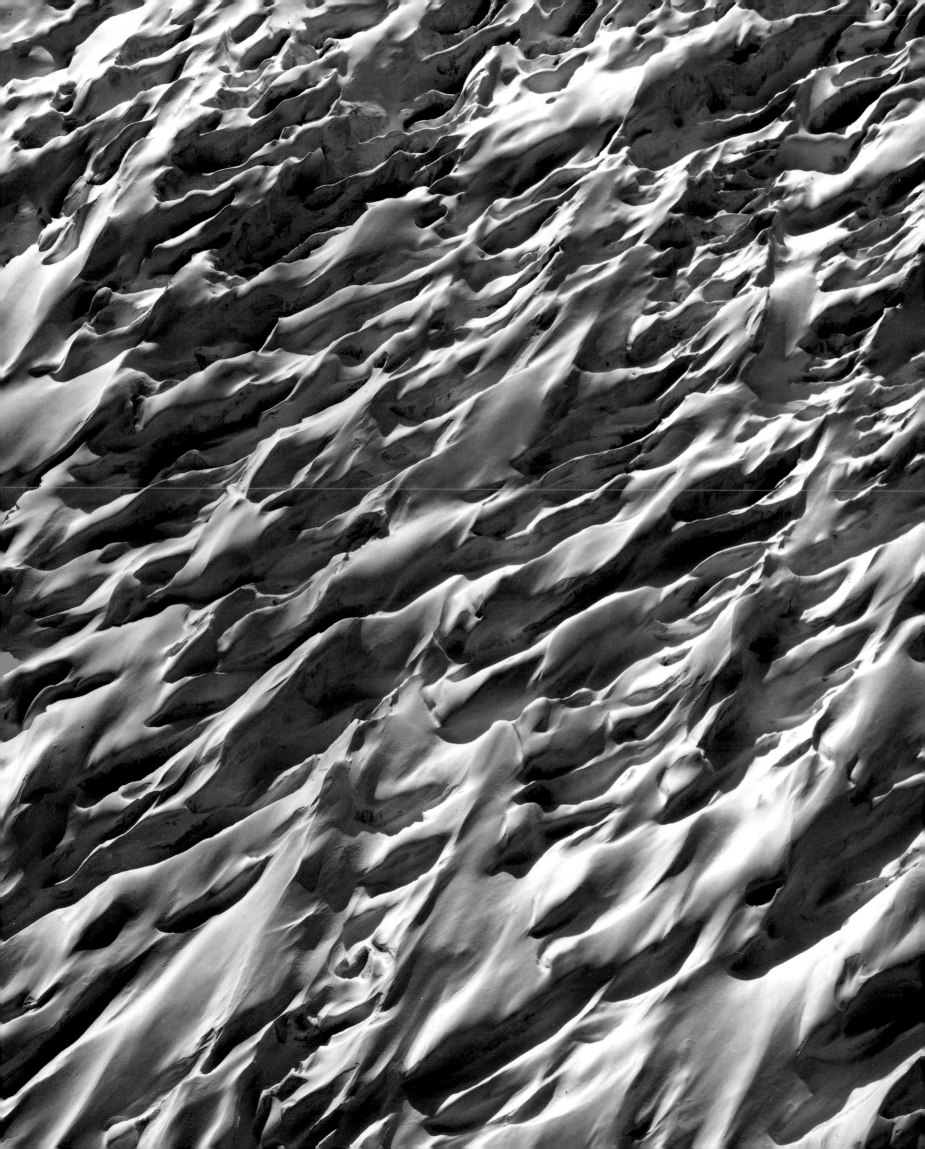

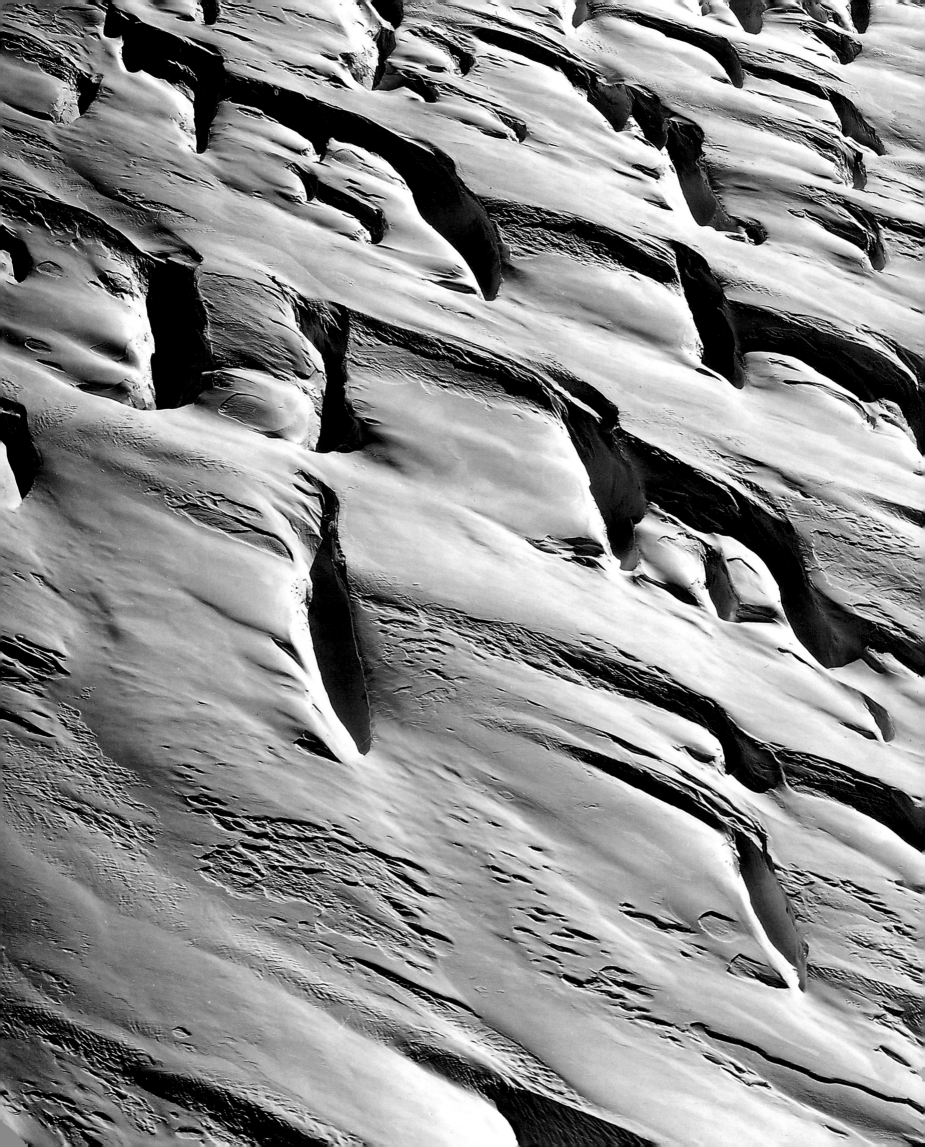

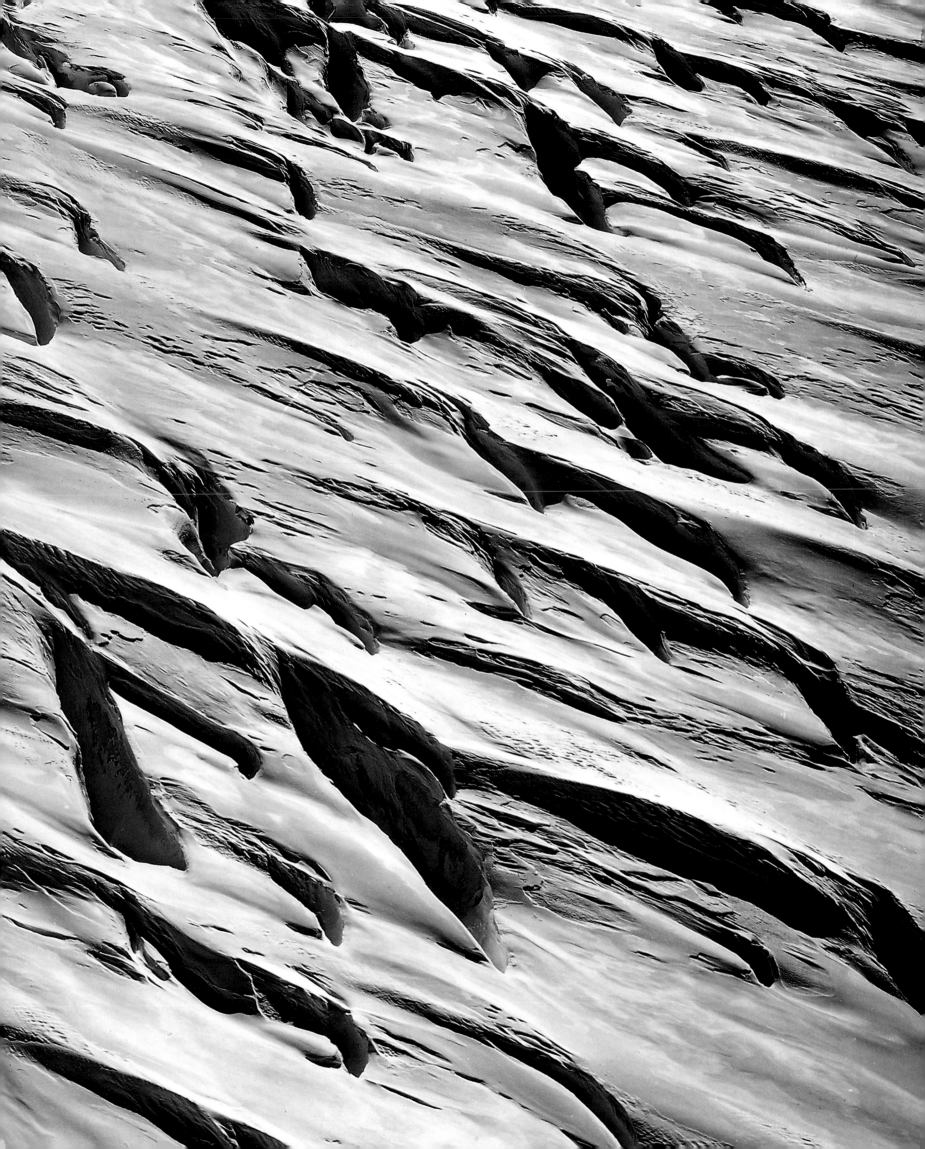

April 10, written on the party's return from McKinley. Nash and Lewis were incredibly tough. They snowshoed far up Cache Creek in search of McGonagall Pass. In fact, they even found the remains of the Sourdoughs' Willow Camp, from which the pass is an easy three-hour hike—but it is neatly hidden by the intersecting ridges south of that spot, and Nash was unable to find it. Frustrated there, the two snowshoed a dozen miles westward, all the way to the Muddy River and decided that its valley was the best way to approach the northeast side of McKinley: it was the same mistake that Judge Wickersham and Cook had made before them.

But Nash and Lewis moved their whole outfit over to the upper edge of timber just below the end of Peters Glacier, backpacking huge loads and assisted somewhat by the three dogs that Phillips had left with them. While Lewis reconnoitered a route up onto McKinley, Nash and Cairns hauled firewood forward by carrying "four or five sticks to a load." Lewis meanwhile dexterously fashioned three small tents out of their big 12-by-14-foot wall tent. They were soon prepared to attack the mountain.

But they never got started. According to reports, Nash thought it would be best if only one man ascended to the mountain camp first, on account of the difficulty of toting up supplies, so, on March 12, camp was pitched among the "white rocky glacier knobs at the face of the great icy spur of McKinley." From this advanced base, Nash explored far up Peters Glacier and simply confirmed the fact already established by Wickersham and Cook, that "it would be absolutely impossible for human beings to climb the north exposure of the mountain, due to overhanging layers of ice reaching at least 100 feet in thickness. These are constantly discharging large sections that go crashing into powder at the foot of vertical walls of rock, a combination of deterrent conditions which would put to naught every device brought to bear against them."

They, therefore, decided to swing to the east, up to what is now known as Gunsight Pass, and attempt McKinley's "Northern Northeast Ridge," which began there. Their plan was to set up a camp at the pass (6,560 feet), then another at 14,000 feet, and from there make a dash to the summit. Firewood and food, however, were running out. Cairns hiked all the way back to the McKinley River "to procure some old cans for packing alcohol" for their stove on the mountain, but while he was there a blizzard halted everything for several days.

When Cairns rejoined his partners at the mountain base camp after the storm, "they had become downcast." Having reconnoitered up the ridge to well over 9,000 feet during moments of decent weather on March 30, the pair had found to their dismay that the route above was blocked by "a group of sawteeth pinnacles"

on its crest. "There was no way of worming around these jagged prongs and no way of going over them." The highest point that they reached was a snowy dome atop the ridge at 9,240 feet, two-and-a-half miles southwest of Gunsight Pass. Here they not only saw that horrible knife-edged ridge ahead but also looked directly down onto Muldrow Glacier, 2,000 feet below them: "We pictured the Parker climbers toiling among the crevasses in the glacier-strewn canyons. All credit to them if they get there!" This entire ridge was not climbed all the way to the top of McKinley's North Peak until 1988. It does not lead to the true summit of the mountain.

That was the end of the *Fairbanks Times* Expedition. "We didn't get there, and that sums it all up. . . . So, down the mountain we started. . . . The return trip was without incident, except that we hated to abandon a lot of perfectly good stuff over on the Muddy." Half-snowblind, they hiked speedily back to Kantishna, where they rested for a couple of days with mining friends. Then they returned to Fairbanks "in six days at an average rate of 26 miles a day."

While the *Times* Expedition was attempting to climb what is now known as McKinley's Pioneer Ridge, exciting things were also happening far to the south of McKinley. Until that time the general public in the East had given little or no thought to Dr. Cook's McKinley claim. But now it was developing into a matter of international interest. Since no one could possibly prove that Cook had reached the precise location of the North Pole in the level arctic wasteland, the relative credibility of what Cook and Peary each said he had done became the only reasonable standard by which to judge their polar claims. Herschel Parker and Belmore Browne were certain that Dr. Cook had lied about his ascent of McKinley: they knew where Cook's "summit" pictures had been taken. They were also certain that there was no "heaven-scraped granite" on top of Mount McKinley. They wanted to take good photographs of the real top—and the way down from it!—and they also still wanted very much to be the first men to reach McKinley's summit.

The North Pole furor in the fall of 1909 now enabled them to finance a new expedition to McKinley with ease. What route would they follow this time? Wickersham and Cook had conclusively shown that the northern and northwestern approaches were very long, and perhaps impossible above 12,000 feet. They knew from their 1910 experiences that an attempt form the southeast made no sense. Brooks, Cook, Sheldon, and Karstens had all believed that the northeastern side offered the greatest hope. Moreover, in 1910 the Sourdough Expedition (if you believed them) had proved that their Muldrow route was feasible—they had just made a terrible mistake and climbed the wrong peak.

So Parker and Browne decided to attempt McKinley again, this time from the northeast. They also knew that others were almost certain to try it soon, so they got a very early start: from Seward, on Alaska's Pacific coast, two hundred miles south of McKinley, on February 1, 1912, when all the rivers were frozen solid and not a single mosquito was in sight. Arthur Aten and Merl LaVoy, their 1910 partners, had already gone ahead and were to haul most of their gear as far as possible up the frozen Susitna and Chulitna and then meet them at Susitna Station—no boats, no swamps, and no horses this time.

Dog-teaming along the route of today's railroad, Parker and Browne rapidly reached the site of Alyeska, then turned northward, away from Turnagain Arm, over Crow Creek Pass and down Eagle River. It was still three years before the railroad tent-camp called Anchorage was to be set up, and this was by far the shortest route to the Susitna. They crossed the frozen Knik River, near today's upper bridge, eighteen days out of Seward, and met La-Voy and Aten at the village of Knik, "a tiny settlement of white men and Indian cabins. George Palmer runs the only store, and there the traveller could purchase all the necessities for a wilderness trip." There the advance team greeted them with good news: they had managed to get all the supplies not only up the Susitna as far as Talkeetna, but onward through the Chulitna Canyon and well past the Tokositna and Ruth glaciers.

At Knik, Parker, Browne, Aten, and LaVoy joined the big dog team that hauled the U.S. mail and made a speedy trip across the lowlands to Susitna Station, at the junction of the Susitna and the Yentna—making the entire trip in a single fifty-five-mile day along the much-used and icy trail.

On February 19, they headed northward up the frozen Susitna, "always passing places that we remembered from our previous trips—now a smooth snowcovered point where a bad rapid had bothered us, or a spruce-covered island where we had camped in the old days. . . . We had at last said the final farewell to civilization, and were dependent on our own resources. . . . The winter silence shut down on us; no sounds but the straining of the dog harness and the rhythmic clicking of our snowshoes broke the absolute silence." Only once did they run into other people—two prospectors, Wells and Coffee, who were freighting supplies to the interior over Broad Pass. They urged Browne, when the party returned to civilization, to tell those folks outside that "we need a railroad and we need it bad!"

The four men continued to move fast, for all their gear was cached far up the river and they were traveling ultra-light. All they had with them, other than food, was "a tiny mountain tent and a frying pan or two." As Browne said, "We were steadily creeping away from the seacoast, and already the still, intense cold was noticeable. The snow was dry and powdery under our snowshoes and steam was rising from men and dogs as we swung along."

The Chulitna Canyon was a pleasure. "In place of the rushing waters of the river, there lay a smooth expanse of untrodden snow." In place of the "sullen roar of the rapids, we now jogged along through an almost oppressive silence. . . . Soon the canyon bluffs fell behind and, towering high in the winter sky, stood Mount McKinley. . . . The Tokosha Mountains, Foraker and Hunter loomed gigantic to the westward—each one by itself a king, but for the overwhelming grandeur of old Bolshaia [the Russian traders name for McKinley]."

At last the four men reached the cache that promised luxury on the trail: a "big tent, stove, axes, bacon, beans, flour, tea, sugar, guns, ammunition." But this all added up to 2,500 pounds and meant much slower sledding and relaying as they headed northward, leaving McKinley farther and farther behind as they searched for a pass across the Alaska Range to the northeast. Their trail worked its way back into a winding canyon again as they followed the ever smaller Chulitna's westerly fork toward its source.

Moving an outfit of that size up the valley would have been impossible without the help of a powerful dog team. "The dogs were splendid animals—hard-working, affectionate and lovable; but among themselves they were savage brutes. Each team was held together by the frail bond of daily companionship and when a fight started, each team would back its favorite to the death. We lost some of our most valuable dogs in these savage fights."

Thirty miles above the Tokositna, however, the party made a serious mistake. Their prospector-friends downriver had told them to follow an "obvious valley to the left," which would take them easily across the range to the Kantishna. But in their eagerness to make that left turn, they forked off the main course of the river too soon, at "a point where the gorge split" and turned directly into the mountains. They should have persevered for another fifteen miles along the Chulitna until it turned sharply northward into the mountains. (This "East Fork" is by far the easiest way to Anderson Pass from the valley of the Chulitna.)

Instead they sledged upward for twenty long miles until their valley (now called Ohio Creek) ended abruptly in a mass of rocky peaks that barred further progress. Miraculously, though, they found a cleft between these peaks at an altitude of nearly 6,000 feet, managed to hand-line their sled and equipment down its steep northern side, and amazingly, emerged in the valley where they should have been, only four miles below Anderson Pass.

This low, 5,400-foot pass, as promised by the prospectors, proved easy to cross. They were now camped at the Great Bend of

Muldrow Glacier and could look directly up it for eighteen miles, all the way to Gunsight Pass. Fresh Dall sheep meat replenished their larder and buoyed their spirits. They could have headed straight for McKinley, then and there, but they wisely felt that the season was still too early and cold for high climbing. They were also eager to have a bit of a rest before returning to the attack, for as Browne described, "the Muldrow Glacier acted as a huge wind-funnel; I have never seen the wind blow with more regularity and fury than it did at our first camp on the northern side of the range." They now detoured downhill to the north, around Muldrow's snout, then westward along the broad valley of the McKinley River toward Wonder Lake and the Kantishna. "We were now in a wilderness paradise . . . Big game was abundant. We were wild with enthusiasm over the beauty of it all."

On April 17, Browne recorded an exciting moment: "Timber! By all the Red Gods! Timber! If anyone ever reads these scrawled lines, I wonder if they will realize what it means to us. First it means success, for we have crossed the Alaska Range 'from wood to wood.' Secondly it means that we have added slightly to the world's geographic knowledge—not an easy thing to do these days. . . . We are in God's country, with the whole majestic sweep of the Alaskan Range towering over us, and culminating in the great, snowy king of mountains, McKinley."

To their astonishment, at the edge of the first spruces they stumbled upon Lloyd's camp, which had in turn just been reoccupied by Ralph Cairns' party. Here was their canvas wall tent, an iron woodstove, plenty of cut wood and fresh, dry shavings ready to make a fire. Although the team didn't realize it, the *Times* party had left this camp only two weeks earlier on their retreat to Fairbanks. Among the treasures they found were copies of the *Times* that Cairns had hoped to carry to the top of McKinley.

Two relatively fresh trails led from their new camp—one northward through the dense spruce timber toward Wonder Lake and Kantishna, the other heading southward. "A careful study of the trail," Browne said later, "convinced me that the men who made it were traveling *from*, and not towards, Mount McKinley." He was right.

The next few days they spent reconnoitering and getting more supplies. Parker and Aten headed off toward Kantishna in search of some staple food that they hoped to buy from the miners who they knew were at work in that general vicinity, only a few miles to the north of their camp. Browne and LaVoy crossed the McKinley River and explored southward into the foothills, not following Cairns' trail, which led southwest and clearly not in the direction of McGonagall Pass. As others had done before, they tried both of the wrong forks of the trident sources of Cache Creek before they finally discovered that the central fork was both the shortest and

the easiest route to Muldrow Glacier, not realizing that it was the one chosen by the experienced Sourdoughs three years before.

On April 24 the team moved all its gear to a new Cache Creek base camp, at 2,600 feet and ten miles to the south of their McKinley River camp. Four days later, the attack on McKinley started in earnest. Their entire outfit now weighed 600 pounds, and in light of what was soon to happen, it is interesting to note exactly what they carried for food and fuel: pemmican (for men), 102 pounds; hardtack (biscuits), 96 pounds; sugar, 30 pounds; raisins, 30 pounds; chocolate, 7½ pounds; dog pemmican, 75 pounds; alcohol (for stoves), 15 gallons.

Aten stayed in the Cache Creek camp while the others headed upward, through McGonagall Pass and along Muldrow Glacier—smooth and cold and marvelous sledding at that time of year. After several close calls, falling into small crevasses, they decided to rope up for every minute of travel along this seemingly innocuous but treacherous glacier.

By May 3 the three climbers had managed to get everything to the base of the Great Icefall, at 8,000 feet above the sea and eight miles above McGonagall Pass. Two blizzards ensued in rapid succession, but the team kept inching their supplies steadily ahead, using the dogs wherever possible and backpacking in the steepest places. Finally they reached the head of Muldrow at nearly 11,000 feet. The nightmare of crossing flimsy snow bridges and constantly falling into unseen crevasses was over, and McKinley towered, incredibly large, directly above them.

On May 7, during another day of bitter cold and wind squalls, they hauled the last dog-team load from the crest of the Great Icefall up the exposed trail to the head of the glacier. There they cached 300 pounds of freight, safely in the middle of the narrow valley, and headed immediately back to base camp battered by ghastly wind, cold, and blowing snow: "For seven hours we struggled against the worst glacier conditions that I have ever experienced. . . . We crept down over six miles of ice and over the whole distance I sounded every foot that we advanced." They were still six miles above McGonagall, "and the driving snow had turned us—men and dogs alike—to dim, white forms." Traveling was getting dangerous, in the midnight twilight, so they bivouacked right where they stopped, dining miserably on two meager hardtack biscuits and one scant ounce of pemmican each.

Back at the Cache Creek camp the next night, they were thrilled by the sight of the first green grass and flowers and running water. "We took the most extravagant delight in our new life, for living on the ice is an unnatural and trying ordeal, and experience does not bring immunity from the dislike of it, as a man must steel himself to every new experience."

For three idyllic weeks they stayed at Cache Creek, reveling in the beauty of the wilderness as the winter finally gave way to spring. They hiked in the foothills, ate sumptuously off fresh sheep and caribou, carefully resting up for the great ordeal that lay ahead. On June 5, almost exactly four months after leaving Seward, the final assault began.

Aten and the dogs went with them as far as the First Icefall. The next morning he headed back for Cache Creek in another blizzard, which pinned down the climbers for three days in their tiny trail tent. When the skies cleared, a tremendous avalanche coursed down the slopes of Mount Tatum, loosened by the 46-degree heat of the afternoon sun. It barely missed their tent, which was enveloped in a massive cloud of snow and ice-dust, reminding them vividly of the great avalanche on the Ruth Glacier two years earlier. They were lucky, and never again camped on the south side of Muldrow.

Two days later they reached their cache, now almost totally buried in the spring snowfalls. Still another blizzard held them here for a day; then they speedily carried their supplies to a camp on the crest of Karstens Ridge, almost exactly where the Sourdoughs had located their tunnel camp three years before. The view was stupendous: a 3,000-foot precipice dropped to the head of Traleika Glacier to the south. Opposite them to the west, across the head of Muldrow, the cliffs and ice slopes of the North Peak and its Pioneer Ridge rose 8,000 feet into the skies, and the 4,000-foot icefall of Harper Glacier tumbled out of the Great Basin in a cataract of blue and green and white ice, as it inched its way over the tawny granite cliffs at the head of the Muldrow valley. Karstens Ridge, the only possible route between this icy Scylla and Charybdis, towered for 3,600 feet straight up above their little tent. "Our breath was taken away by the grandeur of this view. . . . We could not see the depths, for a sea of cold grey clouds rolled ceaselessly one thousand feet below us, and as we stood in awe watching them, a shaft of sunlight stabbed the upper clouds and turned the grey sea to fire." Browne was reminded of the lines of Robert W. Service: "I've stood in some mighty-mouthed hollow that's plumb-full of hush to the brim."

The climb up Karstens Ridge rapidly impressed on them the vast size of McKinley. "It is reared on such a gigantic scale that ice slopes that only look a few hundred feet high may be several thousand!" Climbing the ridge proved a terrible struggle of alternately chopping steps along the airy crest of the ridge and wallowing in the corniced drifts, to move a camp up to the level 12,000-foot shoulder: above this the ridge soared steeply to a sharp granite tower, another 2,500 feet higher. Once at the shoulder camp, they feared that their food and fuel were not sufficient for a task of this ever-increasing magnitude, so down they went again on June 22 to raid the cache at the lower "Col Camp."

"By this time we were awful objects to look at; LaVoy and I were more or less snow-blind from trail-chopping," says Browne, "and our eyes were swollen to slits and ran constantly; we were almost black [from sun and windburn], unshaven, with our lips and noses swollen, cracked and bleeding." They were indeed a sight "to frighten children into the straight and narrow path."

The next day was a tremendous one. Starting from the Col Camp with heavy loads, they climbed past their 12,000-foot camp, up the Coxcomb, and all the way to the foot of the magnificent granite cliff at the top of the ridge (now known as Browne Tower), altitude 14,600 feet. They called it South Gateway Peak because it flanked the entrance of the Grand Basin of Harper Glacier, from which they were certain the summit of McKinley could be reached.

By the night of June 24 they were snugly settled at Browne Tower, having completed the rough haul of all their gear up the last steep slopes of the Coxcomb. Camped there "in the lee of some great granite slabs," they were in "the wildest and most desolate spot imaginable. . . . Below us, all is mist and clouds; it seems as if the earth, thinking we needed her no more, had withdrawn from our lives." The Browne Tower campsite is always like that: lofty, exposed, lonely—and impressive beyond belief. Perched at the very crest of Karstens Ridge, the last thread of connection to the lowlands, a climber is also at the threshold of the vast mysterious valley that leads upward to the summit.

After a two-day tempest at Browne Tower had died down, the men gingerly traversed the steep side-hill snowslope (now called Parker Pass) that leads upward into the Grand Basin, and set up a new camp at 15,000 feet, on the broad, snowy, lower plateau of Harper Glacier.

They were at the gates of victory, but something unusual was happening: none of them could any longer eat their pemmican without suffering terrible abdominal cramps. On the night of June 26, Belmore Browne was deeply concerned: "Pemmican was our staff of life; on it we depended for strength and heat to carry us through the toil and cold of our high climb. Without it we would be reduced to a diet of tea, sugar, raisins and a small allowance of chocolate, which was not enough to keep us warm, let alone furnish fuel for the hardest toil." Maybe they hadn't cooked the pemmican in order to save fuel. In any case, they decided to try cooking it now, and also to push on to one more camp. There they would see if things got better: they *had* to.

But they did not. At 15,500 feet, the temperature was much, much colder—inside their little tent, at ten-thirty on the night of June 26, it was 19 degrees below zero Fahrenheit. The men went to bed with all their clothes on and still slept fitfully, and cold. Down sleeping bags were not a part of mountain outfits in 1912.

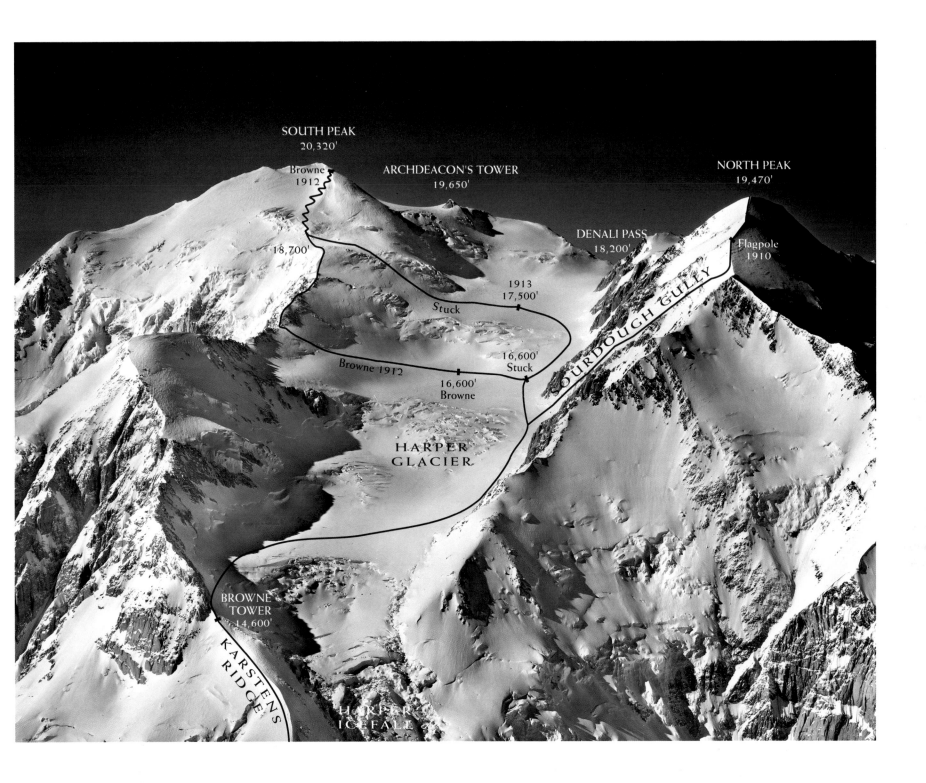

The three early routes to the summit of Mount McKinley.

Somehow the party had to get closer to the top, so their climb would not be too long on that final day. Once more they pushed upward, this time to 16,400 feet, just below the highest icefall in the Grand Basin of Harper Glacier. "We arrived with our last loads after the sun had gone down, and I have never felt such savage cold as the ice-fields sent down to us. . . . On the North the great blue ice slopes led up at an almost unclimbable pitch between the granite buttresses of the Northern Peak. On the South, frozen snowfields swept gently to the rock-dotted skyline" of the ridge "which led in an easy grade to the final or southern summit of the great mountain."

The trio had a frigid time making their last camp and bedded down frozen and exhausted. They felt awful—even cooked, the pemmican was still making them sick. But they slept better that night because the weather was much warmer (only 8 degrees below zero)—a bad omen at that altitude on McKinley, but they didn't realize it.

They took a day of rest on June 28, planning every detail of the next day's summit attack. Browne wrote that nothing but a storm, or that damnable pemmican could stop them now: "We were at last forced to realize that our stomachs could not handle the amount of fat it contained." Pemmican is a compressed ground-up dried mixture of lean meat, often dried fruit, and alas, lots of pure fat. A staple on the sourdough trail through the lowlands, it was eaten by the dog drivers every day in the Yukon. It was a boring diet, the same thing day after day, but it is light and easy to cook, and it works—below 15,000 feet. Up there, however, they had almost reached the altitude where the oxygen supply was half that at sea level, and it takes oxygen to digest fat.

June 29, 1912, dawned cloudless. Up at four, the climbers were off at six. It was cold, but the snow was rock-hard, and they made good time. But as the grade steepened below the crest of the northeast ridge, they began to flounder through deep, loose snow and the going got slower. They stopped for a moment as they passed 18,000 feet and, forgetting the extraordinary ascent of the North Peak by the Sourdoughs, joyfully congratulated each other at breaking the North American altitude record set by the duke of the Abruzzi on Mount Saint Elias fifteen years before. And they marveled for the first time at the magnificence of the view to the south, over the peaks and valleys through which they had struggled in 1906 and 1910. "But the views looking northeastward along the Alaskan Range were even more magnificent."

Finally, the trio passed the last granite ledges on the ridge and emerged onto the 18,700-foot plateau out of which rises the great white snowy summit cone. "It rose as innocently as a tilted, snow-covered tennis court and as we looked it over we grinned with relief—we knew the peak was ours!"

But they now began to pay dearly for those last two warm nights. As they toiled up the summit, the southwest wind slowly but steadily began to pick up. The slope was too steep for the "creepers" they had strapped onto their "dry-tanned" moccasins, and Browne and LaVoy took turns chopping steps—up and up, chop and chop—at 400 feet per hour.

As at last the gallant little team crested the 20,100-foot top of the summit's northern shoulder, there was no more shelter at all, and they emerged onto rock hard, almost level snow. Here, wrote Browne, "I was struck with the full fury of the storm. The breath was driven from my body and I held my axe with stooped shoulders to stand against the gale. . . . As I brushed the frost from my glasses and squinted upward through the stinging snow, I saw a sight that will haunt me to my dying day. *The slope above me was no longer steep!*"

Parker and LaVoy were at a standstill. Browne struggled onward for a few pointless minutes—first staggering, then on his hands and knees. The summit, now only a few hundred yards ahead and only a few feet above them, appeared and disappeared in the vicious waves of wind and blowing snow.

They were almost there, but they could not move another inch.

McKinley had beaten them at the very threshold of victory. Exactly thirty years later a U.S. Army party *strolled* to the top from that spot in twenty easy minutes.

The next day was cloudless and calm—but all three climbers were dead with fatigue and lack of proper nourishment. They were forced to lay over for a twenty-four-hour rest. They were tragically one day out of phase with the weather. On July 1 they made one more desperate attempt, but still another storm hit them, this time at only 19,000 feet. The game was up. They retreated to camp, exhausted, and heartbroken: they had enough food to wait out a half-dozen more days, but they couldn't eat it.

The five-day retreat from McKinley to the lowlands was the darkest experience in Belmore Browne's life, in Parker's, and in LaVoy's. They had conquered McKinley, yet they hadn't made those last few important yards. But in their defeat they may also have been extremely lucky. Just as they reached their base camp and were luxuriating on the warm mossy ground among the first willows of Cache Creek, a tremendous roar arose from the peaks that towered above them to the south. It was the great earthquake of July 6, 1912. Fissures cracked the ground. The men were barely able to stand up. Mount Brooks and McKinley disappeared for an hour in a colossal cloud of avalanche dust. And as the skies cleared and twilight set in, they realized that if they had had good food and waited out that final storm, they would all have perished in those avalanches, and the first ascent of Mount McKinley would have gone unrecorded for history.

Mountaineers have greatly admired Belmore Browne and his gallant companions over the years, not because they set a new altitude record for North America, or for their near-ascent of McKinley—on their own feet up and back, all the way from Seward on the coast—but for the very quality of their undertaking, their daring spirit, their inspiring determination. And the fact that they told the whole simple heartbreaking truth about what actually happened. Even in their tragic defeat, the trio displayed a standard of fairness and nobility that is still applauded by climbers and outdoorsmen throughout the world.

Brad Washburn took this photograph looking north-northeast from the summit of the South Peak (20,320 feet) at 5:15 PM on July 23, 1942. The North Peak (19,470 feet) is at left, two miles away and 850 feet lower than the camera. Bob Bates and Terris Moore are standing precisely where Belmore Browne gave up the ascent in 1912—just above the crest of "Farthing Horn" (the northeast shoulder) and only a 200-yard stroll to the summit in good weather.

81

CHAPTER EIGHT

THE SUMMIT AT LAST

by Bradford Washburn

AFTER ALL THE CREEK CROSSINGS, swamps, mosquitoes, frustration, bickering, lying, contradictions, confusion, and tragedy of the years from 1903 to 1912, the story of the first successful ascent of Mount McKinley is a delightful relief. The party was competent. The best route was chosen. The weather was cooperative. And in the end, there was not the slightest doubt that the summit of the South Peak of Mount McKinley had been reached at last.

Hudson Stuck, archdeacon of the Yukon, then forty-nine years old, had lived and ministered for the Episcopal church throughout central Alaska. He had traveled by riverboat, dog team, and on foot, summer and winter, and was as much at home on the trail as he was at his parish in Nenana. Long before he went to Alaska he had been fascinated by mountaineering. As a youth he had climbed in the hills of Scotland, and as a young man he had made ascents in the Rockies and, when he was older, of Mount Rainier. When he came to Alaska in 1904, he brought all his climbing gear along. For, as he says on the first page of his wonderful book, *The Ascent of Denali*, "again and again, now from one distant elevation and now from another, the splendid vision of the greatest mountain in North America" tempted him: "I would rather climb that mountain than discover the richest gold-mine in Alaska!" For a long time before he climbed Mount McKinley, Stuck had dreamed about the ascent, but his plans did not begin to come into sharp focus until 1911—a year and a half before his expedition actually took place.

The man he picked as his "senior partner" was as superb a climbing leader as could be found anywhere from Fairbanks to Zermatt: Henry Karstens, who was then thirty-two years old. Karstens had ventured to the Klondike at the age of seventeen, meeting his expenses by backpacking gear over the Chilkoot Pass for soft big-city miners. He had mined in Canada and, along with Charlie McGonagall, had inaugurated the first dog-team mail service between Valdez and Fairbanks. He knew McKinley's foothills well, as he and Charlie had also run the mail from Fairbanks to Kantishna at the time of the great gold stampede there in 1906. He had also camped throughout the wilderness north and east of McKinley, summer and winter, in 1906, 1907, and 1908, with Charles Sheldon, the New York naturalist. "With the full vigor of maturity, with all this accumulated experience and the resourcefulness and self-reliance which such experience brings," Stuck said, summing up Harry Karstens, "he had yet an almost juvenile keenness for further adventure which made him admirably suited to this undertaking."

Karstens's right-hand man was Walter Harper, the half-breed son of Arthur Harper of Fort Yukon, one of the foremost of all central Alaska's pioneers. At age twenty-one, the younger Harper had been Stuck's assistant and native interpreter for three years—a dog driver, boatsman, and wilderness camper of great strength and ability. "He took gleefully to high mountaineering, while his kindliness and invincible amiability endeared him to every member of the party."

The fourth and most inexperienced member of the party was Robert Tatum, also just twenty-one years of age, a young minister-in-training who had been in Alaska for only one year. He had dog-teamed on the upper Tanana and surveyed in the summer, and Stuck assigned him the job as expedition cook (although every member of this sort of expedition works as cook or dishwasher at one time or another).

Last but not least were two native youngsters of fourteen or fifteen, Johnny and Esias, who kept the base camp and handled the dog team. They were, according to Stuck, "picked out from the elder boys from the school in Nenana . . . good specimens of mission-bred native youths."

The team's equipment and food were typical for the Alaskan winter trail—tough, simple, and practical. As no crampons or strong ice axes could be bought "outside," they simply had them made by a blacksmith in Fairbanks after the archdeacon's design. All but one of the tents were also made in Fairbanks. Their footgear on the trail was dry-tanned native moccasins with felt insoles and many pairs of heavy woolen socks. On the lower trail and at base camp they cooked with firewood on an iron Yukon stove; up on the mountain, they used a Swedish Primus stove. A luxury never enjoyed on McKinley before were the "down quilts which are superseding fur robes and blankets for winter use because of their lightness and warmth and the small compass into which they may be compressed." Karstens had a huge twenty-five-pound wolf sleeping robe, "of which we were glad enough later on."

Over the course of more than a year these treasures were assembled at the mission in Nenana. In the fall of 1912 Karstens carried most of the gear by boat up the Kantishna and Bearpaw rivers to the head of navigation and cached them safely about sixty miles north of McKinley.

After a busy winter that left them all strong and healthy, the little party headed southwest across the still-frozen lowlands on Saint Patrick's Day, 1913: six men, two sleds, and fourteen dogs. With McKinley's giant profile silhouetted ahead against the clear blue winter sky, they made excellent time along the well-packed trail toward Kantishna. On March 24, the day after Easter, they reached their 3,000-pound cache at the tiny mining town of Diamond City on the Bearpaw, where they bought their dry-tanned moccasins. From there they moved onward, having to divide the huge cache in half and move it forward in relays.

They reached Moose Creek just below Kantishna, then swung southward across the frozen surface of Wonder Lake, enjoying day after day of beautiful cloudless weather, with McKinley always towering ahead of them, ever more impressive as the little party drew nearer and nearer. Once on the McKinley River, two miles south of Wonder Lake, they headed downstream four miles to the mouth of the Clearwater, then swung sharply up its wooded canyon and made their final timber camp there, just at the edge of the last spruces—2,000 feet above sea level and seventeen miles almost due north of McKinley. According to Stuck, this was "the pleasantest camp of the whole excursion."

It took two relays to establish an "advanced base" at the upper forks of Cache Creek, seven miles farther up the valley, at 3,500 feet above the sea. The men next dog-teamed a large supply of dry firewood up to this treeless spot so that their Cache Creek camp would always be warm and comfortable. It would be their last camp on dry land for almost a month. (The stones that held down the sides of their 8-by-10-foot canvas wall tent there are still firmly in place today.)

On April 10 the last freight load was moved up the valley, and the Cache Creek camp was occupied. Stuck paid tribute to those who went before him: "There has been no need to make reconnaissance for routes, since these pioneers blazed the way: there is no other practicable route than the one they discovered." Those who followed Browne, Parker, and LaVoy walked "precisely in their footsteps up as far as the Grand Basin at 16,000 feet, and it is the merest justice that such acknowledgement be made." Every detail of the route was now clear, and this time not a single mistake was made.

Stuck and Karstens's team, unlike Parker and Browne's, did not occupy their camp just to rest and fortify themselves with fresh sheep and caribou meat. They also wisely invested time making their own special brand of McKinley pemmican right on the spot, heeding the lesson taught by the high-altitude food disaster of the year before. "Why should anyone haul canned pemmican hundreds of miles into the greatest game country in the world? We made our own pemmican of the choice parts of this tender, juicy meat and we never lost appetite for it or failed to enjoy and assimilate it. A 50-pound lard can, three-parts filled with water, was set on the stove and kept supplied with joints of meat [caribou and Dall sheep]. As a batch was cooked, we took it out and put more into the same water, removed the flesh from the bones and minced it. [Harry Karstens told me that as much of the fat as possible had been removed and fed to the dogs.] Then melted a can of butter, added pepper and salt to it, and rolled a handful of the minced meat into a ball about as large as a baseball. We made a couple of hundred of such balls and froze them, and they kept perfectly. When all the boiling was done, we put in the hocks of the animals and boiled down the liquor into five pounds of the thickest, richest meat-extract jelly, adding the marrow from the bones. With this pemmican and this extract of caribou, a package of Erbswurst and a cupful of rice, we concocted every night the stew which was our main food in the higher regions."

The respite at Cache Creek camp was used for other important final preparations as well. Stuck was determined to secure a precise altitude reading for McKinley's summit, so they carefully checked their mercury barometer, two aneroids, and boiling-point thermometer. Johnny and Esias completed the hauling up of firewood from timberline on the Clearwater, and Karstens carefully adjusted the team's ice creepers (crampons) to fit the moccasins just bought at Diamond City. They also had to "roughlock" their snowshoes to keep them from slipping backward on the steep lower slopes where the snow is soft and deep. "Roughlocks"—a length of half-inch rope tied at the front of each runner and carefully twisted around it in a spiral to the back—are often used on dogsleds to prevent their getting out of control on steep downhill trails. Snowshoe roughlocks are fashioned of either thick cord wrapped around the edge of the shoe or, if the grade is steeper, such a cord plus a bar of hardwood lashed crosswise under the foot.

One day while all this activity was going on, the men were surprised to hear dogs barking outside. There they found a native man and woman who had traveled over sixty miles, all the way from Minchumina via Kantishna, to have their baby baptized.

After five busy days, all the firewood was hauled, the pemmican was all made, and most of the men's other gear had been dog-teamed or backpacked to the crest of McGonagall Pass, three miles farther up the valley and 2,200 feet above the camp—at an altitude of 5,730 feet. On April 15 the little party said good-bye to Esias, and he headed down the valley alone with the dogs over one hundred miles along the muddy, rapidly deteriorating winter trail, a routine assignment in those exciting days for a fifteen-year-old native boy who had been born and brought up in the heart of Alaska.

SOUTH PEAK
20,320'

NORTH PEAK

EAST
BUTTRESS

MT. FORAKER
17,400'

WICKERSHAM
WALL

PIONEER RIDGE

Dog team
reached here
10,800'

THE
GREAT
ICEFALL

Where Cairns stopped
1912

HILL
OF
CRACK

GUNSIGHT PEAK
7,460'

LOWER
ICEFALL

MULDROW GLACIER

McGONAGALL
MOUNTAIN
6,560'

McGONAGALL
PASS
5,720'

CACHE CREEK

Stuck's base camp
1913 →

BROWNE
TOWER
14,600'

NORTH PEAK

HARPER
ICEFALL

MT. KOVEN

12,200'

11,000'

FLATIRON
SPUR

MT. CARPÉ
12,550'

AVALANCHE
DANGER

Old route
1910, 1912,
1913, 1932

Route since
1947

GREAT
ICEFALL

8,500' campsite
(1947)

PIONEER RIDGE

Left: Cache Creek, McGonagall Pass, and the first route to the summit.

Above: Muldrow Glacier's Great Icefall, showing the climbing routes: the early routes have been abandoned in recent years because of the danger of avalanches from the steep snowslopes of Mount Carpé at the left. This is the most treacherous part of the Muldrow route because of its complex systems of huge crevasses, usually buried deeply beneath a veneer of fresh snow.

The party kept two small sleds and six dogs at base camp to use on the glacier, and the next few days saw feverish activity. Johnny and Walter used the dogs to relay still more supplies up to the cache at McGonagall Pass, and Karstens and Tatum broke and marked five miles of trail up-glacier, right to the foot of the Lower Icefall (6,600 feet). There they set up their first glacier camp, with the magnificent ice-clad cliffs of what is now known as Mount Tatum towering 4,500 feet above them, at the beginning of Muldrow's superb upper canyon.

Johnny and the dogs relayed small sled-loads of firewood and other supplies up to the glacier camp from the McGonagall cache, and the others, led by Karstens and Harper, broke trail over the Lower Icefall, across the dangerous dome of the Hill of Cracks and up to the foot of the Great Icefall, where they made another cache, at 8,000 feet. Trail-breaking here was a complex and often hair-raising job for, as Parker and Browne had discovered, Muldrow's enormous crevasses are one of McKinley's most effective defenses.

Muldrow's Hill of Cracks was so named because of its intricate crisscrossing network of crevasses, which are often almost completely covered with snow.

It took several days of work on snowshoes to prepare a safe, firmly packed trail that the two small dog teams could negotiate safely. Even then, in the steep spots, it took a lot of pushing and hauling by the men as well as the dogs to make any progress. The crevasses were continual challenges. Stuck recalled: "Sometimes a bridge would be found over against one wall of the glacier, and for the next we might have to go clear across to the other wall. Sometimes a block of ice, jammed in the jaws of a crevasse, would make a perfectly safe bridge; sometimes we had nothing upon which to cross save hardened snow." Occasionally they even made bridges in order to avert long detours, "excavating blocks of hard snow with the shovels and building them up from a ledge below."

Muldrow's crevasses have to be seen and grappled with to be believed. "Some of the gaps were narrow, some yawning chasms. Some of them were mere surface-cracks and some gave hundreds of feet of deep blue ice with no bottom visible at all." (A friend of mine once fell through a flimsy layer of snow into an enormous Alaskan crevasse on Peters Glacier. The rope caught him at his shoulders, his legs dangling below in nearly a hundred feet of free air: "I felt like a roofer," he said, "who had just fallen through the dome of St. Peter's in Rome!")

Once "Snowball," their favorite dog, fell through a weak bridge. His harness broke, and he tumbled another twenty feet before he hit a snow-covered ledge. Karstens had to lower Walter on a rope to rescue the dog—scared stiff but unhurt!

This loose surface snow on Muldrow is so deep that an ordinary ice axe is useless in probing ahead for the crevasses. A light pole at least six or eight feet long is more practical. "In bright weather it was often possible to detect the crevasses by a slight depression in the surface or by a faint shadowy difference in tint, but in the half-light of cloudy and misty weather these signs failed, and there was no safety but in the ceaseless prodding of the pole."

The number of hours that the party toiled and the amount of ground they covered is remarkable. One day, for example, Walter worked for twelve hours hauling freight and building bridges, and then he took one of the small sleds and three dogs all the way down to the Cache Creek camp, ten miles away, to spend the night with Johnny, who was taking a day off there. Then he was up again at five in the morning to head right back up the glacier with a load of firewood and willow twigs. These priceless twigs were stuck in the snow beside the trail all the way up the glacier, both to mark the location of the crevasses and to help the climbers find their way along the intricate route in fog or drifting snow.

On Ascension Day, May 1, at nearly 8,000 feet, the noon sun was so hot that it was a day of toil and penance, according to Stuck. "I trudged along all day, panting and sweating through four or five inches of new-fallen snow, while the glare of the sun was terrific. It seemed impossible that, surrounded entirely by ice and snow, with millions of tons of ice underfoot, it *could* be so hot." That day they hauled their first load all the way to the head of Muldrow—over six miles of snowshoeing, pushing, and hauling, and an increase in altitude of 4,000 feet.

On the following afternoon, between two relays, the midway cache at the bottom of the Great Icefall caught fire. Miraculously, the men saw the smoke and rushed down to it, but not in time to prevent a disastrous loss of supplies: "All our sugar was gone, all our powdered milk, all our baking powder, our prunes, raisins and dried apples, most of our tobacco, a case of pilot bread, a sack full of woolen socks and gloves, another sack of photographic films." Fortunately, their high-camp food—the pemmican, Erbswurst, chocolate, tea, and figs—had not yet been hauled up there. But it was a terrible loss, not the least because it stymied the use of the archdeacon's excellent camera. Almost all of the pictures after that had to be taken with Walter's little vest-pocket Kodak on just a half-dozen rolls of film. All because of a carelessly-tossed match after a trail lunch and pipe smoke a few hours before.

On May 3, the party moved everything forward to the head of Muldrow and established their highest dog-supported camp—exactly where Parker and Browne had the year before. It was a long, steep struggle up and over the Great Icefall and then along the seemingly endless snow valley above it. Walter Harper describes it succinctly and powerfully in his tiny diary: "The sun was very hot and we made a slow time doing it. After we pitched the tent we broke up all the boxes we had and put the boards on the snow underneath us to serve as a floor. After this was all done we set to work making a cache of hard snow blocks, putting one on top of another in a shape similar to an igloo. Just as soon as the sun went behind the north ridge of the North Peak of Denali, the thermometer went down to 26 below zero."

Everything now ground to a brief halt as the losses in the fire were carefully weighed and supplies were readied for the ascent of Karstens Ridge to Browne Tower—neither feature, of course, yet named. Having lost all shelter but their big wall tent in the fire, they set to work with characteristic sourdough ingenuity, and sewed two small new tents from the "soiled and torn" sled-cover canvas.

Finally, on May 9, Johnny left for base camp with all six dogs. The archdeacon and Tatum accompanied him down to the first camp to see him safely through the bad crevasses. He was to care for the camp and the dogs until the climbing party returned, in a couple of weeks, they said.

And now the attack on Karstens Ridge began. If the fire had been Disaster Number One, this foray certainly was Disaster Number Two. Instead of being a "steep but practicable snow slope" as Browne had reported, the ridge was a nightmare. Below the 13,000-foot level it was "a jumbled mass of blocks of ice and rock in all manner of positions." And the floor of the glacier beside the bottom of the ridge "was strewn with enormous icebergs." Suddenly it dawned on them: the earthquake of 1912! "What a providential escape these three men, Parker, Browne, and LaVoy had!... Had their food served, they had certainly remained above, and had they remained above their bodies would be there now." What had been an easy climb in 1910 and 1912 turned into a ghastly struggle—nearly three weeks of arduous step-chopping and backpacking along the ridge's shattered remains.

Starting the work on May 11, they were not able to camp up to the level 12,000-foot shoulder until May 25—normally an easy two-day job. (And we must not forget that each time they moved forward at this stage in the climb, they were carrying about 300 pounds of food, fuel, and tentage. Stuck described the process with his usual conciseness: "Put a 40-pound pack on a man's back, with the knowledge that tomorrow he must go down for another and you have mountaineering in Alaska.... It is going down and doing it all over again that is the heartbreaking part of climbing.") It was not until May 30, after a stretch of miserable weather, that the rugged little group negotiated the steepest part of the shattered ridge and finally set up camp at Browne Tower (14,600 feet). Harry Karstens and Walter Harper cut that unbe-

lievable staircase—and that is why it is known today as Karstens Ridge.

At the crest of the ridge their little tent was nestled between the granite blocks just below Browne Tower and, for the first time in over a month, they saw the summit of the South Peak—a lofty silver cone that looked just a stone's throw away, but in reality, was still three miles ahead and over a vertical mile above them. The weather cleared early the next morning and they were speechless at the view—as is everyone who has ever visited that incomparable spot: "We went to sleep in a smother of mist; we had seen nothing as we climbed; we rose to a clear, sparkling day. The clouds were mysteriously rolling away from the lowest depths; the last wisps of vapor were sweeping over the ultimate heights."

Tatum and Harper volunteered to go partway down the ridge and haul up the last of six relays of supplies that were needed to make that camp complete. "So down that dreadful ridge once more the boys went," while Karstens and Stuck broke trail across the steep side hill into the "Grand Basin". Harper described the day: "The wind was so strong that in several places on the narrow ridge I nearly lost my balance with the heavy pack on my back— we had had morning service [it was Sunday] before we went down the ridge, and tonight while we were having our evening service it was so cold that we had to wear our parkas" in the tent.

Browne Tower, though aesthetically breathtaking, is a sort of wind tunnel in a cold chamber. After twenty-four hours there, a climber's one thought is when and how to get out of it—up or down, as fast as possible. At eight the next morning, after a frigid breakfast (down to one teaspoon of sugar each, because of the fire) the four men packed up and headed across Parker Pass for their next camp, at 15,000 feet, halfway across the Lower Plateau of Harper Glacier. For the first time in three weeks they were in the Grand Basin and on level ground, no crevasses to cross and no steps to cut—a huge relief.

After the tent was up, Harry and Walter left the other two men to organize things in camp and headed across to the base of the Sourdough Gully, where there is always an easy way around the huge crevasses of Harper Glacier's Lower Icefall. As they turned the corner and headed straight up the slope, to their amazement, they came upon the tracks of Parker, Browne, and LaVoy, still clearly etched in the ice surface of the windblown crust.

This year, the weather cooperated with the climbers' timetable. After three weeks of snow and fog on the ridge, the skies cleared and stayed clear for one blessed week. "From time to time," Stuck reported, "there were fresh descents of vapor, and even short snowstorms, but there was no general enveloping of the mountain again."

But clear weather on Harper Glacier means *cold*. It was cold even in the sunshine, with a "nipping and an eager air." In clear weather, even in June, when the sun sets behind the breathtaking granite cliffs of the North Peak, the thermometer plunges almost instantly to well below zero. "At night it was always cold, 10 degrees below zero being the highest minimum during our stay in the Grand Basin and 21 degrees below zero our lowest."

The cold in the Grand Basin (now known as Harper Glacier) day and night is always the topic of conversation. The only way to be really warm up there is to be in bed. If you are not in bed, you have to crowd around the stove. As Stuck described: "It was disgraceful overcrowding, but it was warm. The fierce little Primus stove, pumped up to its limit and perfectly consuming its kerosene fuel, shot out its corona of beautiful blue flame and warmed the tight, tiny tent. The Primus stove, burning seven hours on a quart of coal-oil, is a little giant for heat generation."

All the way up the lower part of McKinley a climber longs to overcome the problems of Muldrow Glacier and Karstens Ridge: the Grand Basin is nirvana. It is a stunning and beautiful place. The gentle grade hides all the lower part of the mountain from view. All that one can see are the cliffs of the North Peak, the summit, and the distant lowlands, usually hidden below a sea of glittering clouds. It is a beautiful but lonely place, totally cut off from our regular world—magnificent but brutally stark. And once one is there, a sudden new yearning seems to hit almost everyone—a yearning to get up to the top and back down to the lowlands just as quickly as possible.

The little party capitalized on the superb weather. Stuck and Tatum were beginning to feel the listlessness of high altitude, so Karstens and Harper took charge. On June 3 camp was moved upward about a mile to the gently sloping plateau between the two icefalls—almost exactly the location of Belmore Browne's final camp—at 16,600 feet. Here the North Peak towered directly above them, its vertical cliffs of tawny granite topped with layers of black metamorphic rock, according to Stuck, "as though a gigantic ink-pot had been upset." The photograph of this camp shows it surrounded by huge white blocks of avalanche debris, grim reminders of what would have happened to Parker, Browne, and LaVoy if they had persevered only a few days longer in that normally safe spot.

Then came a moment of great excitement: "We fell to talk about the pioneer climbers of this mountain who claimed to have set a flagstaff near the summit of the North Peak—as to which a great deal of incredulity existed in Alaska. . . . All at once Walter cried out 'I see the flagstaff!' eagerly pointing to the rocky prominence nearest the summit—the summit itself is covered with snow—he added, 'I see it plainly!' " Out came their field glasses

and in no time everyone saw it clearly. The Sourdough ascent of the North Peak was confirmed at last.

Two nights in that magnificent but desolate spot were more than enough. On June 5 they toiled up the last steep crevasseless slope, packed hard as rock by the wind, and set up their little tent slightly above the crest of the Upper Icefall, at 17,400 feet. They were convinced that the 1912 party had camped too far from the top, leaving too long a climb for the final day. Once more avalanche debris surrounded their camp on every side, mute evidence of the terrible force of the earthquake. What devastation that convulsion had wreaked on an otherwise peaceful and gently-contoured scene.

The superb weather held. But, still worried about the magnitude of the final climb, they decided to pack up camp and move it just once more, a bit higher and a little farther toward the middle of the glacier, 2,800 feet below the top, now barely a vertical half-mile to go. "The end of our painful transportation hither was accomplished; we were within one day's climb of the summit, with supplies to besiege. . . . If we had to fight our way step by step and could advance but a couple of hundred feet a day, we were still confident that . . . we could reach the top."

On the night of June 6 it was 21 degrees below zero inside the tent. They only "lay down for a few hours." The combination of cold, altitude, and excitement made sleep impossible. Then, too, they had downed a triumphal banquet of Dall sheep pemmican and lots of half-cooked noodles. Everyone but Walter was sick all night. He "alone was at ease, with digestion and somnolent capabilities proof against any invasion."

June 7, 1913, dawned cloudless. Despite the miseries of their brief rest, they were up at three o'clock—the pink light of the sun just touching the summit cone of McKinley as they started up the final slope. "The sun was shining, but a keen north wind was blowing and the thermometer stood at four below zero. We were a rather sorry company. Karstens still had internal pains; Tatum and I had severe headaches. Walter was put in the lead and in the lead he remained all day."

They circled gently to the east, planning to climb the summit cone by Browne's route—since the direct ascent from camp, though crevasseless, was very, very steep. "Our progress was exceedingly slow. It was bitterly cold, all the morning, toes and fingers were without sensation, kick them and beat them as we would. We were all clad in full winter hand and foot gear—more gear than had sufficed at fifty degrees below zero on the Yukon trail . . . yet until high noon feet were like lumps of iron and fingers were constantly numb. That north wind was cruelly cold, and there is no possible question that cold is felt much more keenly in the thin air of nineteen thousand feet than it is below.

Karstens Ridge, the key to the first ascent of Mount McKinley.

. . . Not until we had stopped for lunch and had drunk the scalding tea from the thermos bottles, did we all begin to have confidence that this day would see the completion of the ascent."

The slope steepened and the snow hardened, packed and re-packed by centuries of hurricane-force winds. Twenty steps, then a rest. Another twenty steps, and another rest. The horizon crept above the top of the North Peak. The grade lessened, then for a short distance became level. A little ridge lay just ahead. Its crest looked like the top. Not quite, but beyond a tiny wind-scoured hollow *was* the final summit drift.

Stuck described the final moments: "With keen excitement we pushed on. Walter, who had been in the lead all day, was the first to scramble up; a native Alaskan, he is the first human being to set foot upon the top of Alaska's great mountain, as he had well earned the lifelong distinction. . . . As soon as wind was recovered, we shook hands all round and a brief prayer of thanksgiving to Almighty God was said, that He had granted us our heart's desire and brought us safely to the top of His great mountain."

Next the instrument-tent went up. The mercury barometer was erected on its little tripod, "the boiling-point apparatus was put together and its candle lighted under the ice which filled its tiny cistern." The temperature stood at 7 degrees—a tropical day for the top of Mount McKinley.

Their work completed, the men allowed themselves to be stunned by the magnitude and magnificence of the view. Stuck recalled: "Never was nobler sight displayed to man. . . . What infinite tangle of mountain ranges filled the whole scene, until gray sky, gray mountain, and gray sea merged in the ultimate distance!" It was 100,000 square miles of Alaska in one incredible sweep. As Robert Tatum said later: "It was like looking out the windows of Heaven!"

Stuck described another feeling, which has been shared by everyone who has stood on that lonely and lofty spot: "Yet the chief impression was not of our connection with the earth so far below, its rivers and its seas, but rather of detachment from it. We seemed alone upon a dead world, as dead as the mountains of the moon. . . . Above us the sky took a blue so deep that none of us had ever gazed upon a midday sky like it before."

The four reached the top at one-thirty—and left at two minutes past three. Just before they headed down, they gathered in a little group and said the *Te Deum* together. Many who have reached and left this wondrous spot over the years, even the toughest and most experienced mountaineers, find tears streaming down their cheeks at the magnificence of it all. Said Stuck: "All the way down, my thoughts were occupied by the glorious scene my eyes had gazed upon and should gaze upon never again." (I have had this infinitely religious experience three times; and each time it touches the depths of one's soul.)

The next morning they started down the mountain. "Perhaps never did men abandon as cheerfully stuff that had been freighted as laboriously as we abandoned our surplus baggage at the eighteen-thousand-foot camp! . . . The Grand Basin was glorious in sunshine, the peaks crystal-clear against a cloudless sky, the huge blocks of ice thrown down by the earthquake and scattered all over the glacier gleamed white in the sunshine, deep blue in the shadow. . . . We wound our way downward, passing campsite after campsite." Browne Tower at 1:30: it was cloudless, *hot*, and there was not a breath of wind. As they plunged over the edge and said good-bye to the Grand Basin, Stuck named the glacier for Walter Harper and his father Arthur, "the pioneer of all Alaskan miners." Harper Glacier, Parker Pass, Browne Tower, and Karstens Ridge—all named by Stuck—names that have remained to this day; all are appropriate, deserved, and perfect.

Karstens Ridge was a nightmare of deep new drifted snow, jumbled blocks of ice, and delicate passages—every vestige of their old trail had disappeared. The climbers finally reached the 11,000-foot camp at 9:30 P.M. "Our hearts filled with thankfulness that the terrible ridge was behind us," Stuck recalled. The next day brought mile after mile of the same deep new snow, which had mostly buried their trail markers. Then came miles of rotten slush, pools of water, and miserable moraine: as Hudson Stuck exclaimed, "the lower stretch of a glacier is an unhandsome sight in summer!"

At last McGonagall Pass, dry land, and tiny flowers: "If a man would know to the utmost the charm of flowers, let him exile himself among the snows of a lofty mountain during fifty days of spring and come down into the first full flush of summer." Soon, exulted Stuck, they had their "hands full of blooms, like schoolgirls on a picnic."

They were two long weeks overdue and worried about little Johnny, alone at camp with the dogs, wondering, worrying, and waiting. But they gave one joyous shout, and he bolted out of the tent. All was well. The first ascent of Mount McKinley had come to a happy end.

Looking southwestward from the top of the South Peak: the South Face plunges nine thousand feet to the Kahiltna Glacier in the left foreground. Mount Foraker rises above the clouds in the background.

Overleaf: McKinley from 40,000 feet, looking eastward up the backbone of the Alaska Range.

Brad Washburn and pilot Estol Call made a flight over McKinley in August 1937 to reveal its magnificence in a violent southwest windstorm. The few flights made before then were in calm, cloudless weather. *Right:* In a later photograph both summits are overwhelmed by a full gale.

Looking west–southwest over McKinley's summit just before a summer thunderstorm with Mount Foraker in the background and Denali Pass at right.

Above: South Peak

Overleaf: Looking southeast across McKinley's summit

Second overleaf: The summit, seen from the air almost exactly over Denali Pass

CHAPTER NINE

NEGLECT, REDISCOVERY, AND TRAGEDY

by David Roberts

THE WHITE HEAT OF EXPLORATION and controversy that had been generated by McKinley for more than a decade suddenly chilled. Since the turn of the century the Alaska Range had been the epicenter of the most intense mountaineering competition the world had yet seen. After Stuck's retreat from the heights in 1913 nobody would set foot on McKinley until 1932.

In the long course of mountaineering history this rejection is unique. After Whymper's victory on the Matterhorn in 1865, not only was the peak climbed by the Italians three days later, but mountaineering throughout the Alps became more and more popular—and this interest has never stopped increasing. Since Everest's first ascent in 1953, the Himalaya have been overwhelmed by expeditions, and official permission from Nepal and China to attempt Everest now must be secured years in advance. Although World War I brought exploration of all kinds to a standstill throughout the world, the 1920s became a fervid decade for alpinism—in the Alps, Canada, and even the Himalaya. The first three attempts on Everest came during these years, bringing climbers to altitudes above 28,000 feet without oxygen, and in the Alps technical standards rose at a dizzying pace.

There are other peculiarities about the early campaign for McKinley. Almost without exception it was waged—appropriately so, given the demands the mountain made—by men who were explorers or prospectors first, climbers second if at all. Among the ten expeditions culminating in Stuck's ascent, there was not a single mountaineer even close to the caliber of the duke of the Abruzzi or his guides, who had made the first ascent of Mount Saint Elias. In an important sense, the main currents of mountaineering would not affect Alaska until the 1930s. The quest for McKinley had owed its impetus to the turn-of-the-century passion for the arctic as much as to anything. And after Peary's apparent success at the North Pole in 1909 and Amundsen's at the South Pole in 1911, the polar passion had died equally quickly. When Shackleton tried to organize a team for his last antarctic expedition in 1914 (the survival ordeal chronicled in his classic book *South*), he had difficulty finding volunteers; only three years earlier, he could have picked his men from the best in the British navy.

There is one other anomaly about McKinley. Despite the scores of months of hazardous toil undergone by even the speediest of the early McKinley expeditions, not one of the teams had suffered a fatality. In fact, there had not been so much as a single incapacitating accident or illness. Any contention that Alaskan mountaineering was a safe business, however, would soon be contradicted. By 1990, the fatality rate for climbers on McKinley stood at far more than that on the Grand Teton or Mount Rainier.

The nineteen years of neglect, ironically, bore witness to the establishment of Mount McKinley National Park (its headquarters in a lowland hollow eighty miles from the mountain) and the construction of the Alaska Railroad, which cuts through the great range to link Fairbanks and Anchorage. For the first time, McKinley was accessible without a month-long overland journey, which until then had presented the greatest barrier to success.

As fortune would have it, when climbers returned to McKinley in 1932, two separate teams arrived at the same time, both wanting to climb the same route—the Muldrow. One used the traditional means of approach, dogsled. The other was boldly innovative: it planned to land on the glacier in an airplane. When the two expeditions learned of each other's designs, they resorted to a highly unusual stratagem: cooperation. Thus the dogsledders hauled 800 pounds of scientific equipment to the Muldrow for the airplane party, which planned to attempt the first high-altitude cosmic-ray observations ever made in the far North.

The ski-equipped dogsled expedition was the brainchild of a wealthy businessman and skiing enthusiast, Alfred E. Lindley of Minneapolis, and of McKinley Park Superintendent Harry Liek. Starting from park headquarters was a vast improvement over mushing all the way from Fairbanks, and the Lindley-Liek party performed its trek every bit as smoothly as Stuck's had done. By the early date of April 20 they were already well established at 11,000 feet on the Muldrow route. Lindley and a Norwegian skiing instructor named Erling Strom, who were experts at the craft, had convinced their teammates to use skis on the lower part of the glacier—another McKinley first. It was Lindley's conviction that the long boards considerably lessened the dangers of crossing Muldrow's enormous crevasses, although at higher windswept elevations the going proved to be much too rough and icy for the practical use of skis.

The party slowed to second gear on knife-edged Karstens Ridge, where the Muldrow route skirts the huge Harper Icefall. On May 7 the entire four-man group stood on top of McKinley, having pulled off a textbook second ascent. They were in such

102

good shape physically and logistically that two days later they also climbed the North Peak. The party reported no sign of the earlier ascents of either summit, but of course both peaks are capped by deep mantles of snow, and the Sourdoughs' flagpole was planted several hundred yards below the top of the North Peak on the opposite side from the Lindley-Liek route of ascent.

While these events were taking place, the vanguard of the cosmic-ray party had safely landed at McGonagall Pass and was well on its way up the mountain. Its leader was a thirty-eight-year-old Bell Laboratories scientist from New York named Allen Carpé. Here at last was an alpinist of the stature of the duke of the Abruzzi: Carpé was, in fact, probably the finest American expeditionary mountaineer of his day. He had climbed extensively in the Alps and the Canadian Rockies, and had led the first ascents of Mount Logan (Canada's highest peak) in 1925, Mount Bona in 1930, and Mount Fairweather in 1931—the last being a major Alaskan peak that was significantly more difficult than the others to climb.

The rest of Carpé's party of five, however, was very weak, and only Theodore Koven, whose credentials consisted of little more than belonging to the Sierra Club, would play any sort of role in advancing the group up the glacier. They too were using skis because Carpé had been most impressed by the speedy way in which his partner on Mount Fairweather, Terris Moore, had performed on them during their approach to the mountain the year before.

Skis had been used in the Alps and the Rockies for years. But the idea of flying in to land on a glacier was quite radical in 1932; it had never been done anywhere in the world before. This fact seemed not at all to bother Joe Crosson, however. Then Alaska's best-known bush pilot, Crosson installed a pair of landing skis on his single-engine Fairchild 71 and put down on the frozen river at Nenana to pick up Carpé, Koven, and Edward Beckwith on April 25, 1932. An hour and a half later, after circling over the Muldrow to give it a good look, Crosson performed the world's first mountain ski-landing, at 5,700 feet, opposite McGonagall Pass. Carpé enthusiastically pumped Crosson's hand; the bush pilot seemed to think the landing routine and promptly lit up a cigar before he climbed back in his plane to return to Fairbanks.

The trio watched as Crosson's big Fairchild lumbered up the valley into the wind. They saw it wobble into the air, then disappear behind a bulge in the glacier. They waited for an all's-well pass on the pilot's way out, but no airplane returned. Fearing the worst, the trio donned skis and started up the Muldrow. After a while they spotted Crosson, snowshoeing downhill toward them. Not having enough power to clear the surrounding ridges, the nervy pilot had made a controlled uphill emergency landing on the smooth glacier, which was still blanketed with winter snow.

The next day, after much pulling and pushing by the assembled forces, Crosson got his airplane into position to take off again. This time he headed down-glacier, as the wind had luckily changed, and he rose speedily into the air. With him was Beckwith, who, it had been decided overnight, should return to Nenana with Crosson, buy some much needed forgotten supplies, and return to the glacier a week later with the last two members of the party, soon due on the train from Seward.

Exactly a week later, Beckwith and his two partners, Nicholas Spadaveccia and Percy Olton, were ready to head for McKinley. But spring was already far advanced in Fairbanks. To find smooth ice for their heavily loaded takeoff, they had to move everything thirty miles out of town to Birch Lake, which was still frozen solid but covered with pools of meltwater. Crosson was also worried about too heavy landings on Muldrow, so this time the party flew to the glacier in two aircraft—the heavy, powerful Fairchild 71 and a light Stearman biplane in which Crosson had made the second flight over McKinley's summit less than a year before. Pilot Jerry Jones flew the small plane with Beckwith as passenger. The other two men and most of the freight went in the Fairchild.

Once more the landings on Muldrow were perfect. Crosson even agreed to fly Beckwith up the glacier to 12,000 feet in order to drop five boxes of supplies to Carpé and Koven, who now occupied an advance camp at the head of Muldrow.

After this virtually flawless start, troubles began. Beckwith soon got a violent case of ptomaine poisoning that time did not cure. The team's progress ground to a halt right at base camp. Without radio nobody could be informed. Spadaveccia started on foot through the slush for help at park headquarters ninety miles away, while Carpé and Koven, frustrated by waiting for the arrival of their companions, started down-glacier to see what was wrong.

At 2:00 A.M. on May 12, Beckwith and Olton were awakened at McGonagall Pass by Lindley's party, which had just descended the Muldrow in a single push through the night. At a frantic daybreak conference, they told the two men of their tragic findings near the head of the glacier.

While high on McKinley, the Lindley-Liek party had heard and seen Crosson's plane as it dropped the supplies to Carpé. On May 11, as they descended to the bottom of Karstens Ridge, they approached a pair of tents obviously pitched by Carpé and Koven. Anticipating a jubilant meeting, the descending party was surprised to find the tents empty. They found Carpé's and Koven's diaries, dated through May 9, and concluded from entries in them that, worried about their three teammates lagging behind, Carpé and Koven had headed down to see what the problem was.

With a feeling of dread, Lindley's team continued its descent. Here and there they found recent ski tracks, but new snow had obliterated most such signs. A mile and a half below the empty tents, the descending team saw a black spot on the trail ahead. As Erling Strom described the discovery:

There in front of us with his face turned down was the body of a man lying in the snow. It was Theodore Koven. He was partly covered with snow, and appeared to have been lying there for several days. A wound in the head and a bad wound in the leg showed that he had fallen into a crevasse. He was not wearing skis. We concluded that these were broken when he fell, that he then had been able to climb out, but on account of loss of blood and exhaustion had not survived very long.

The Lindley party searched fruitlessly for Carpé, then tried to haul Koven's body down the glacier on an empty sled to where an airplane could land. But this is an extremely dangerous part of Muldrow, gutted by enormous crevasses. They had gone only a few hundred yards when Grant Pearson, unroped and pushing the sled, fell forty feet into an enormous snow-covered hole. Miraculously his big pack jammed in the narrowing crack and he dangled there precariously, far above its bottom, until he was rescued by Strom and Lindley.

It was now the gray twilight of arctic night. The descending party held a speedy conference. Koven was dead. There was no sense in risking more lives to evacuate his frozen remains. So they lashed his body securely to the sled and planted it upright in the soft snow—to be found later by a "rescue" party if the body were to be retrieved. Securely tethered all together, the Lindley-Liek team now headed for McGonagall Pass as fast as their exhausted legs could carry them, weaving their way downward through the rat's-nest of crevasses in the Great Icefall. These cracks were "of

such dimensions," wrote Strom, "that a whole railway train might disappear into them."

Lindley's team skied and hiked all the way to park headquarters to sound the alarm. Airplanes on skis took off from the grassy Fairbanks airport, which had been flooded with water by the fire department to make the takeoff possible. One of them broke its axle on landing and was repaired on the Muldrow with dropped parts. The ailing Beckwith was finally flown to safety, and Olton and Spadaveccia walked out through rain and mosquitoes.

Three months later a recovery party, financed by Koven's mother, reached the still-frozen body—located by a mere eight inches of the sled's gee-pole protruding above nearly ten feet of new snow. This retrieval was engineered by Andy Taylor, a tenacious Alaskan sourdough who was a close friend of Carpé, and Merl LaVoy, veteran of the Parker-Browne expeditions of 1910 and 1912. (As they dug out the body, an airplane piloted by Crosson circled above them to scatter the ashes of a wealthy Texan who had wanted to have his remains brought to McKinley.)

Carpé's cosmic-ray data were also recovered and declared to be very useful by Arthur H. Compton, distinguished professor of the California Institute of Technology. Carpé was an excellent photographer as well as a top scientist. Exposed film left in the empty tents was successfully developed. The pictures showed Carpé and Koven skiing unroped up the Muldrow, their camp, Crosson's airdrop, and even an excellent view from the crest of Karstens Ridge.

Carpé's body was never found.

At the close of 1990, 64 climbers had lost their lives on Mount McKinley. Allen Carpé and Theodore Koven were the first in a long and ever growing list. Two beautiful snow peaks that tower above the scene of the accident have been named in their memory.

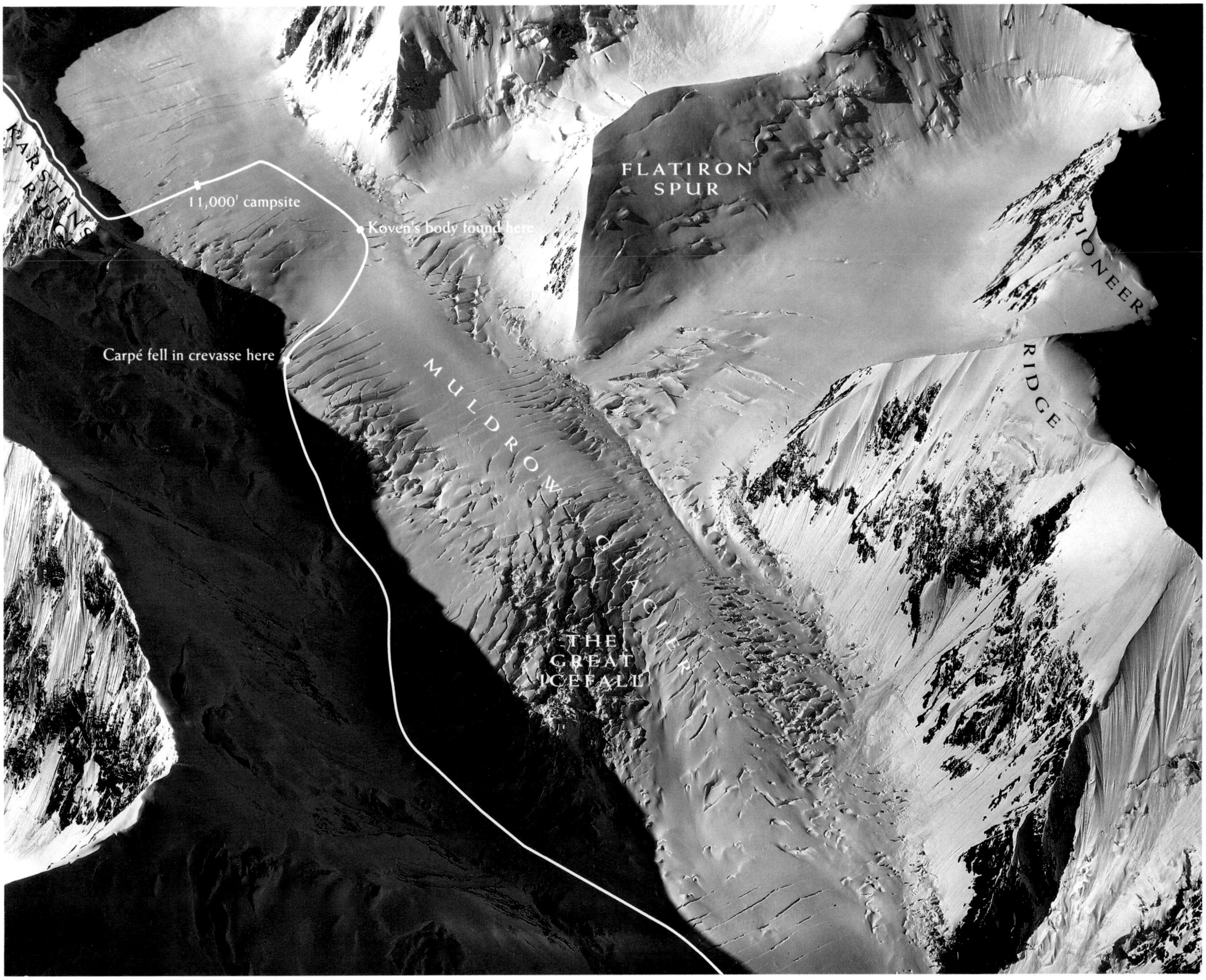
KARSTENS RIDGE
11,000' campsite
Koven's body found here
FLATIRON SPUR
PIONEER RIDGE
Carpé fell in crevasse here
MULDROW GLACIER
THE GREAT ICEFALL

The Upper Icefall and its deceptive array of hidden crevasses lead to the head of Muldrow Glacier and the bottom of Karstens Ridge (extreme upper left): this is where Carpé and Koven met their deaths.

CHAPTER TEN

THE AGE OF WASHBURN

by David Roberts

ONLY TWO YEARS AFTER THE DEATHS of Carpé and Koven the last old-fashioned expedition to a great unclimbed peak in the Alaska Range took place—the ascent of Mount Foraker by a five-man party led by Charles Houston.

Foraker, standing fifteen miles southwest of McKinley, had been known to the natives of the interior as Denali's Wife. At 17,400 feet, it was the highest unclimbed peak in North America and thus a great mountaineering prize. Even when seen from Anchorage, 140 miles away, Foraker is an enormous mass, rivaled only by McKinley and equally impressive in its snowy grandeur.

Charlie Houston, only twenty-one years old, had been a key member of Bradford Washburn's attempt on Mount Crillon in the Alaska Coast Range the year before. Despite his youth he had already made difficult climbs in the Alps and was one of a handful of dynamic young men who were to distinguish themselves in both Alaska and the Himalaya during the decades that lay ahead.

Houston's expedition to Foraker was old-fashioned only in that it used a lengthy overland approach by packtrain. But the Alaska Railroad opened access to McKinley Park station in a day and a half from Anchorage, and the new road across the park from the station now extended southwestward for sixty-six miles. This road, over which Lindley's party had dog-teamed two years before, brought Houston to within thirty-three miles of McKinley at the end of an easy two-hour drive, at roughly the same spot that Parker and Browne had taken seventy-six days to reach in the winter and spring of 1912.

There, on July 3, 1934, the party met Carl Anderson, an Alaskan horsepacker as experienced and affable as Fred Printz had been in the era of Brooks and Herron. Only four days later, after a fifty-mile trek across the tundra, the team was camped at the end of the Foraker Glacier. Not even a good sketch map of the area existed in 1934, so it took them nearly two weeks to reconnoiter a feasible route and reach an advanced camp at the head of the glacier, 6,000 feet high and fifteen miles above the limit of pack-train travel. Houston's powerful team started the real climb, which, in the mild midsummer weather, moved rapidly upward without a hitch.

Houston's experience was augmented by the presence of T. Graham Brown, a Welshman who was at that time, along with Frank Smythe, one of Britain's two most experienced expedition climbers. Two young men, Charlie Storey and Chychele Water-

ston, provided the backpacking punch that kept camps moving steadily upward, and on August 6, after the now familiar struggles with deep fresh snow and fickle Alaskan weather, Houston, Brown, and Waterston stood triumphant on Foraker's domed summit.

In Houston's own words: "We moved slowly but steadily, and it seemed as though nothing could stop us, until I remembered Belmore Browne's famous description of the storm that turned them back within a few hundred feet of the top of McKinley. We had a short piece of step-cutting, crossed another false skyline, kicked steps up some big frost-feathers. Surely we must be on the final skyline! The slope was gentler suddenly, the wind rose, we joined arms and walked onto the summit together!"

Brown found a tiny cluster of frost feathers that seemed a bit higher than everything else and they crowded together on it. "It was fearfully cold and windy. The little thermometer read minus 4 F and it was nearly five in the afternoon. . . . McKinley was incredibly big and had the color of old silk. . . . The whole area south and east of Foraker and McKinley is a wilderness of snow and ice and rock, and I've never seen a more inhospitable land. . . . It looks an impossible country to explore, or at least a difficult and dangerous one."

Four days later, from the same high camp, the team climbed Foraker's South Summit, which dominates the prodigious cliffs and knife-edged ridges that would see extraordinary ascents forty years later. As they paused there, looking down on a "climber's nightmare, a gloomy tumbled waste of ice and rock," they were "literally standing in the sunset which colored all the snow around us a deep red!—McKinley stood out like a ghost in the pale evening light."

The three highest peaks in Alaska had now been climbed—McKinley, Saint Elias, and Foraker—but a whole new age was opened: one of intensive exploration, mapping, scientific research, the ascents of the satellites to these huge mountains, and repeated assaults on ever-more-difficult routes to their summits.

The days of massive logistics and interminable approaches were over, and a new climbing aesthetic lay ahead: going light and going fast, with an increasing dependence on the airplane for airdrops and glacier landings, and on the radio for increased safety and efficiency. But good maps are prodigiously expensive and take years to make. Before these speedy climbs and approaches could become a reality, a new and less costly alternative to the map had to be found—and that need brought a new face onto the McKinley scene, Bradford Washburn of Boston.

While Houston had been climbing Foraker, Washburn, Adams Carter, and Waldo Holcombe had made the first ascent of Mount Crillon, a stubborn and isolated peak on the Alaskan seacoast a hundred miles west of Juneau. In 1936 the *National Geographic* offered Washburn one thousand dollars toward actualizing his scheme for speedy, inexpensive high-altitude aerial photography, with which to explore and record every nook and cranny of the Alaska Range in large format (7 x 9″). Pan American Airways had just initiated scheduled flights to and from Fairbanks during the previous summer, and, using one of their sleek new twin-engined Lockheed Electra aircraft (to be used the next year by Amelia Earhart on her tragic world flight), Washburn made three flights over and around McKinley in July 1936, scru-

A huge wooden film drying drum was set up in Washburn's field photo lab in an abandoned building in Valdez, Alaska. The rolls of Kodak aero film were 120 feet long and 9½″ wide.

Washburn sits in the door of Bob Reeve's Fairchild 71 holding his 50-pound Fairchild K-6 camera. He is roped to the other side of the cabin to keep him from falling out in turbulent air. (Russell Dow)

pulously returning a forty-dollar unspent balance to the *National Geographic* from its thousand-dollar outlay.

Washburn's detailed pictures and others taken on additional flights in 1937 and 1938 laid bare all of the previous mysteries of the intricate inner reaches of the Alaska Range, and established Washburn as the leader of a new group of mountaineers who used air reconnaissance, airdrops, and airplane landings as essential gambits in their wilderness climbs. This system had worked on Crillon in 1934. It also worked for Washburn on 17,000-foot Mount Lucania in 1937, Mount Marcus Baker in 1938, Mount Bertha in 1940, and Mount Hayes in 1941. Here was a string of mountaineering successes that could be said to be unequaled on any continent.

The Lucania expedition perhaps best exemplified the brilliance of this new lightweight style. Bob Reeve, an exceptional bush pilot who flew a ski-equipped plane off the mud flats at Valdez, lifted Washburn and his partner Bob Bates across 250 miles of rough wilderness from Valdez to the 8,500-foot level on the Walsh Glacier, the highest and most remote glacier landing then accomplished in North America. Reeve had an even tougher time getting back into the air than Crosson had had on the Muldrow. His Fairchild 71 was mired for five days in oceans of unanticipated summer slush on the glacier, and he barely got out, by throwing away his tool kit and even his emergency equipment. Reeve refused to bring in Washburn's two additional climbing partners, who were waiting in Valdez for the second flight. Washburn and Bates were trapped in the middle of one of the most complicated wilderness areas on the earth.

The two men made the most intrepid possible response to their plight. They climbed as fast as they could up to the top of 17,150-foot Lucania, making its first ascent; then traversed over 16,644-foot Mount Steele, for its second ascent; and forced their way out across the flooding Donjek River until they reached a trading post on Kluane Lake after a frantic trek of over a hundred miles with no air support. To save weight, Washburn and Bates threw away all unnecessary gear, one of their two sleeping bags, and even cut the floor out of their tent. For the last two days they lived on mushrooms, a rabbit, and a squirrel. By the time they reached Kluane, they were each twenty pounds lighter than they had been the month before. Never before or since has a party whose urgent need was simply survival managed to make a major first ascent along the way.

During these years Washburn first studied, then taught wilderness surveying at Harvard's new Institute of Geographical Exploration, which provided him with the best of modern equipment for mapmaking, aerial photography, and radio. Gradually he refined his aerial technique to produce the unique images of mountain topography for which he would become world famous. He used a series of secondhand Fairchild cameras made deliberately rugged and heavy for military and commercial aerial photography. He would hold these cameras, the lightest of which weighed well over fifty pounds, on his lap and shoot out the opening made by removing the airplane's door, which was left behind at the airport. A pilot himself, Washburn would choreograph his pilots' passes around the mountains he wanted to photograph. The work involved constant exposure to cold and high wind. Usually Washburn operated with a mitten on his windward hand, a glove on the other. To keep from falling out of the airplane, he would tie or chain himself to a structural support behind him in the cabin.

It was not until 1942, however, that Washburn set out to climb McKinley. With ten major expeditions behind him, he had arrived at the ripe old age of thirty-two. He had also become director of the New England Museum of Natural History (now known as Boston's Museum of Science), making him the youngest man in the country to head a major museum. In 1940 he had married Barbara Polk, who has been his partner and companion in almost everything that he has done ever since.

The immediate incentive for the 1942 McKinley expedition was, curiously, the bombing of Pearl Harbor. The office of the U.S. Army Quartermaster General, in something of a panic as World War II approached, had set up a team of experts in the fall of 1941 to help in a frantic program to redesign all of the army's World War I "doughboy-type" gear to meet the needs of an oncoming global conflict that might necessitate U.S. troops' fighting anywhere from the poles to the jungles of the equator. Bob Bates, Terris Moore, Ad Carter, and Washburn, all friends from Alaskan exploits in the thirties, were among the key members of this new McKinley team.

By the time new equipment was designed and ready for production, it was the spring of 1942—too late for winter testing even in the northern states. Although the army trusted the ability of its team, which consisted of experts on mountains, deserts, and jungles from all over America, it still insisted on a hard-boiled field test somewhere. When asked where constant subzero cold could be encountered in North America in midsummer, the experts could nominate only two spots as sure bets: Mount McKinley in Alaska and Mount Logan, the highest peak in Canada. The choice was simple. Logan, though possibly colder than McKinley owing to its geographic position, was ruled out because of its isolation in a remote corner of the Yukon Territory. McKinley, exactly halfway between major military installations in Anchorage and Fairbanks, was selected as the ideal spot for the extraordinary U.S. Army Alaskan Test Expedition.

In terms of the small-party style that Washburn and Moore had perfected, the seventeen-man expedition that went off to Alaska in the summer of 1942 was a veritable circus. It included not only representatives of the United States Army and Air Corps, but also experts from the Canadian Air and Ground Forces. Yet from start to finish, it depended constantly on all the expertise gained during the Alaskan expeditions of the thirties.

By 1937 an eighty-seven-mile dirt road had been completed from McKinley Park headquarters to Wonder Lake, shortening the northern approach to McGonagall Pass to less than twenty miles. It was now a matter of only a two-day hike for the party to reach Muldrow Glacier and set up a huge base camp. The point of the expedition was not to climb but simply to get to a high altitude quickly and to work every day in the extreme cold: to eat special food, to live in new tents and wear special clothing—in short, to use it all and report on what was good and what was bad.

With liberal airdrops to support them, seven team members, including Washburn, Moore, and Bates, made their way as quickly as possible to 17,800 feet, where they set up a research camp, higher on Harper Glacier than either Stuck's or Lindley's camps had been. This was the most powerful and experienced team yet to set foot on McKinley. Most of the high-altitude party spent three continuous weeks above 15,000 feet—far longer than any of their predecessors had stayed. And on July 19 and 20, 1942, all seven of the team performed an almost routine third ascent to the summit of McKinley.

For its combination of wind and low temperature, the upper part of McKinley has been called by more than one expert the coldest place on earth except for the poles. Here Browne's, Stuck's, and Lindley's parties had fought grimly just to hold their own. One of Washburn's main hopes was to come back with really good pictures of and from the summit. Stuck's only picture of the top had been a triple exposure; Lindley, too, had failed to get a good shot. With six years' experience photographing out the open door of a plane and a decade of securing good pictures on climbs, Washburn had no trouble getting his photographs this time, on an almost cloudless and windless afternoon. His summit picture, published soon in the *American Alpine Journal*, made it obvious to all who cared to know that the top of McKinley looks nothing at all like the place where Frederick Cook had photographed Edward Barrill holding the American flag.

Washburn and his friends were as usual in terrific shape that summer. In one fifteen-hour push, he and Moore, both carrying sixty-pound packs of tested equipment, descended from 17,800 feet to 5,700 feet at McGonagall Pass, covering the entire fifteen miles of the Muldrow route in a single dash. This was a feat that few are likely to repeat, as was the almost ridiculous experience, one morning at the high camp, of hearing Colonel Marchman, their commanding officer, address the party by radio from base camp with the order: "Mount McKinley will be climbed today!"

Five years later, in 1947, Washburn returned to McKinley, again with what was for him an uncharacteristically large party of seventeen. The impetus came this time not from the army but from RKO Radio Pictures, which was planning to make a movie called *The White Tower*, based on James Ramsey Ullman's melodramatic mountaineering novel. The movie would be made in the Alps, but RKO wanted to shoot several thousand feet of "background film" in much bigger and more impressive scenery than could be found anywhere in Switzerland. RKO persuaded the trustees of Boston's Museum of Science to cosponsor this expedition—provided that RKO paid the entire bill. The movie studio also agreed to fund a broad scientific program. This included cosmic-ray observations, geologic collecting, surveying, weather and glacier-motion studies, as well as further testing of equipment for the military.

The 1942 U.S. Army equipment-testing team rests briefly at Browne Tower. The South Peak looks deceptively near, but is still three and a half miles away and nearly 6,000 feet higher.

The party included George Browne, Belmore's son, who was eager to settle an old family feud with McKinley; Bob Craig of Aspen, who in 1982 would lead an expedition to Everest; Grant Pearson, the McKinley Park ranger who had reached the summit in 1932 with Lindley, Liek, and Strom; Capt. Bill Hackett, who represented the Army; Jim Gale of the Air Force; and Barbara Washburn, who thus had the opportunity to become the first woman to climb McKinley.

A complex airlift transported most of the party in a single hop from Anchorage to the Muldrow Glacier in March, while another small contingent traveled by dogsled from park headquarters. As the group worked its way up the Muldrow, Pearson and Washburn agreed that the crevasses were much worse than they had been in either 1932 or 1942. The team had two deep falls into these huge holes but no injuries. For the first time a McKinley party relied heavily on igloos rather than tents for high camps. "They were wonderful," Washburn wrote later. "They did not flap in a gusty wind. They did not have to be dug out after a heavy snowfall.

Almost best of all, they were up for weeks. They were cozy little motels as long as the weather stayed cold." On a very cold night, the party learned, the temperature in a tent would drop to minus 20 degrees F., while the temperature in a neighboring igloo with two men sleeping in it would stay just below freezing.

Washburn has always had a great talent for logistics. In 1947 he managed to get reliable support from Earl Norris and his dog team all the way to 11,000 feet. He was also confident in the ability of the Air Force's Tenth Rescue Squadron to airdrop five large cartons of food on the wind-packed snow of Harper Glacier, just below the 18,000-foot Denali Pass, to be retrieved three weeks later by the advance team of the party. Marked aerial photographs taken in 1942 showed the fliers exactly where to locate the drop.

The vanguard of the party reached Browne Tower at 14,600 feet on May 16, climbing the last 2,500 feet "in dense, impenetrable fog." Above Browne Tower "the weather became perpetually fierce" and the party broke up into three units. Seven men remained at 11,000 feet, Barbara Washburn and two companions stayed at the Tower, and Brad Washburn and Gale pushed upward in an effort to get a foothold in Denali Pass. On May 17 a furious nine-day storm set in. The wind was so savage at an emergency igloo occupied by Washburn and Gale at 16,500 feet that "a 60-pound pack was blown a hundred yards down the hill" and the men at 11,000 feet "held onto the cooktent to keep it in place."

The wind and cold were constant and debilitating. Building the 16,500-foot igloo in a full gale at zero degrees F. was, Washburn would report, "as unpleasant an afternoon as I have ever experienced." Between April 10 and June 30 there were only five days "on which the summit could possibly have been attained with any degree of enjoyment." Once, as they sat out winds of 100 mph, the climbers talked by radio with park headquarters, where, they learned, there was a "heavy warm rain and buds coming out on the trees."

In a brief lull, Washburn and Gale managed to reach Denali Pass and locate four of the five cartons of rations that had been dropped from a B-17 on the windswept surface of Harper Glacier. They pitched a tent there, and the storm descended upon them with renewed fury: "Just talked to Barbara on the radio and she says their camp is half blown away with wildest winds to date."

In early June the weather lulled for three days, and the entire team moved speedily upward to the frigid "beachhead" at Denali Pass. On June 6 they seized another brief break in the weather to go to the top. Eight members made it, including Barbara Washburn, but everyone was saddened when Grant Pearson, worried by a misbehaving heart, decided to turn back just above 19,000 feet. On the summit it was 20 below zero with a stiff southeast wind, but just as he had insisted on getting good pictures there five years before, Washburn now set up a bone-chilling survey station to measure angles for the map of McKinley that he had decided to make. It took his fingers two hours to rewarm after working for fifteen minutes on the steel tangent-screws of his theodolite.

The next day dawned cloudless and calm. "Fortified by a monstrous breakfast of frozen Bird's-Eye mixed fresh fruit, oatmeal, bacon and coffee," the team climbed the North Peak and again put up a survey station, this time in the uncanny stillness of a day without the slightest breath of wind. In forty-eight hours Barbara Washburn had become the first woman to climb both peaks of McKinley, and her husband the first man to climb them twice.

The skillful parachute team of the Tenth Rescue Squadron kept dropping supplies near Denali Pass to equip the party during its stay. In addition to fuel and fresh frozen fruit and vegetables, they sent down an 800-pound pre-fab plywood cosmic-ray lab and quantities of the latest army cold-weather gear for testing. Washburn, however, vehemently vetoed the drop of one item that RKO wanted to have parachuted to the highest camp and photographed on the summit: a full-color, life-size dummy of Rita Hayworth dressed in an exceedingly scanty bathing suit.

The 1947 expedition spent an unprecedented ninety days on McKinley, many of them in the high Harper valley between the North and South summits. The prolonged camping in cold and thin air could well have frayed everyone's nerves to the breaking point. But Washburn later reported the expedition as "one of the most perfect social experiences I have ever had in the mountains." Nearly all the party's goals were accomplished. Among the many scientific projects, only the glacier-motion study had to be scrapped, after an initial finding that the Muldrow, even in its steepest part, was advancing only fifteen inches a day—too little for the planned hourly motion experiments.

Shortly afterward, the fifth and sixth ascents of McKinley were made, also by the Muldrow route. Meanwhile, Washburn's aerial photography had become a serious occupation, and in his many flights around the mountain he was always on the lookout for new routes. Already in the 1947 American Alpine Journal, he had proposed two alternatives to the old Muldrow line of attack: one up Wickersham Wall, first tried by the judge himself in 1903, the other via the West Buttress on the other side of the mountain, which could be seen in its entirety only from an airplane. "Both routes," he closed the article, "are magnificent climbs that represent a real challenge to the mountaineers of America."

Not surprisingly, the first person to respond to one of these challenges was Washburn himself, who joined his three-man party with a five-man Denver team in 1951. Half the group reached the mountain from Wonder Lake by packtrain, making the first ascent of Peters Dome on the way. The other four, including Washburn, landed by skiplane at 7,650 feet on the Kahiltna Glacier. Their pilot was none other than Terris Moore, who had by then become president of the University of Alaska as well as a top bush pilot. A few days later, Moore made a landing at 10,000-foot Kahiltna Pass to set a new altitude record for Alaska. (In subsequent years, by landing on the summits of Mounts Wrangell and Sanford, Moore would push his own record up first to 14,160 feet and then to 16,240 feet.)

While waiting for the Denver group to arrive from Wonder Lake, Washburn and his old partners Jim Gale and Bill Hackett carried out precise surveying observations from the nearby summit of 12,500-foot Kahiltna Dome, making its first ascent easily in the process. Year by year new data were being gathered that would finally make possible Washburn's beautiful 1960 map of McKinley.

With his usual determination, Washburn led the party up the West Buttress. He was, in effect, following his own dotted line— the one he had drawn on the photo published four years earlier. Never before had a major new route anywhere in the world been entirely reconnoitered from the air rather than on land. The only climbing difficulty lay in a steep ice slope between 15,000 feet and the top of the West Buttress proper. Here the party had to hack an 800-foot staircase in exceptionally hard ice, then make the slope safe for backpacking with a strong fixed handline.

A cozy igloo was built by Washburn, Gale, and Hackett on July 9 atop a broad snow shelf at 17,200 feet. July 10 was supposed to be a day of rest, but the weather was so beautiful that the three couldn't resist an immediate attempt on the summit. The going proved to be even better than their highest hopes. Reaching Denali Pass at noon in only two hours, they located their old cache of four years before, then pressed on up the ridge, deliberately taking their time so that a cloud cap would dissipate by the time they reached the top in late afternoon. It did, and despite a frigid gusty wind, they marveled once more at the staggering magnificence of the view. Both Washburn and Gale later admitted that tears had streamed down their cheeks as they left the summit, knowing that it was unlikely that they would ever be there again. That night, before the descent, they feasted on still-frozen delicacies left at Denali Pass in 1947.

Never one to exaggerate his own deeds, Washburn declared in print that the new route was safer, shorter, easier, and warmer than the Muldrow route, and he recommended it to future parties. In 1951, however, it was impossible for him to imagine just how popular the West Buttress would become. Four decades later nearly six hundred climbers, most of them landed by skiplane on the Kahiltna, crowded up it to McKinley's summit in a single summer.

Far left: Norman Bright is dwarfed beneath a huge ice-block just east of Silverthrone Col. Striations of annual brief summer thaws and deep winter snows mark this block like the rings of a tree.

Left: Jake Stalker looks out from Mount Deception's ice cascade.

Above: Two members of an Air Force accident investigating team take a brief rest in the shelter of a gigantic cornice on the shoulder of Mount Deception; November 1944.

Above: The forbidding, avalanche-swept North Wall of Mount Carpé towers a vertical mile above climbers as they rest on the 7,500-foot plateau of Muldrow Glacier.

Top right: Grant Pearson and Jim Gale carefully test a bridge across one of Muldrow Glacier's snow-filled crevasses.

Bottom right: Earl Norris and his powerful team haul a load over the crest of Muldrow's lower Icefall.

Above, and at right: The contorted ice-blocks of Mount Carpé overshadow the camp at 8,500 feet on a snow shelf halfway up Muldrow Glacier's Great Icefall; April 1947. To the right of the camp, a dog team starts up the steep upper part of the icefall with a light load of supplies bound for the expedition's advance camp at the head of Muldrow, still two miles ahead and 10,800 feet high.

Opposite: Barbara Washburn looks over a precipice that drops 4,000 feet to the head of Muldrow Glacier from the camp at Browne Tower (14,600 feet) at the top of Karstens Ridge. Great clouds of the late May thaw hide the lowlands to the north.

Left: Brad and Barbara Washburn rejoice atop the South Peak; June 6, 1947.

Below: The highest survey station ever occupied in North America. Brad Washburn sights the angle downward to the top of the North Peak as Shorty Lange records the figures.

Jim Gale and Hugo Victoreen build a perfect igloo just east of Denali Pass. The summit rises two thousand feet above them at the head of the Grand Basin.

Overleaf: The West Face of Mount McKinley on a glorious summer day; note the foot trail.

Terris Moore stands beside his special Super Cub 150 fitted with ski wheels. When this photograph was made, June 25, 1951, this was the highest airplane landing ever made in Alaska. The place is the 10,000-foot Kahiltna Pass advanced base camp of the West Buttress mapping expedition.

Bill Hackett gingerly tests a huge cornice near Kahiltna Pass to look down for the first time on the upper reaches of Peters Glacier; June 1951.

Overleaf: McKinley's West Buttress (left) and the extraordinary snow shelf (right center) where Don Sheldon made his rescue landing in June 1960

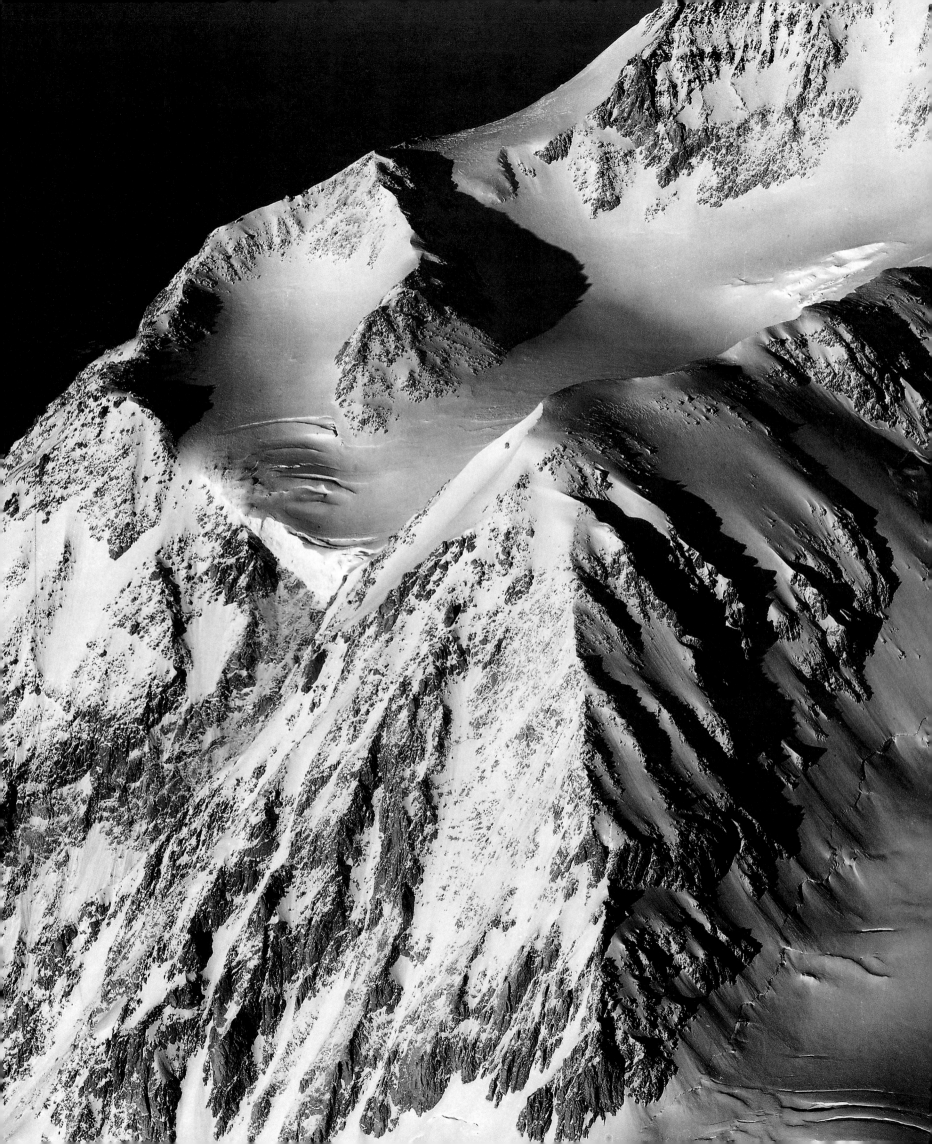

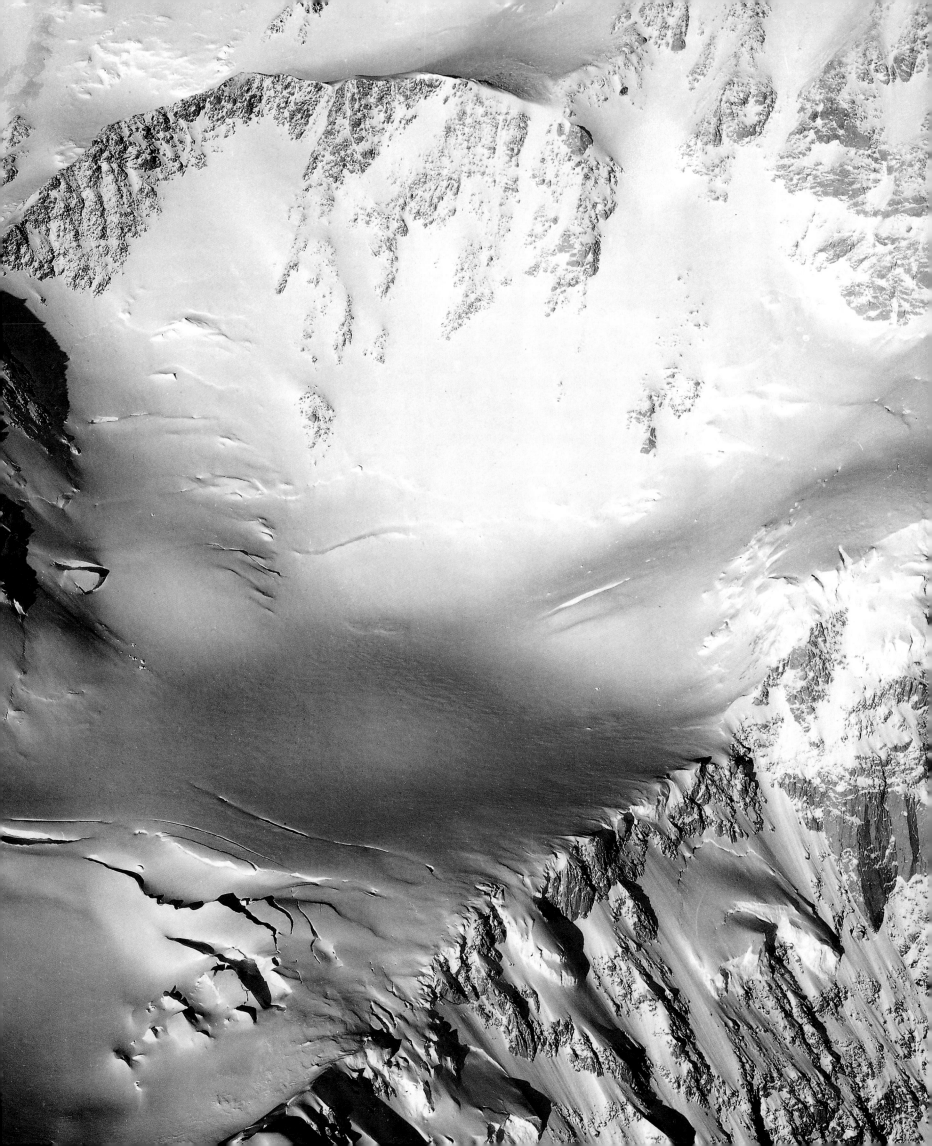

Left: Bill Hackett and Jim Gale approach the 18,000-foot level on the first ascent of the West Buttress of McKinley; July 10, 1951. The snow pass above the climbers is 18,200-foot Denali Pass, still half an hour from the climbers. The black crags of the North Peak tower to the left. McKinley's summit is hidden far above and to the right.

Above: The summit of Mount McKinley from the northwest: Denali Pass is the snow collar at center and the snowy 17,200-foot plateau of the West Buttress lies in the foreground. The thrilling events of the first winter ascent of McKinley took place in this lofty and exposed spot.

129

At 4:45 P.M., July 10, 1951, Jim Gale and Bill Hackett approach the summit of Mount McKinley to conclude the first ascent of the West Buttress. The scale is, as usual, deceiving: the top is still nearly a quarter of a mile away. The steep slope of rock and ice at the right drops 9,000 feet to the East Fork of the Kahiltna Glacier.

July 10, 1951: 5:30 P.M. Hackett and Gale atop McKinley. This was the sixth ascent of the peak and the first over the West Buttress. Washburn recalls that it was a beautiful evening, "temperature just below zero, wind from the west at about fifteen miles an hour, and a view that none of us will ever forget."

Overleaf: July 10, 1951: The view from the top, looking southward across Mount Hunter and the winding 33-mile course of Kahiltna Glacier.

THE LEGACY OF WASHBURN

by David Roberts

BY THE TIME HE CAME OFF MCKINLEY in 1951, Bradford Washburn was forty-one years old. He had focused a very large part of his adult life on Alaskan exploration and the testing of new techniques in exploratory mountaineering, cartography, and photography. In his future were many more wilderness ventures, including no fewer than eighteen to the Alaska Range to complete his map and to intensify his aerial photographic studies of McKinley and its approaches. But the West Buttress expedition was his last with mountaineering as its chief aim.

Not that Washburn would ever settle comfortably into an easy chair. As climbing itself became less important to him, he transferred most of his enthusiasm to Boston's Museum of Science, where his full-time responsibilities as director were growing in direct proportion to the institution's emergence as one of the great American teaching museums. In 1960 his map of McKinley, one of the most precise and beautiful wilderness charts ever published, was printed in Switzerland. Although Washburn tends to regard his photography as of primarily scientific or documentary interest, over the years its reputation has grown as a body of work of considerable aesthetic value. In 1983 the magazine *American Photographer* honored it with a full-length profile, as did New York's International Center of Photography with an exhibition. Washburn photographs are also in the collections of New York's Museum of Modern Art, Tucson's Center for Creative Photography, and George Eastman House in Rochester, New York..

From a mountaineering point of view, Washburn's significance has continued to be profound. Many a great climber, when he finally takes off his boots, adopts a suspicious and defensive attitude toward the younger generation. He dismisses their exploits as the folly of daredevils who hold life cheap; secretly he hopes they will fail when they set out to repeat or surpass his own climbs. Washburn, to the contrary, has done everything he could to broadcast his unmatched knowledge of fine Alaska routes waiting to be climbed. Even more important, he anticipated the dramatic rise in difficulty that would soon find mountaineers attempting walls and ridges his own generation had regarded as impossible or too dangerous to attempt. He himself was often the first proponent of climbs on which, traditionally, only the young and crazy would have set their sights.

I still vividly remember the first time I met Washburn. It was an evening at his house in Cambridge in February 1963; he had invited seven of us Harvard boys over to discuss new routes on McKinley. Our ambitions were fairly modest, but Washburn brushed aside our demurrals and urged on us a "line" he had scouted from the air that went straight up the east-central section of McKinley's 14,000-foot Wickersham Wall. He slapped down a pair of his exquisite photos and a stereo viewer and invited us to look. At first, he was the only person in the room who believed we were up to the challenge of the route. Gradually his enthusiasm rubbed off onto us, and the climb that had been a dream of many years for him became a reality for us.

Between 1954 and 1963 nine great new routes were climbed on McKinley. Those nine lines did not exhaust the possibilities on the mountain, but in the two decades since 1963 climbers managed to add relatively little in the way of genuinely original pathways. Writing in 1983 in the British journal *Mountain*, Ben Read observed: "During the last five years, three new routes have been put up on Denali. They are good routes; alone on the respective faces they would be great. But like the sometime brilliant variations described in the three volume guide to Chamonix (the *Guide Vallot*), the recent lines are eclipsed by the stature that clings to their predecessors."

Every one of the nine new routes was first proposed by Washburn. At regular intervals of two or three years, the *American Alpine Journal* would publish his articles with such titles as "Challenges in Alaska and the Yukon." Climbers all over the world have written to Boston's Museum of Science requesting photos and suggestions for new routes; Washburn has given unstintingly of both. His landmark article in the 1956/7 edition of the Swiss anthology *The Mountain World* was solely responsible for arousing the Alaskan interests of some of the best European climbers. Washburn has often said that the joy he gets vicariously from seeing others succeed on difficult new routes he'd discovered during stereo-study of his aerial photographs was almost as great as if he'd done the climbs himself.

The first of these new routes was McKinley's South Buttress, a long and complicated but technically moderate route that had been the way Belmore Browne had hoped to climb McKinley after his penetration to the very head of the Ruth Glacier in 1910. In 1954, it was the goal of a well-organized party of four young Alaskans led by McKinley Park ranger Elton Thayer. In April, with a heavy snow cover still on the ground, the group started on snowshoes from a whistlestop called Curry on the Alaska Railroad. Ginny Wood, a first-rate pilot and the wife of one of the men in the party, airdropped supplies to them after they had covered the fifty miles to Ruth Glacier's Sheldon Amphitheatre—fifteen miles from McKinley's summit and 5,000 feet above the sea. From there they relayed supplies for another ten miles up the Ruth's winding upper canyon to its head at 10,000 feet, Parker and Browne's limit in 1910.

The biggest problem with the South Buttress is its tremendous length and the fact that eight miles of the route lie higher than 15,000 feet. All the hard climbing lies in the middle of the route, so that a huge amount of supplies must be backpacked up difficult terrain just to put a party in position to go for the summit. Compounding this logistical challenge was the Thayer group's intention to descend by the Muldrow route and thereby complete the first *traverse* of McKinley. Only one of the party had ever been on McKinley before—Morton Wood, Ginny's husband. Fortunately, he had been on the Muldrow and knew the mountain's approaches from Wonder Lake.

The four Alaskans, who had become very fit, managed to cut their way rapidly up the icy defenses of the South Buttress. On May 14, after deftly circling McKinley's massive cone so that they could attack it from the northeast, they made their final camp at 17,000 feet. The next day was superb, and they reached the summit, following almost precisely in the footsteps of Belmore Browne's final 1912 attempt. They had been up high for so long that they had no problem with altitude. The next day they started down the Muldrow route.

It is a particularly trying experience to descend a route that you have not climbed up. Even if you've climbed it before, without a beaten trail to follow if the weather sours and lack of knowledge of current snow conditions always causes problems. On Karstens Ridge, the steepest part of the Muldrow route, the four men kicked steps cautiously as they descended over the tricky snow, too soft for ice pitons but too hard for the shaft of an ice axe. They negotiated the wind-packed Coxcomb without a hitch, then started out onto a narrow icy step in the ridge at just below 13,000 feet. This was the only bit of technical climbing on the whole descent. A five-thousand-foot wall of ice and rock plunged to the Traleika Glacier on the right. Two thousand feet of steep snow-slopes dropped to the Muldrow's head on their left. Harper's magnificent ice cascade glittered in the midday sun at their left elbow.

All four men were roped together. In this arrangement the man coming last has the critical job. They were wallowing waist-deep in loose, drifted steep snow underlaid by solid ice. The going was tricky, but not difficult. In only a few yards the men would be back on the easy crest of the ridge below the step. Suddenly, the

key last man, Elton Thayer, tripped. Like dominoes the other men, one by one, were pulled off after him. For a moment it was a mere slide in loose snow, but nobody could arrest the fall. Out of control they accelerated, tumbled, bounced, and slid eight hundred feet to a tiny snow shelf that miraculously stopped them before a final thousand-foot plunge all the way to the Muldrow.

As soon as the least-injured man got to Thayer, he discovered that the leader of the expedition was dead, his back apparently broken. George Argus was badly injured with a dislocated hip. In the middle of a potential avalanche slope, Les Viereck and Morton Wood pitched a tent and got Argus inside. There they waited and waited, each day hoping that Ginny Wood would see them and mount a rescue.

She flew over, exactly as had been scheduled, but failed to see the minuscule tent—off the ridge where it was not supposed to be, on that precarious shelf. After six days the food and fuel situation became critical. Argus was in terrible pain. There was no easy solution.

Viereck and Wood managed to drag Argus down steep snow slopes to the head of the Muldrow—exactly where the Sourdoughs and Stuck had camped forty years before. Food was scant for three men, but for one there was enough for about a week. Only a quart of fuel remained. Wood and Viereck made Argus as comfortable as possible, then set out to hike to Wonder Lake. By walking all day and all night, the men got there in only forty hours. Argus's life was saved a week later by an extremely competent rescue, which evacuated him by sled to McGonagall Pass and thence to civilization by helicopter.

The tragedy of Thayer's death obscured the team's fine accomplishment in making the first traverse of the mountain as well as ascending a new route. It was the third death of a climber on McKinley, occurring a stone's throw from the disaster of 1932.

During the same month, on the opposite side of the mountain, a very experienced group of five, led by Donald McLean, made the first ascent of the Northwest Ridge of the North Peak, the route on which Cook had reached about 11,000 feet in 1903. The climb was a particularly cold one, as the vast bulk of the mountain eclipsed the sun until 11:00 each morning. McLean's team got up the mountain without incident, although the trip was enlivened by the surprise appearance of the party's pilot and his wife at base camp in Peters Basin. On a check flight, the pair had been caught in a downdraft and crashed. They were unhurt, but the wreckage of the plane still lies swallowed up in the crevasses of the Tluna Icefall.

The most difficult bit of climbing on the Northwest Ridge came at the relatively high elevation of 15,000 feet. Here Fred Beckey, one of the great American mountaineers of the century, drove the first rock pitons ever placed on McKinley. To get supplies to their high camps, team members had to make several trips up and down a number of delicate sections of the route. To make these trips safer, "fixed" ropes were left in place for use as handlines and even for rappels on the way down, exactly as Washburn had roped the steep pitch on the West Buttress. Increasingly during the next two decades, as the routes on McKinley and other big mountains became more and more difficult, "fixing" became the standard mode of operation. Some mountaineers came to regard the total number of feet of rope that was fixed as a measure of the seriousness of a climb. But fixed ropes soon deteriorate into trash. Many a fine route has been spoiled by the accumulation of rotting ropes left in place on it, and many serious accidents have resulted from climbers attempting to use the weak or damaged handlines left in place by previous expeditions.

In 1952 Washburn looked over his aerial photographs of the Kahiltna and had another idea. In the 1953 *American Alpine Journal*, he announced, "Mount Hunter (14,580′) is the highest unclimbed peak in the Alaska Range and doubtless the most outstanding virgin peak in Alaska." The article included four aerial photographs that showed the proposed climb in detail.

That was all that was necessary. In Fairbanks in 1954, Fred Beckey and Henry Meybohm, the strongest members of the party that had just climbed McKinley's Northwest Ridge, met Heinrich Harrer, one of the world's most distinguished alpinists, who had made the first ascent of the Eiger's famous North Wall. The three restless experts were fascinated by the challenge of Mount Hunter. They quickly teamed up and phoned Don Sheldon, a young Talkeetna pilot who had flown Washburn on a survey trip to the snout of Ruth Glacier in late 1951 and who, tempted by Terris Moore, had just bought a pair of ski wheels for his tiny Piper Super Cub airplane.

This veteran team, airlifted by Sheldon in his first glacier landings, speedily made the first ascent of extremely difficult 12,500-foot Mount Deborah, 125 miles east of McKinley. Then, plucked off by skiplane, they made a brief stop at Talkeetna and landed on June 29 right at Mount Hunter's back door on the surface of Kahiltna Glacier. This was the first small, uniformly experienced team of alpinists ever to climb in the range. In six days they had conquered Hunter's West Ridge almost exactly along Washburn's suggested line. Instead of being flown out, the rugged trio simply hiked forty-odd miles down the rough Kahiltna.

The 12,000-foot shoulder of Karstens Ridge, showing the location of the tragic accident of 1954.

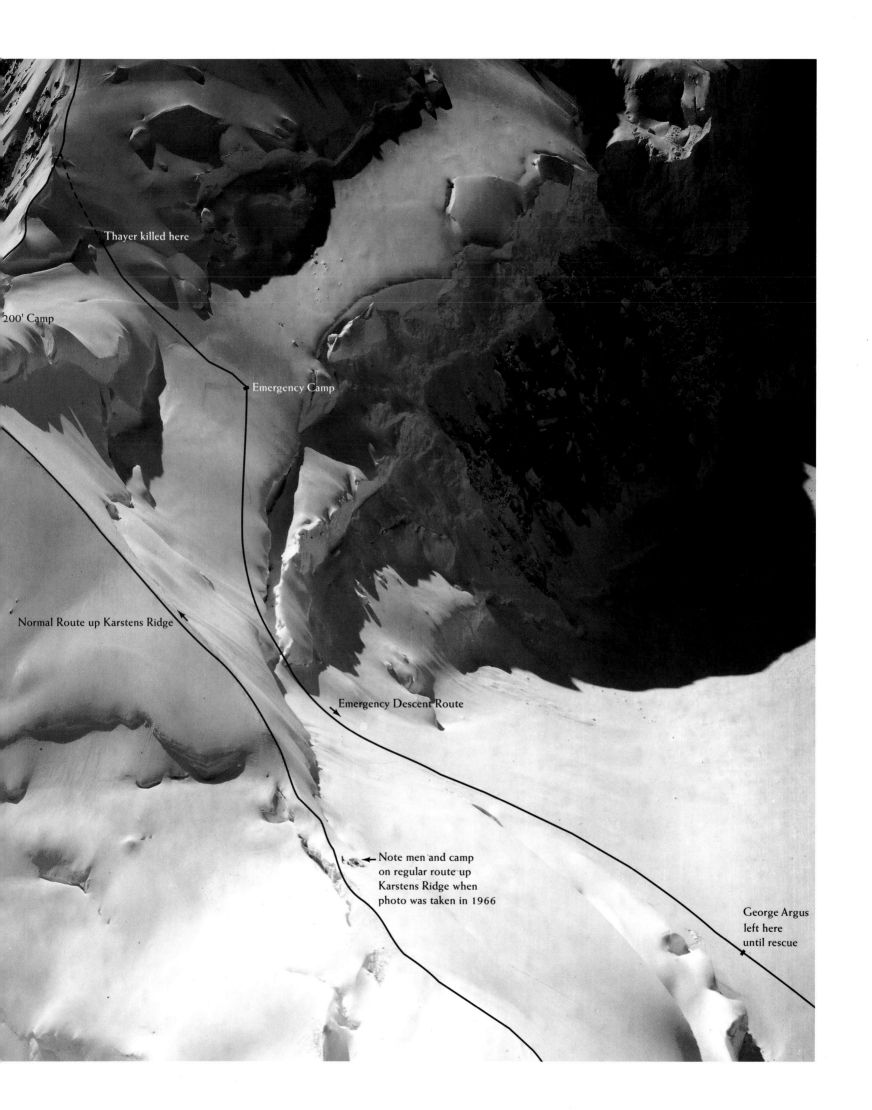

Thayer killed here

200' Camp

Emergency Camp

Normal Route up Karstens Ridge

Emergency Descent Route

← Note men and camp
on regular route up
Karstens Ridge when
photo was taken in 1966

George Argus
left here
until rescue

Hunter's ascent was not only a great climb, which had set a new standard of difficulty against which to measure the accomplishments of others; it also marked the first *commercial* airplane landing on the Kahiltna. This level, snowy "airport" was to become the gateway to McKinley, and Don Sheldon was soon to become its main pilot. Each year more climbers used that "airstrip," and hauling climbers into and out from the mountains soon became the principal business of Sheldon and his Talkeetna competition, the Hudson brothers, Glenn and Cliff.

Five more years passed before another new route up McKinley was forged. One evening, after a good climb in the Tetons, four young Dartmouth climbers decided to try McKinley's South Face. Technically they were the strongest party to visit the area since Harrer and Beckey: Jake Breitenbach, Barry Corbet, Bill Buckingham, and Pete Sinclair. The route that they chose to tackle in June 1959—the West Rib of the South Face—was by a considerable margin the most demanding yet attempted on McKinley. The team was blessed with day after day of good weather, something Washburn in all his months on the mountain had never enjoyed. Furthermore, while the rock on the Northwest Ridge is the badly shattered, unstable black schist that caps the northern side of McKinley, that on the West Rib is the solid, rough-grained pink granite that is the ancient core of the main mass of McKinley— and these four talented friends were the first climbers to encounter it.

The happy quartet that pioneered the West Rib route, averaging only twenty-three years in age, stood at the peak of their careers that year on McKinley. A mere four years later, Breitenbach would be killed by the collapse of an ice pinnacle in Everest's Khumbu Icefall, and shortly after that, Corbet would be paralyzed for life in a helicopter crash.

During the late fifties more and more parties each year climbed McKinley by the West Buttress route, which was slowly coming to be known as the "best way up." And Don Sheldon and Glenn Hudson, ferrying the climbers from Talkeetna to the mountain, were turning the Kahiltna Glacier landing strip into something of a glacial taxi stand. Merely getting to the top of McKinley by the fastest, safest, and easiest route was no longer a sufficient incentive for the best mountaineers.

The first of these brilliant new climbers was a four-man party from the Pacific Northwest which wanted to set a new speed record on McKinley. (It had taken about a month to make the climb via the Muldrow, about three weeks via the West Buttress.) Before 1960, nobody in Alaska had ever thought that the time he spent on a mountain was a criterion of excellence. Three of this impatient foursome were top-notch expedition veterans. The fourth was a wealthy Oregon rancher named John Day. Having

taken up climbing late in life, Day was possessed with a passion to set speed records on big mountains. The veterans were, in effect, his guides.

The four men did indeed reach the summit by the West Buttress in only three days from their base camp. However, on the way down, just below Denali Pass, one man fell, pulling the whole team down the icy slope, just as Thayer had done while descending Karstens Ridge. They slid nearly eight hundred vertical feet before they came to a stop at the bottom of the hill, just above the level 17,200-foot shoulder. Two of the leaders were knocked unconscious. John Day's leg was broken. Fortunately, another party that was descending just ahead of them came to the rescue. After rushing down the steep ridge to their 16,400-foot camp, the leader, Paul Crews, dashed back up the ridge in the middle of the night (without a moment's rest, despite the fact that he had just climbed McKinley too) with a tent to shelter the injured men.

This party of Alaskans had a good two-way radio, and they sounded the alarm to Anchorage. In the midst of all this, Crews' teammate, Helga Bading, who was attempting to become the second woman up McKinley, became seriously ill with pulmonary edema. That morning she had felt too weak to make the climb and had urged her four partners to leave her in camp and go to the top. When they reached her after the accident she was in desperate shape. Both parties needed outside help—and fast.

Instantly a fifty-man rescue team was organized at park headquarters and in Anchorage. Experts flew up from Seattle to help their injured friends. Overnight the rescue on McKinley burgeoned into a front-page drama from coast to coast. And once more Brad Washburn became deeply involved, from over 4,000 miles away. He recalls the maneuvering that led to an extraordinary rescue:

That evening Barbara and I were attending a Pops concert in Boston and the people in front of us asked if we'd heard on the radio about a big accident on Mount McKinley. We hadn't. It was sweltering hot in Boston and an hour later, while we sipped some ice-cold ginger ale in our kitchen, I telephoned Talkeetna at midnight to see if I could help. Amazingly, Don Sheldon was on the line in a couple of minutes. When there was an accident or crisis, Don was always at the focus of the action. He was refueling to bring additional rescuers to join the throng already assembled at the 10,000-foot landing-spot where our party had had its base camp nine years before. Don outlined the problem. The weather was "socked in" above 12,000 feet but promised to clear in the morning. They were frantically trying to drag Helga Bading down the steep ice-slope to the 14,000-foot plateau where she would be nearer to the rescuers. Did I know of any spot where he could land closer to Helga before it was too late?

I knew the area intimately. Don and I had repeatedly made skiplane landings on McKinley together—but never that high. I thought I had an answer.

'Yes, I think I know exactly where you can land. Because of the potential danger of motor-failure on all my photo-flights I've pinpointed three high-altitude emergency landing-spots on McKinley, all above 12,000 feet. I've never had to use one, but the best one is exactly where you need it.

When it clears, instead of landing at your 10,000-foot rescue camp, get up to 15,000 feet and fly straight north, *right over it*. When you are exactly over it, turn 90 degrees to the right. Directly in front of you, you'll see a perfect snow-capped pyramid with granite ribs outlining it. You can't miss it. That's the West Buttress—precisely two miles ahead of you as you finish that turn, and exactly 16,000 feet high.

Fly level and straight at that pyramid until you don't dare to get any closer. Then turn sharp to the right, throttle back, give her full flaps, and as you round the corner of the Buttress you'll see a perfect landing spot right ahead of you, half a mile away and 14,000 feet high. I know you can set down there, but increase your power as you near the ground and land as steeply up the gentle slope as you can, so you'll get the longest possible takeoff run when they turn you around.'

The weather broke the next morning. Don followed my suggestions exactly, made a perfect landing, and flew Helga back to safety. She recovered rapidly and completely. Lots of God-given natural oxygen is the best medicine for pulmonary edema. This thrilling incident further cemented my friendship with Don Sheldon. Don and I had enormous faith in each other. I knew that Terry Moore had landed a Super-Cub almost exactly like Don's on top of 16,000-foot Mount Sanford the year before. I knew that the plane could handle a 14,000-foot takeoff, and I also knew that Don was the only pilot in Alaska who could handle this crisis—and do it with style!

Later that same day, Link Luckett flew his Hiller helicopter, stripped of everything (including even the starter-battery), to the 17,200-foot shoulder and plucked off John Day. On May 21 he similarly rescued Pete Schoening. Both landings dramatically broke all Alaskan altitude records for helicopter operation. The other participants in this remarkable episode trudged down to Kahiltna Pass and were evacuated in less dramatic fashion.

The Day-Bading accident profoundly changed the attitudes of many of the climbers who were setting their sights on McKinley. Before 1960, no one who went to the mountain would ever have thought he could be rescued if he got into trouble on its slopes; neither would he have dreamt that someone else might pay the bill for saving him. After Sheldon's and Luckett's daring flights, however, it was evident that rescue was an option, last ditch or not. In the 1980s, according to Talkeetna pilot Jim Okonek, climbers had been known to radio for rescue when they were in no emergency at all, simply to save themselves a long walk down a glacier. As Washburn ironically remarks, "After all, the Coast Guard spends millions every year rescuing thousands of folks who get into trouble on level, unfrozen water—people are now insisting that the same rules should apply to this game where the water is frozen solid and tipped at an angle!"

At the end of his widely read 1957 article in *Mountain World*, Brad Washburn had suggested a central route up McKinley's South Face: "This method of approaching Mount McKinley directly from the south is so continually steep and difficult, and so exposed to the full force of the great southwesterly storms that none but the most uniformly experienced and powerful team of climbers should even think of attempting it. But I mention it here in conclusion because to omit it would be to sidestep the greatest remaining pioneer ascent in North America."

To Riccardo Cassin, the finest Italian mountaineer of his generation, this was tantamount to a gauntlet thrown down; and he immediately started a correspondence with Washburn. Pictures were sent from Cambridge to Italy, in addition to suggestions for equipment and air support (Don Sheldon) and warnings about McKinley's violent storms and intense cold. In the spring of 1961 Cassin traveled to Alaska with an excellent team of Italian alpinists, spending the night in Cambridge with Brad and Barbara on the way.

Between July 5 and 20, 1961, Cassin worked out a very steep route on snow, ice, and rock, directly up the middle of McKinley's South Face. For the first time, pitches that would have rated a fairly high standard even on some sunny cliff in the Dolomites were tackled at high altitude on the world's coldest mountain. Despite the fact that the U.S. Board on Geographic Names refuses to name anything for a person who is still alive, this magnificent ridge, now one of the world's classic climbs, is fondly known as "The Cassin."

Though Cassin had consulted endlessly with Washburn before the expedition, he seriously underestimated the climate of the

Alaska Range. His men went into battle wearing the knickers, knee socks, and single boots they would have used in the Alps. The conditions they found impressed them strongly. Once at the top, according to Cassin, they could not utter "a word in the intense cold. A short, silent embrace by six frigid men, tried by fatigue, ends the short moment on the summit. We must descend. The satisfaction will come later." All the men suffered frostbite, one of them a quite serious case. On the way down, unable to fit his swollen feet into his boots, he was saved by a teammate who gave up his own larger pair and completed the difficult downpitches of rock and ice wearing only several layers of heavy socks to protect his feet.

Cassin's own words convey the drama of that descent:

Jack Canali's condition was really frightening. I was in fact afraid that if we waited any longer [in a terrific storm] he would not be able to put his feet on the ground, and we still had to cross the steep ridge, upon which it would be impossible to carry a man. . . . Groping in ever-thickening mist and near darkness we reached Camp I where we could at last stop and sleep. . . . I massaged Jack's feet which hurt him terribly. We all spent a horrible night. Only at dawn did we manage to rest a little, while it went on snowing outside. . . . [Later] it was another horrible night for all three of us. Jack constantly moaned because of the unbearable pain and that made us suffer too. After 75 hours of continuous snow we finally saw the sun on the morning of July 23.

Cassin's expedition was a triumph. Telegrams flooded Talkeetna from everywhere, even one from President Kennedy that concluded, "Our nation is proud to have witnessed within its own borders this conquest which has served to strengthen the ties between the United States and Italy and to earn the admiration of all the world."

Cassin's party had been the first crack European expedition to visit Alaska since the duke of the Abruzzi had tackled Mount Saint Elias in 1897. Washburn now stepped up his efforts at needling the French to come to McKinley. He had done most of his own apprenticeship among the great peaks of the French Alps and had for many years been a member of their Groupe de Haute Montagne. At last his letters to Lucien Devies bore fruit. Lionel Terray, France's premier alpinist and veteran of the first ascent of Annapurna, picked up the correspondence. In 1964 he came to Alaska.

Terray and his French team wanted to climb directly up the middle of McKinley's South Face, a much steeper, more difficult route than Cassin's, but the weather was unusually cold. They decided to "warm up" by making the first ascent of Mount Huntington, McKinley's satellite—a stunning 12,200-foot peak of ice and rock that flanks Ruth Glacier eight miles south of McKinley.

A 12,000-foot mountain seemed to pose no special problem to such a powerful and experienced group, and on May 7 Don Sheldon swiftly airlifted them to their base camp, right at the foot of Huntington. As Washburn had told Terray, "You can land so close to the climb that you could rope up in Talkeetna and start the ascent right out of the airplane!"

Terray was at once visibly moved: "Without transition we had been plunged into the great bath of adventure. The site was grandiose, the peaks as impressive and majestic as the most beautiful of the Himalaya. Unfortunately the thermometer hovered stubbornly around minus 10 degrees F. and the wind whipped up enormous eddies of powder snow. Under these conditions we installed Base Camp in the heroic surroundings of a polar expedition."

It did not take long for the party to realize that Huntington was no warm-up, but presented a complex challenge involving some of the most difficult pitches of ice and rock these climbers had ever seen. At one point Terray himself fell and dislocated his shoulder. For a while it looked as though the whole attempt would collapse. Then, in a magnificent surge of strength and valor, he returned to the action and, with his right arm in a sling, accompanied his teammates to victory on May 25–26.

No mention was made of the South Face plan when the party left Anchorage for the return flight to Paris. Wrote Terray, "On this proud and beautiful mountain we have lived hours of fraternal, warm and exalting nobility. Here for a few days we have ceased to be slaves and have really been men. It is hard to return to servitude." Lionel Terray, like Riccardo Cassin, had seriously underestimated the severity and magnitude of the mountains of Alaska. He returned to Europe with a new respect for the remote and frigid peaks of faraway North America.

Until the 1960s, American climbing languished in the shadow of British, French, German, and Italian standards. Then all at once, the word leaked out that a tiny band of unknown young Americans, experimenting on the granite precipices of Yosemite Valley, were probably becoming the best pure rock climbers in the world. At the same time, Alaska became securely fixed on the map of world mountaineering.

The early sixties saw an unprecedented wave of activity on McKinley. On the heels of Cassin's triumph, a Canadian party had made the first ascent of the steep upper part of the North Peak's Pioneer Ridge. Two years later the complex Southeast Spur fell before a carefully planned attack led by Boyd Everett.

In 1963 the last three of the nine major new routes were climbed. The first to be completed was the extremely long and arduous East Buttress, in late May by a strong group of Teton and Rainier guides. (It was one branch of this buttress that Cook had ridiculously claimed as the route of his and Barrill's ascent in 1906.) Three weeks later a group of Canadian guides succeeded on the right-hand edge of Wickersham Wall, the route attempted by the judge in 1903. A party had been avalanched off this route in 1961, and the Canadians felt that safety lay in getting up the mountain fast. This they did, but at the price of severe altitude-sickness. They descended by the West Buttress, using short skis to advantage in the deep snow.

A party of seven Harvard students, including me, arrived at McKinley Park in June 1963. We learned immediately that the Canadians were already on Wickersham Wall. Our dismay vanished, however, when we realized that their route lay a full three miles to the southwest of ours, and that the two overlapped not a single step. The route Washburn had talked us into was the longest in terms of altitude gain possible on McKinley, or indeed anywhere in the western hemisphere—a full 14,000 feet from bottom to top.

We ran into some difficult rock climbing and considerable avalanche danger low on this route. In one camp falling rocks drilled holes in the roofs of our tents, and ice axes planted nearby were swept away by snowslides. But we got high as quickly as we could and soon found better going on long and continuously steep slopes of snow and ice.

As we waited out a week's storm at 17,400 feet, Don Sheldon, checking our progress, flew through the clouds and saw our footsteps lower on the wall disappearing into avalanche tracks. Alarmed, he put out the word that we were missing and feared dead. An intensive search occupied the next three days; all we knew of it was that we heard a lot of airplane engines through the dense clouds that obscured everything above 12,000 feet.

The press rapidly picked up the story across the country. Brad Washburn bluntly stated that he had full confidence in us, that he had repeatedly holed up and patiently waited out storms far longer than this one on McKinley.

When the skies finally did clear, it was Sheldon himself who first spotted us. We reached the North Peak a few days later on July 16 in a full blizzard. Of the view from this lofty and magnificent point, Washburn had written in 1947: "We realized that we were looking down one of the greatest precipices known to man." We wrote our names on a slip of paper, added the last half of Washburn's sentence, stuck the note in a bottle, and cached it there. It wasn't a 14-foot pole, but we were proud as sourdoughs.

TRIUMPH AND TRAGEDY

by Bradford Washburn

AFTER THE GREAT 1963 ASCENTS of the East Buttress and Wickersham Wall, only three really tempting major pioneer climbs remained on McKinley: the South Face direct, the Catacomb Ridge of the East Buttress, and the fearsome East Face. While a number of top climbers pondered these challenges, a small group of Alaskan climbers began to hatch an "ultimate" McKinley scheme—to climb the mountain in the dead of winter. The initial idea was suggested to Art Davidson of Anchorage by Shiro Nishimae, a Japanese climber from Osaka who had climbed McKinley in 1965 and had become a fast friend of many of the Anchorage climbing fraternity. Art and Shiro sold the idea to Dr. George Wichman, an Anchorage surgeon who loved to ski and climb. Then the three enthusiasts tried to locate anyone else who wanted to set foot on McKinley during the winter. At first their efforts were in vain. McKinley was frigid enough in midsummer. The danger of horrific storms and virtually certain frostbite made winter climbing in Alaska far too risky to tempt anybody. And in addition to the cold, the extremely limited hours of midwinter daylight made this expedition a more-than-grim proposition. Finally, their persistent search led them to Gregg Blomberg of Colorado. He was an expert mountaineering-equipment manufacturer and had just led a new route up frigid Mount Logan, Canada's highest peak and at 19,850 feet only a trifle lower than McKinley. After considerable prodding, Blomberg agreed to be the leader.

He promptly wrote to me for advice, and I responded with enthusiasm. But I warned him of the terrible combination of wind, cold, and darkness and urged him to give up the use of tents and rely solely on igloos. I also pointed out that a Coleman mantle lantern used in an igloo is a marvelous source of light, heat, and morale at minimal cost of fuel consumption. The bright, warm light would be a vital asset if the party was jammed together through scores of hours of darkness in one of McKinley's outlandish winter blizzards—and even the lantern's constant purr would be a morale-builder.

Reassured, Blomberg stayed with the project and by the fall of 1966 had added four more men: Dave Johnston, John Edwards, a Swiss climber called Ray Genet, and Frenchman Jacques Batkin. Batkin was the only really crack mountaineer in the eight-man group, having been the first man atop Mount Huntington two years before, as a member of Lionel Terray's French team. Genet, though physically very strong, had had little previous climbing experience. He was, however, destined to play a significant role in McKinley's history during the next seventeen years.

It was 30 degrees below zero in Don Sheldon's hangar in Talkeetna on the night of January 29, 1967, as the men tried to sleep on the eve of flying in to the Kahiltna. By the following night, they were ecstatic at their progress. The wind-packed surface of the glacier was as hard as concrete, and they had made wonderful headway carrying their first loads upward toward Kahiltna Pass. In fact, the going seemed so safe that nobody had bothered to rope up.

But safe the Kahiltna was not. Three months of terrific winter storms had not only packed its surface to rock-hardness, but had also neatly and smoothly drifted over its lethal network of crevasses. Some were hidden by only a deceptive mantle of powder.

On the second day, the weather was exceptionally fine and morale sky high. The men were stretched out, hundreds of yards apart, climbing unroped in single file up the almost level glacier. Some had already reached the team's first advance camp. Those on the trail were looking down as they methodically trudged along at dusk. Nobody saw Jacques Batkin fall into a completely hidden crevasse. In fact, it was several minutes before anyone even looked up and realized that a man was missing.

Everyone dashed to the point of crisis. All was total silence. A small hole in the middle of the trail was the only sign of the tragedy. Johnston valiantly roped down fifty feet into the crevasse where Batkin lay, crumpled and motionless, on a tiny shelf between the converging walls of deep blue ice. He was alive but unconscious when the team hauled him to the surface, and, despite frantic efforts at mouth-to-mouth resuscitation, he died.

Utterly demoralized, the team considered abandoning the climb. They descended to base camp to radio for help but could not make their transmitter work. It was several days before a plane happened to fly by and spot the team's message, "LAND," stamped in the snow.

Two hours later Don Sheldon was there. Out went poor Batkin and his friend Ray Genet, to telegraph the sad news to France and face the press. Within a few days, however, Genet returned, and the morale of the team strengthened again. They pushed onward up McKinley.

It took them most of a month to fight their way up the lower part of the West Buttress route. First up the long, easy glacier to Ka-

Don Sheldon circles before landing with a load of climber-passengers at the Kahiltna Glacier "airport." His tiny airplane is silhouetted against a cloud that drifts in front of the gigantic Eastern Face of Mount Foraker. (Olaf Soöt)

hiltna Pass; then the steady grind of snow slopes, past Windy Corner, and up the steep pitches of ice and broken rock to a snow cave camp on the shoulder at 17,200 feet. There, on the last day of February, the men awoke to find the temperature at minus 43 with a slight breeze. The sky was cloudless. "Hell, let's go for the summit!" exclaimed Genet. In no time at all five of the seven men decided to climb to Denali Pass. Wichman and Edwards remained at the snow cave. At 18,200 feet, the party planned to pause briefly to cache emergency food and three sleeping bags. If it was not too windy up there, they would head on for the summit.

At Denali Pass, Blomberg, exhausted, decided to descend, and Nishimae gallantly went with him. It was still cloudless and windless. Johnston, Genet, and Davidson pushed ahead. Climbing with their headlamps lighted into the early darkness, they reached the summit at seven o'clock. There, in the inky blackness of the arctic night, they encountered a twenty-mph wind gusting up the South Face and a bone-chilling temperature of 58 below F. As Davidson recalled, "We had looked forward to the view from the summit, but there was only darkness in every direction. After a few moments, Johnston spotted a faint glitter of greenish light way to the south. 'Wow,' he sighed, 'they look like specks of phosphorescent plankton in a black sea!' "

After all it had taken for them to get up there, the only things they could see clearly were the lights of Anchorage 150 miles away.

"Confidently, I started down the ridge," Davidson's account continues. "Our headlamps illuminated about ten square feet; beyond this area everything was black. As expected, the route was traceable only by our bootmarks in the snow. Wherever the snow thinned, I had to stop to search for the next mark in the snow. Over and over I warned myself to forget the summit, to forget my relief. It's just beginning, I told myself. I tried to bolster up all my powers of concentration—each of us was well aware that, should anyone slip, we would all tumble down through the darkness to the basin five hundred feet below."

Exhausted, but in remarkable control of a critically dangerous situation, the trio worked its way cautiously downward through the night and safely reached their cache at Denali Pass near midnight. Johnston wanted to continue down to the cave at 17,200 feet, but the other two persuaded him that they should all rest a few hours in their sleeping bags, then renew the descent at dawn. The first two hundred yards of that slope below Denali Pass were steep blue ice—unwise to attempt in the pitch dark, exhausted, at 50 below zero.

But what seemed to be an intelligent decision nearly cost the three men their lives. Somehow they survived that night in stupefied, intermittent catnaps—with no shelter of any sort, huddled in their sleeping bags, dressed in all their arctic clothing, boots on, and wrapped together in an old parachute from the 1947 cache. Thank God that Shiro Nishimae had insisted on their carrying up those sleeping bags, a stove, and a bit of gasoline as far as the pass.

It was the sound of the parachute flapping in a wild wind that woke the men at dawn. In those few hours the blessed calm of midnight had been transformed into an all-out blizzard. Johnston was for descending at once, but when he left the pathetic shelter of the parachute for only a few moments, he realized that to abandon the bivouac would mean almost certain death. With fingers already frostbitten, the trio dug a tiny cave in the icy snow just east of the rocky crest of the pass and crowded into it, numb with cold and apprehension. A nearly foodless bivouac in a winter storm at Denali Pass was almost too terrible to contemplate.

With four lunches and three cans of ham and peas from the old 1947 cache, however, they survived not only that day but five more after it. Davidson's detailed account of that incredible week, *Minus 148°*, is a classic book. The thermometer never rose much above 40 below zero and the winds screamed through the pass, day after day, at well over a hundred miles an hour. (Later they calculated the wind chill at 148 degrees F. below.)

They soon ran out of both food and fuel. Without water they would die. Genet managed to crawl out into the blizzard and found a gallon of gasoline that Johnston had cached on the pass three years before. They melted cans of snow. Soon after that both Genet's and Davidson's hands became numb and useless, and Johnston had to perform all the manual tasks for the trio.

Day after day, night after night, the storm continued. At one point, Blomberg and Nishimae climbed up from the cave at 17,200 feet to attempt a rescue. Nishimae managed to poke his head a trifle above the crest of the pass but dared not try to go an inch farther for fear that he would simply be blown away. Only a few yards ahead of him he saw the sleeping bags sticking out of the entrance of the miserable little cave that the men had dug. He was sure that his three friends were dead, but to keep Blomberg's spirit from cracking, he did not tell him what he had seen.

At last the wind let up. The men were almost too weak to stand up, but in a frenzy Davidson attacked an old cache with his ice axe. Under layers of discarded and frozen gear, he found dried potatoes and raisins, at least fifteen years old. They ate again, then settled in for the night as the wind subsided and the clouds lifted. Davidson had nightmares: "I dreamed that a kindly man cut off my feet every time they grew too large. There would be several minutes of relief each time he sliced them off and set them on a shelf, but always my feet, growing a bright chartreuse, would swell again to the size of basketballs and ache as if about to burst until they were cut off. I was lying in a small, dark cellar, and before long the shelves that lined the walls were filled with huge, luminous, green feet."

On the seventh morning, Davidson, Genet, and Johnston tottered down the icy, windswept slope below Denali Pass, their packs blown away and no equipment left but their sleeping bags draped over their shoulders. The cave at 17,200 was deserted, but in one corner was a precious cache of food and fuel. Blomberg and Edwards had first headed down the mountain to radio for a helicopter rescue; Nishimae and Wichman had followed soon after.

The trio at the cave gorged on "the most favored delicacies" that their teammates had left there: "sausages, coconut balls Gregg's wife had made, and some of the fruitcake my grandmother had baked for us." Then, all of a sudden, the thrilling sounds of rescue filled the air. Don Sheldon's silver Cessna 180 flew low over them and dropped a radio—which didn't work. Nevertheless, their battered bodies responded to the certainty that others were nearby and helping.

Down the rocky ridge they staggered and then down those 800 feet of glare ice, along the fixed ropes below the 16,000-foot shoulder, barely able to grip that critical lifeline with their swollen, throbbing hands. Into a sea of clouds, blessed warmth—only 20 below. Two more empty igloos and another glorious feast: "It seemed irreverent to leave any food uneaten." Then welcome sleep in a snow home with walls and a roof.

At dawn it was like summer again—only 16 below. As the battered little team started downward, a jet roared past, then a massive U.S. Air Force four-engine plane. Help seemed so tantalizingly near yet still just beyond reach. Then, a parachute, and a radio that *worked*. Their teammates were okay. Three hours later the three were plucked off 13,000-foot Windy Corner by an Air Force helicopter: "God bless those wonderful guys for landing it just at the edge of the impossible!"

Safe in Talkeetna, they had made the first winter ascent of McKinley—a miracle of fortitude and determination. They had been through the worst survival ordeal in McKinley's history. Johnston spent forty-five days in the hospital and lost three toes. Davidson, confined to a wheelchair for eight weeks, lost one toe and the use of three others. Ray Genet lost nothing. But the genial, powerful Genet was to die of exhaustion seventeen years later, descending from the summit of Everest after a long, successful career as McKinley's first professional mountain-guide.

In July 1967, just four months after this extraordinary winter ascent of McKinley, came the worst disaster in the entire history of Alaskan mountaineering. At that time, in order for a team to attempt the ascent of McKinley, it was necessary to file a formal application and receive permission for the climb from the superintendent of Mount McKinley National Park. As a part of the application, each leader was required to describe in considerable detail the previous climbing experience of all the party's members as well as to provide a medical clearance signed by a physician for each person.

Of the expeditions that had applied for permission that spring, two presented the Park Service with unusual problems. One of the teams, composed of four experienced men, initially received approval, but the permission had to be rescinded when one of the climbers was injured in an automobile accident too late to be adequately replaced: at that time, four was the minimum number of climbers allowed on a team. The other group, a party of nine men, appeared too loosely knit and had only marginal previous experience, with none in high-altitude snow-and-ice climbing. No one in either party had ever climbed in Alaska before.

The Alaska Rescue Group and the Park Service suggested that the two parties join forces, but neither was eager to lose its own identity. It was then proposed that the teams climb near to each other and share expensive special equipment such as radios. When the two groups started for Alaska, the form that this relationship would take was still very unclear.

But in mid-June, when all twelve men arrived at McKinley Park Headquarters, they were finally persuaded to climb as a single team, though unfortunately without anyone who was thoroughly qualified—and clearly acknowledged—to be leader. And, unfortunately too, mountaineering arithmetic is a different variety from what we learned in the classroom: a party of twelve is not necessarily four times as strong, or as safe, as a party of three. What took place during the next month on Mount McKinley is well documented by Howard Snyder in his *Hall of the Mountain King*. Although a few succinct paragraphs could easily summarize those events, it is still worthwhile to go into more detail here, as one truth comes through loud and clear: Mount McKinley can be a savage customer if a large party of average experience climbs too high, too fast, and then fails to identify the time-honored signs of an approaching storm.

The ascent this time was by way of the historic Muldrow route. The men started out on foot, aided by Berle Mercer's packtrain from Wonder Lake. Despite the lack of any discernible homogeneity among the twelve climbers, things went along rather smoothly during the first phase of the climb. Then they reached the lofty valley of Harper Glacier and entered surroundings that none of them had ever experienced before.

On the night of July 11–12, climbing through the subarctic twilight, the entire group, in two teams, moved camp from 12,000

feet on Karstens Ridge all the way up to the broad lower plateau of Harper Glacier, 3,000 feet higher on the mountain. Eight men stayed at this camp. Four promptly returned to the lower shoulder of Karstens Ridge and, after only a few hours' rest, climbed right back up again, through the next night, arriving at 15,000 feet as July 13 dawned.

This was the expedition's fourth consecutive cloudless, windless day, and every moment of it was devoted to frantic activity. One party reconnoitered a route upward to 16,500 feet; another made an exhausting final relay down to Karstens Ridge and back up again.

The clear weather held on July 14. Four of the men, worn out by day after day of constant pressure and beginning to feel the effects of altitude, decided to rest for a day. The other eight, fired with enthusiasm to reach the top, which was now in clear sight above, pressed on with heavy loads to erect a final camp at 17,900 feet, just half a mile below Denali Pass. They arrived there, exhausted but jubilant, at seven in the evening, the weather still beautifully calm and clear. The summit beckoned devilishly, a tempting snowy dome barely a mile away as the crow flies and only 2,400 feet above them. From that spot, it looks as if you can simply reach up and touch it. Nothing in the world could be more deceptive.

After a blustery night, the skies dawned clear again on the morning of July 15. The weather was too good to be true. Getting a late start, four men made it to the top that day in a tremendous ten-hour effort. The four others in the high camp, dead tired from continual stress and high altitude, rested all day. Just as the climbing team returned from the summit, the quartet from 15,000 feet staggered into camp, and all twelve were united briefly once more.

Everyone relaxed on the sixteenth—providentially, as a brief but violent storm swept the mountain—but now the sinister effects of pushing too high too fast began to take their toll. The next morning, in order to save food and fuel at the high camp, the four men who had already reached the summit decided to drop back down to 15,000 feet. One of the four was too weak and ill even to roll up his tent; two of the other three were vomiting. Just as they were leaving, a fifth man threw in the towel and joined them, already so weak from altitude that he doubted his capacity to make the top.

This splendid photograph of one of McKinley's vicious lenticular "cloud cap" storms was taken by Ed Cooper near the Eielson Visitor Center. Two hours earlier, only a small veil of cloud lay over the top. Climbers who know Mount McKinley and its meteorology well know that this formation occurs during the mountain's most violent weather.

They headed down at noon and as the weather continued to moderate, six of the seven men still in camp decided to take their crack at the summit—the seventh was feeling too ill to join them. They made him comfortable in camp and then headed for Denali Pass and the summit at about three in the afternoon of July 17. Mare's tail clouds streaked the sky and a very high gray overcast was beginning to drift in from the southwest.

The remainder of the story is told by piecing together facts related by the climbers who had descended to 15,000 feet, interwoven with taped radio conversations between the summit team and the Park Service crew at Eielson Visitor Center, 17,000 feet below and thirty miles to the northeast.

At eight that night, the men at 15,000 feet reported a return to clear blue skies overhead, but a "curious mantle of mist" was settling down over McKinley's crest. "The cloud was a strange motionless veil that covered the summit, the Archdeacon's Tower and the upper part of the ridge above Denali Pass." At the same time, the climbing team radioed to Eielson that they were less than an hour from the top, but in thickening mist.

At 10:00 P.M. they were clearly in deep trouble. Their frigid radio batteries were much weaker, but their message was still received at Eielson: "We're floundering around. We don't know whether we're on the summit ridge or not. We don't know whether the summit ridge is supposed to be 'wanded' or not. . . . We're just floundering around in the dark here. Visibility is about 300 feet." "Wands" are thin yard-long wooden trail markers or willow twigs that have been used for years in Alaska to mark indistinct snow trails about every hundred feet on the way up, so that they will be apparent on the way down in fog or storms. Most of the party's wands had been left behind by mistake at 15,000 feet, and the summit team two days before had had only a handful to mark their entire route. The storm of the sixteenth had doubtless blown most of these away and, of course, wiped out all foot tracks.

A crisis was developing.

The men clearly had no idea where they were. Although they had brought sleeping bags for emergency because of their late start, they had little else but trail rations. The call to retreat should have been sounded then and there, but the summit continued to beckon. They were sure that they were almost there and decided to bivouac in the open—at a place that turned out in the light of dawn to be *at least 800 feet below the top.*

At sunrise on July 18, the shroud of mist lifted briefly, and one of the men, seeing the magnitude of their error, decided to wait there in his sleeping bag. The summit team was reduced to five. Cold batteries warmed in someone's pocket made the radio work again, and at 11:30 A.M. the little party reported that they were on the summit—in dense fog. They announced their five names, and

Eielson, immediately adding them to that of the man they knew was in his sleeping bag at 19,500 feet, asked where man number seven was. The response came faintly: "He didn't feel good at all, so he stayed in camp at 17,900. He's probably wondering where we are at the moment." At 11:45 A.M. the summit team agreed to radio again at 8:00 P.M. As they left the top, they spoke the last words ever heard from them: "Thanks very much; KHD6990; Unit one clear."

During that day the clouds rapidly thickened and lowered. By nightfall a tremendous blizzard swept McKinley. All the next day the team at 15,000 feet was unable to move an inch. The radio reported nothing. On July 20 the five tried to climb back up to the high camp to see what was going on—as Eielson continued to report total radio silence aloft. But a three-hour struggle with a renewed tempest of windblown snow drove them back, and the storm continued with unabated fury for two more days.

On July 22, with three of the men at 15,000 feet too ill to climb and all five increasingly concerned about the situation, they radioed that they could not go upward again for rescue, investigation—or indeed, for anything. On the twenty-fourth, numb with illness and apprehension, they broke camp and started down Karstens Ridge. There, at 12,000 feet, they fortuitously encountered an experienced climbing party of the Mountaineering Club of Alaska.

Dry tent, ample food, and tender loving care rapidly restored the battered team, and Grace Hoeman, a doctor with the Anchorage crew, selflessly descended with them the next day to Wonder Lake—still a rugged two-day trek away, concluded fortunately with a brief ride over the boiling McKinley River in an emergency helicopter.

A few days later Bill Babcock's strong and experienced Mountaineering Club team reached the 17,900-foot campsite in perfect weather. One tent was blown away, another almost buried, and the frozen corpse of one lone man sat weirdly in the snowy desert, leaning against a nonexistent tent pole. Farther up the mountain, guided by a message dropped by Don Sheldon, they found two more frozen bodies around 19,000 feet on the northern flank of the Archdeacon's Tower, far to the north of the regular route of ascent. McKinley's unforgiving snows hid every other vestige of that heartrending retreat from its summit.

No tragedy of this magnitude has befallen another Alaskan expedition since, although almost every year lesser crises occur, often involving much more experienced teams than this dozen men.

It is often easy, at a distance and in less harsh surroundings, to analyze in retrospect the problems that surround any accident.

But the extraordinary combination of serious tactical errors and bad luck that plagued this party from the very start is so typical of McKinley that a few words of analysis may help others who contemplate this climb.

In the appraisal of the many factors that influence the success or failure of expeditions to remote parts of the world, three seem too rarely to be highlighted: luck, patience, and resourcefulness—and these factors, interrelated with experience, stamina, and judgment, are probably more important than any others.

In recent years, as a result of the steadily increased pressure to remove restraints from almost all aspect of our lives, permission is no longer required to attempt the ascent of Mount McKinley. The Park Service is infinitely relieved. Now all that it must do is try to reason as effectively as possible with those who clearly appear to be unqualified to make the climb. While it is relatively easy to identify an excellent party or a weak one, it is often very difficult to evaluate a team that lies near the dividing line between these two extremes. The Park Service intensely disliked being forced to make these decisions, as there always seemed to be an implied responsibility in case an accident occurred. Furthermore, over the years, just about as many experienced climbers have been involved in bad accidents as have inexperienced, occasionally because of bad luck but usually by pressing forward beyond the limits of their strength or abilities.

Although luck, good or bad, is a factor that is shared by all, patience and resourcefulness are, to a lesser degree, characteristics that develop with experience. It is my view that a climber or explorer in his or her thirties is more likely to succeed than one in his twenties, simply because the former is more mature—and competence, patience, and resourcefulness tend to develop with maturity.

Many inexperienced climbers are tempted to try Mount McKinley because of the ever-increasing number of expeditions with poor or marginal competence that reach the top each year with little or no pain. Word goes out that it's easy. But this situation is frustratingly misleading, for in large measure the success of these inexperienced parties was based on a well-beaten trail and uniformly good luck with the weather. Also, everyone climbing the easy West Buttress route has come to count on the existence of the remarkable medical research station that has operated there at 14,000 feet every year but two since it was founded in 1982.

Often parties that run into violent storms halfway up the mountain make the climb with the most success and enjoyment, because they were forced inadvertently to spend longer on the mountain and acclimatize properly to altitude. If these climbers then encounter a violent storm above 16,000 feet they are physically well prepared to cope with it. McKinley, in perfect weather and on one of the easier routes, can be disarmingly pleasant. In bad weather it can be a relentless, brutal adversary.

Looking at the great tragedy of 1967 with these things in mind one experiences a number of if-only pangs: If, for example, these ambitious and strong young men had had a single leader who was familiar with the ways of high-mountain weather, particularly on McKinley, they would have heeded the signs of a violent approaching storm that were seen and recorded all over central Alaska on the day before that second summit climb. Mare's tail clouds approaching from the southwest must always be watched with concern, and there is no more typical or sinister portent than the veil of fog that mysteriously draped the summit of McKinley the night of their final bivouac.

Regardless of the team's experience, had that big storm struck either one day earlier or one day later, the story would have been a very different one. If anyone on that second summit team had climbed the final ridge before, he would have known full well that the group was thwarted in the vicinity of the Archdeacon's Tower, nowhere near the summit ridge, and a retreat—not a bivouac—would have taken place that night. If the party had moved less rapidly above 12,000 feet, acclimatization would doubtless have taken place, and a strong, healthy team would have weathered the storms and reached the summit a week later.

A few caveats arise out of all this—and they are as old as the history of high-altitude mountaineering:

Unless your party is uniformly powerful and experienced, employ a guide who is both—or at least have one member of your team who knows McKinley well and has a deep respect for every inch of it.

Don't climb too fast, even if the weather or the nearness of the summit tempts you to hurry. If you are ill at high altitude, go down three or four thousand feet. It's amazing what the very natural medicine of a bit more oxygen will do to heal the ills and worries of Denali Pass.

And last, if you are caught on the trail in one of the McKinley's fiendish blizzards, don't push on, no matter how near the summit may be. Go back to camp or settle down in a well-equipped bivouac. Have a good sleep and try it again when the weather clears.

Overleaf: The South Face of McKinley: most magnificent mountain wall in North America, seen over the snowy crest of the South Buttress.

Right: The upper 3,000 feet of McKinley seen from a Learjet flying just below 20,000 feet on a crystal-clear morning. The Archdeacon's Tower and upper part of the Southwest Rib are at the left and the final pitches of the Cassin Ridge rise to the South Peak from the lower right-hand corner.

Below: A snug campsite near 16,000 feet on McKinley's formidable South Face. (Dennis Eberl)

Overleaf: The Catacomb Ridge of McKinley's East Buttress, a symphony of ice and rock, has been climbed only once (1969) by the steep snow ridge to the left. The entire knife-edge to the right has never been traversed. This is one of the longest and most difficult of McKinley's approaches—the route that Dr. Cook would have had to take to reach the summit with Ed Barill in 1906.

Second overleaf: The West Ridge of the North Peak at left and the West Buttress on a crisp winter morning.

Below: Nearing the summit of Peak 12,380, one of McKinley's most spectacular little satellites. (Alan Kearney)

Right: Mount Foraker peeks over the shoulder of McKinley's summit.

Overleaf left: A tremendous avalanche plunges down the 5,000-foot granite headwall of Ruth Glacier's northwest fork. (Peter Lev)

Overleaf right: Above Denali Pass a superb display of high cirrus clouds signals an approaching blizzard. (Roger Robinson)

Above: An exquisite snow arête—one of the first major pitches of the Cassin Ridge. (Harold Hunt)

Opposite page—above left: A breathtaking traverse on Mount Hunter's North Face. (Paul Aubrey); *above right:* Climbers negotiating the rock steps on the French Ridge of Mount Huntington. (Roger Robinson); *lower left:* Challenging a granite overhang with a 50-pound pack. (Roger Robinson); *lower right:* Threading the needle through Mount Dickey's western ice-wall.

Overleaf: Looking northwestward over the West Buttress—McKinley's South Face and summit are at right.

CHAPTER THIRTEEN

EXPLORATION'S END

by Bradford Washburn

AT THE SAME TIME THAT TRAGEDY was unfolding on McKinley's northern slopes, one of the most significant new routes in its history was climbed on the eastern crags of its magnificent 10,000-foot South Face. Jake Breitenbach and his stellar crew had climbed the extreme western rib of the South Face. Riccardo Cassin had pioneered the direct central route squarely up the granite rib that splits the face in half. Until the summer of 1967 nobody had yet attempted to scale the eastern side of this southern wall—although Lionel Terray had studied it carefully and fully intended to make its first ascent immediately after completing his "warm-up climb" of Mount Huntington.

In late July and August 1967 Boyd Everett, who in 1962 had mastered the long and arduous ascent of the Southeast Spur, put three powerful parties onto the mountain simultaneously—one on the Cassin Ridge, one up the western flank of the South Buttress, and the third directly up the steep ice slopes and vertiginous granite crags that crested the eastern edge of the South Face. These assaults were so carefully planned, so well manned, and so well executed that they received little attention amid the chaos that surrounded the tragic drama on the other side of the mountain.

McKinley was now the central focus of Alaskan mountaineering attention and its few remaining virgin routes were "firsted" one after another—all but one. In 1969 the magnificently corniced eastern ridge of the East Buttress (which afterward was aptly christened Catacomb Ridge by its conquerors) was ascended in mid-July by a strong and experienced six-man team. The climb, which involved extremely difficult segments of rock, snow, and ice, took this expert group thirty days to negotiate, one way, after an airplane landing right at its base—an almost amusing fact, given that this East Buttress is clearly the route by which Dr. Cook and Ed Barrill were supposed to have made their thirteen-day round trip first ascent of McKinley, starting at a point twenty-five miles farther away, with no air support or maps.

Then in 1970 three records fell in quick succession. On July 5, Kazuo Hoshikawa and Tsuyoshi Ueki made the first ski descent from the South Peak. The next day, a six-woman party made the first all-female ascent of McKinley—Arlene Blum, Margaret Clark, Grace Hoeman, Dana Isherwood, Faye Kerr, and Margaret Young. Then, on August 26, Naomi Uemura made the mountain's first solo ascent. Tragically this magnificent Japanese explorer-mountaineer was to lose his life descending McKinley

fourteen years later after making its first winter solo ascent on February 12, 1984.

This rapid-fire series of extraordinary climbs ended in 1972 with the ascent of the long Traleika Spur by a six-man team who skied and walked all the way to the top from park headquarters. The spur was the last unclimbed ridge on McKinley. The only virgin part of the mountain that remained was its fearsome East Face.

As the possibilities for major new achievement on McKinley dwindled, other areas of intense activity developed. Some climbers began to focus on the magnificent ridges of McKinley's satellites—with special attention to Foraker, Hunter, and Huntington. Others, with ever higher standards of competence and new techniques, forged one new route after another up the unclimbed faces and well-nigh impossible ribs of both McKinley and these satellites. The three magnificent faces of beautiful Mount Huntington were successfully ascended, one after another. All of Hunter's ridges have now been climbed, but few of its dangerous and precipitous faces. The same is true of Foraker, on which some of the southern ridges and ribs are Himalayan in grandeur and difficulty. And the top experts are still busy threading new and mind-boggling lines directly up the ever smaller vestiges of virgin rock and ice on McKinley. The Isis Spur on McKinley's South Buttress, the East Face of the nearby Moose's Tooth, and the North Pillar of the Rooster Comb, as well as the Infinite Spur on Foraker's South Face, and Hunter's Moonflower Buttress—to name a few climbs that could not have been anticipated in anyone's wildest dreams in 1951.

And while all this was going on, McKinley's easiest and safest routes became the targets of a horde of mountaineers who came to Alaska from every corner of the world—simply for the satisfaction of climbing the highest peak in North America. By the end of 1963, fifty years after Hudson Stuck's first ascent, 174 individuals had stood on its summit. By the end of 1990, by the best count of the Park Service, well over 6,000 climbers had reached the top. And in a single day in July 1976, nearly 80 people crowded up onto the summit in one massive Bicentennial surge. In the spring and summer of 1989, for the first time more than a thousand climbers attempted the ascent—but with a success rate of only 51 percent.

At times camping space was at a premium on the West Buttress, and the Park Service had to begin warning climbers of the

Late afternoon at 17,000 feet—a lone climber starts his descent of the West Buttress. (Jonathan Waterman)

serious sanitation problems along this crowded route, where one team was melting snow for water that was already polluted with another's sewage and garbage. The pilots from Talkeetna were running a big business taxiing one group after another to the "Kahiltna International Airport," and Talkeetna itself has developed into a boom town during the spring and summer months of every year.

During the last fifteen years McKinley has been circumnavigated on skis, climbed by dog team, and descended by both hang glider and parasail. In July 1986, Gary Scott, a volunteer park ranger from Australia, made the round trip via the West Buttress in a single day. In 1988, Vern Tejas, a brilliant McKinley guide, climbed the same route, successfully and solo, in the dead of winter, followed the next year by an equally extraordinary and speedy winter ascent of the West Rib by Dave Staehli. And recently climbers have begun to discover that "parasailing" is an easy but risky way to descend even Alaska's greatest peak. There seems to be no limit to the extraordinary new ways in which the challenge of McKinley can be approached, up or down.

A quarter of these climbs are now being made with professional guides, the first of whom was Ray Genet, who climbed McKinley twenty-four times before his tragic death on Everest. Now the government's only restriction to climbing on the mountain is to hold the number of guiding services to less than ten, but there is little doubt that this dam will soon break under the extraordinary pressure that seems to mount year after year.

As one stops to reflect about the great changes that have swept over the Alaska Range in the last century, one must at least remember, with no little joy, that although people can tear pathetically away at the edges, they are unlikely to be able to leave permanent scars on this magnificent peak. Every few days, even in midsummer, the tracks on its slopes are swept away by wind or buried by blizzards—and for nearly half of each year its faces are pristine and virtually free of the visiting hordes. Except in a few areas of intense activity, McKinley's arctic cold, its great altitude, and its cataclysmic storms will effectively preserve the primeval beauty of its slopes and crags.

To this day only a handful of persons have ever set foot on the great central ice slope of McKinley's South Face. Its fierce climate and the complexity of its protective crags and ridges are likely to keep this marvelous aerie a spot where few will ever venture. Douglas Scott and Dougal Haston, two of Britain's foremost mountaineers, both of whom had climbed Everest, first reached it during their *direttissima* of McKinley's South Face in May 1976. The words that they wrote about this experience express, better than any others I know, the thrill of pausing for a moment in the midst of McKinley's magnificent wilderness.

Says Haston: "As we were traversing at about six in the evening towards where we could strike upwards into the final couloir, a miracle seemed to take place. The wind stopped; the clouds rolled away, revealing a staggering view of the Alaskan wilderness. In the evening sun we brewed a hot drink beside an ice block and sat there marveling. Though the peaks below were less high and less spectacular than those seen from the top of Everest, the loneliness and wilderness made this just as impressive. White and black; no other color relief. Rock, snow, and glaciers like frozen rivers stretched for hundreds of miles in all directions. I felt that we had a right to be there. Our compact, homogeneous twosome was still playing the survival game and playing it well. We cramponed out of the sun into the vicious pre-night cold."

And the next afternoon he wrote: "We had climbed . . . forever into a revived storm and relentless wind. Everything was cold, even our souls. Frostbite was waiting to jump at the slightest weakness. . . . We were drawing heavily on all our Himalayan experience just to survive, and it was a respectful pair that finally stood on the summit ridge."

GOING TO EXTREMES

by Bradford Washburn

THE EXPLORATION OF THE GREAT mountains of the world passes through a series of phases that seems to be identical on every continent and in every range.

At first, the mere investigation of the region around a virgin peak and the approaches to its base requires months or years to complete. During this basic reconnaissance, the pioneers constantly study the heights in hopes of locating the weakest spots in the mountain's armor. Often when great peaks are studied this intensively by an experienced team, several climbable routes and approaches may be found. When the job is done, the team always reports the shortest, easiest, safest route as the one by which to attempt the first ascent.

This first approach is usually along a ridge, as ridges are by their very nature the safest routes—and often the shortest. You can fall off a ridge, but if you are climbing along one, you are usually safest from avalanches, the objective dangers over which you have no control no matter how good a climber you are. Here the judgment of the leader or whoever makes these primary decisions is of vital importance to the safety of the whole party.

When a peak has been climbed once, its attraction diminishes dramatically for those who enjoy only virgin ground. (These people are having less and less enjoyment in the mountain ranges of our world today.) For most of those who savor real adventure, however, almost all of the world's mountains, large or small, have several ridges leading to their summits. When one of these has been climbed, the next one is likely to be the shortest and safest of the remaining unclimbed routes.

Once all of the ridges have been climbed, attention tends to center on the valleys and faces between them, unless at the very start one of the valleys proved to be the best route of all. On McKinley the wisest route turned out to be a combination of two valleys linked by a very safe ridge: Muldrow Glacier, Karstens Ridge, and Harper Glacier.

As the focus moves to the faces that lie between the obviously safe routes, the accident potential increases enormously. Some faces are relatively safe, but those that are dominated by unstable walls of ice or snow are lethal trouble spots. Here the climber's safety is no longer in any way related to competence. His life depends on whether or not an avalanche sweeps his route while he is on it. This sort of Russian roulette is being played more and more frequently throughout the world today. Many shrewd players of this chancy game study the walls they want to climb for days or weeks, trying to determine how often they are swept by avalanches. If the face of the ice wall that dominates the route regularly falls off only once each week, then the safest time to enter the corridor of death is immediately after the last avalanche. Then the big problem is how long the climb will take.

Such a situation exists today on McKinley's magnificent East Face—a 9,000-foot wall of granite ribs, dominated by several very active walls of unstable ice. The great Traleika Icefall at the bottom of this face is so steep and moving so fast that it epitomizes the roulette game. Only one party has ever tried it, in 1971. Miraculously, its members managed to thread their way up through the icefall—and back down—without accident, but on the descent they repeatedly found sections of their uphill route wiped out by the collapse of huge ice pinnacles. The climb was so uniformly dangerous that the team did not want to risk relaying supplies up through the 3,000 feet of this icy Niagara to the safer going above, from which a successful summit attempt would be possible. Now we have superbly detailed stereo pictures of every inch of this route and they have been thoroughly studied by top climbers, as McKinley's East Face would be a great prize. But nobody has yet wanted to make a second attempt at that icefall—and nobody has yet wanted to set foot in the great avalanche-cones above it that guard the approaches to the dramatic yet climbable and safe granite ridges that separate them. History, however, is certain to repeat itself. Someone, probably soon, will climb that wall, complex and dangerous as are its approaches.

The climbers today who are attempting these new routes up McKinley and its satellites are an extraordinary breed. Although they come from all over the world, many of the very best are from America's West and Alaska. Certainly, they all have better clothing, food, and equipment than the "pioneers" of only fifty years ago. They have also learned how to use this new gear with superb effectiveness. But most of the new routes that they are forging today are so steep and technically so difficult—even when they are safe—that none of the best climbers in the last generation would have considered them at all possible. In fact, they would not have even thought of attempting this sort of climb.

Twenty years ago none would have dared to apply California's Yosemite techniques to the frigid walls of Alaska's peaks or the Himalaya. If there were no little ledges or shoulders where you could camp for the night on one of these walls, you simply did not try to climb them. In Yosemite it is possible to bivouac for the night slung in a featherweight hammock hitched to a few pitons hammered judiciously into the oft-overhanging rock—but not in Alaska. Nevertheless, it is now being done on all these Alaskan walls, sometimes in the winter. And so, one by one, new routes are being climbed successfully today by a handful of experts whose ability, physical stamina, and resourcefulness transcend the wildest dreams of the leaders of only a few years ago.

But what drives people to do this sort of thing? As a big peak is finally dissected to a point where virtually all the basic routes have been climbed somehow by somebody, others begin to attempt what the French call *variantes*. These routes follow the majority of the path that has been climbed before but then fork off up a new gully or a succession of hitherto unclimbed ledges to rejoin the old route higher up on the climb. All of these variations are incredibly difficult, some very exposed and some dangerous. Their divergence from the basic first ascent is often too brief to rate them as a new climb, but they give a special sense of achievement and joy to those who do them.

The psychology behind all this is very simple: those of us who compete want to do our thing a bit better than or a bit differently from those who have gone before. Whether it's the individual who strives to whittle a second off the record for the mile run or the person who climbs Everest alone in five days without oxygen, this drive for what is different, or new, or better is an integral part of the human psyche. As the limits of possibility accepted by each generation are overcome and new goals replace them, the elite group that is pressing at these frontiers becomes smaller, ever more competent, and often far more willing to put their lives on the line to achieve success.

If a virgin peak may be considered to be in its youth, McKinley is now approaching old age in this scheme of things. As possible new routes on its slopes have dwindled to a handful and involve more unavoidable danger, climbers have turned to its satellites for new challenges—the undeniable thrill of climbing on rock and ice that nobody before has ever touched, of experiencing vistas that no one in all the passage of time has seen. This thrill of discovery lies at the heart of all human endeavor and in the mountains it is no different from anywhere else—except that the game, if played to the extreme, involves danger as well as difficulty and those who play the game out at the pioneer fringe of the Alaska Range can no longer do so unless they are endowed with extraordinary skill, stamina, and judgment.

And why does McKinley tempt the world's top mountaineers, when the Alps, the Andes, or even exciting parts of the Himalaya are far easier to approach? What tempted Riccardo Cassin, Lionel Terray, Doug Scott, and Dougal Haston? Why did Barbara and I devote half our lifetimes to charting this range and delving deeply into its secrets?

The answer is simple. There are few mountains of any size, anywhere on earth, that share McKinley's pristine beauty or offer the fascination of its rugged and exquisite wilderness approaches, its lush lowlands and rushing, icy rivers, its flora, and its as-yet-unspoiled wildlife. Whether you first glimpse it at dawn from the gateway of the Chulitna Canyon or at twilight across Wonder Lake, you are caught spellbound by its grandeur and its aloofness from everything else that surrounds us in the hectic confines of our lower world.

Why do people want to struggle through the wilderness to McKinley's summit, knowing well in advance the inevitable physical miseries and downright dangers the struggle will involve, from the mosquito-ridden tundra of its approaches, through its crevasse-gutted glaciers, to the last granite crags that support its drifted peak?

The magnets that draw people to McKinley in ever-growing numbers, year after year, are different for everyone. Hudson Stuck, who had lived and worked in its shadow for years, said that he would rather climb it than discover the richest gold-mine. Pete Anderson and Billy Taylor climbed it to win a miners' bet. Dr. Cook attempted it because its conquest would bring him the fame that would finance his trip to the North Pole. Belmore Browne loved the struggle with the wilderness in any form, forest or glacier, ridge or canyon: McKinley epitomized this love. Hemmed in by the increasing complexities of civilization, we all feel a special joy in coming face-to-face with the best that nature has to offer.

And every one of us who has climbed to the crest of McKinley's final windswept drift will remember Robert Tatum's very personal thrill of pausing there to look "out the windows of Heaven."

Two thousand years ago, Aristotle understood better than most of us do today each person's ceaseless urge to press forward the frontiers of our knowledge:

The Search for the Truth is in one way hard,
   and in another easy,
For it is evident that no one of us
Can ever master it fully, nor miss it wholly.
Each of us adds a little to our understanding of Nature,
And from all the facts assembled arises a certain grandeur.

Right: McKinley's "Ridge of No Return."

Overleaf: The Great Gorge—mists rise after a blizzard.

Second overleaf: The 5,000-foot granite East Face of Mount Dickey.

Above: Mount Huntington's mile high North Face.

Right: A detail of the same face.

Overleaf: Mount Huntington in late afternoon mists.

Second overleaf: The vast and forbidding East Face of Mount McKinley.

Third overleaf: Mount Hunter.

176

ACKNOWLEDGMENTS

by Bradford Washburn

AN ADEQUATE EXPRESSION of thanks to all of those who, in one way or another, have made a significant contribution to making this book a reality is utterly impossible. As the selection of illustrations was completed and the manuscript went to press, I assembled a vast array of little notes, memos, lists, and "don't forgets"—which, all neatly arranged, added up to more than a hundred and fifty individuals and institutions who have played an important part in this little enterprise since I first started to think about it more than forty years ago.

Its first roots were in the National Geographic Society, with which I have had a warm and wonderful relationship for exactly sixty years.

The need for a good map of McKinley arose from that trip, on which we had no map at all. The adventures that produced the new map resulted, inadvertently, in this book. Year after year, the map took shape with help from Harvard's Institute of Geographical Exploration, Boston's Museum of Science, the Swiss Foundation for Alpine Research, Wild-Heerbrugg, and the Swiss Federal Institute of Topography. (It was inspired by Dr. Edouard Imhof of Zurich.)

To me Mount McKinley is people—not just a mountain. The scores of members of our climbing and surveying teams made McKinley an exciting and inspiring place in which to live and work. These people, many of whom became lifelong friends, were often truly beasts of burden, helping to haul endless tons of food and fuel and shelter and mapping and photo gear—some of it more than once—to the very top of McKinley. They built the igloos, cut the steps, and pulled each other all too often out of Muldrow's crevasses. They helped make the photographs on these pages possible.

Then come the pilots and the aircraft—every conceivable size and type—that brought us to the mountain or dropped our supplies in such outlandish places—and the mechanics who kept them all in the air. And the National Park Service kept an ever-faithful watch over where we were and what was happening long before today's amazing network of reliable featherweight radios.

I can't resist singling out a few individuals among these expressions of thanks: the faith, generosity, advice, and prodding of these stalwarts brought this book into existence: Gilbert Grosvenor, Hamilton Rice, Kari Weber, Ernst Feuz, Albert Schmidheini, Simon Bertschmann, Ernst Huber, Daniel Chervet, Othmar Gurtner, Carl and Dorothy Fuller, Norman and Helene Cahners, Din and Terre Land, Terry and Katrina Moore, Bob Bates, Jim Gale, Bob and Miriam Kinsey, Roy, Augusta and Arthur Little—and the members of the 10th Rescue Squadron of the U.S. Air Force.

My special thanks go to the gifted photographers, young and old, whose added pictures do so much to bring our text to life—and, like the mechanics who kept our airplanes flying, the lab technicians who brought my negatives to life: Ted Wood, Bob Keller, John Glynn, Gus Kayafas, Panopticon, and Northeast Color. We must also remember the many who submitted superb pictures for which we couldn't find space to print. Nobby Clark and Kodak's Research Laboratories gave me years and years of wise advice and all sorts of exciting new kinds of film to test. Jim Baker and Fred Macone designed and built a wonderful zigzag viewfinder for my aerial camera. Jim Greenwood and Learjet, Rowland and Liberty Mirror produced an incomparable optical glass photo window through which so many of our pictures were made. Legible texts could not exist without typewriters and word processors, and love and thanks go to those wondrous women who plied them so selflessly: Priscilla Smith, Mary Morgan, Jean Buitekan, Jessie Gugino, and Esther Fich.

To this ever-growing but special group I must add David Roberts whose climbing and writing skills are so important to these pages—and Bob Morton, Doris Leath and Maria Miller, Christine Liotta and the Abrams team that put it all together so beautifully—and Ad Carter, Carolyn Jakeman, Madeleine Gleason, and Bill Hackett whose infinite patience and competence helped me with the intricacies of our bibliography.

Without those memorable evenings with my heroes of the past there would have been no tales to tell: Ansel Adams, Albert Stevens, Edouard Imhof, Belmore Browne, Bobby Dunn, Charlie McGonagall, Harry Karstens, Chris Christensen, Grant Pearson, Joe Crosson, Don Sheldon. How lucky I have been to be able to count them all as close friends.

Last and most important of all: my gratitude is boundless for the patience, wisdom, partnership, and guts of my beloved Barbara, who has brilliantly weathered the fifty years of cameras, negatives, tripods, theodolites, houses jammed with camping gear, pictures, boxes, and duffelbags—which all eventually brought these pictures and text into reality.

The Moose's Tooth, seen through the granite Gateway of the Great Gorge.

Kuskokwin River
(South Fork)

Brooks 1902

Cook 1903

Dillinger River

Tonzona River

Kuskokwim River (Swift Fork)

Browne
June 30, 1906

MT. RUSSELL
11,670'

MT. FORAKER
17,400'

Cook 1903

MT. DALL
8,756'

DALL GLACIER

YENTNA GLACIER

LACUNA GLACIER

MT. HUNTER
14,570'

RAINY PASS

Yentna River (West Fork)

Yentna River (East Fork)

KAHILTNA GLACIER

Brooks 1902

Kichatna River

MT. KLISKON
3,940'

Lake
Chelatna

Dutch Hills

Cook-Parker-Browne 1906

Skwentna River

1902 & 1903

1906 (horses)

1906 Base Camp
(limit of boat travel)

YENTNA RIVER

Kahiltna River

Peters Hills

Tokositna River

1902, 03, 06 (horses)

Swan Lake

Skwentna River

1906 (boat)

1902, 03, 06 (horses)

YENTNA RIVER

Cook 1906

SUSITNA RIVER

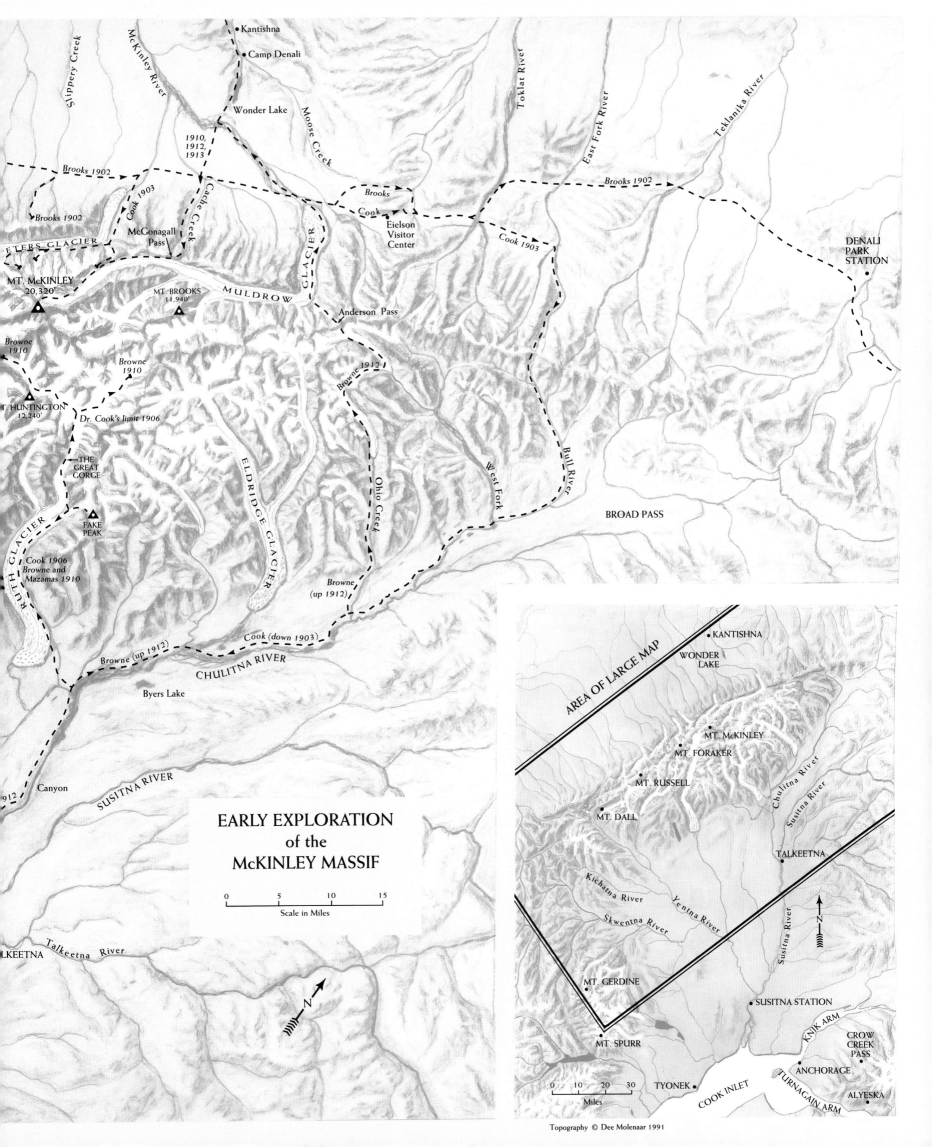

EARLY EXPLORATION
of the
McKINLEY MASSIF

Scale in Miles
0   5   10   15

N

Large map labels:

Kantishna
Camp Denali
Wonder Lake
1910, 1912, 1913
Brooks 1902
Brooks 1902
Cook 1903
McGonagall Pass
ELERS GLACIER
MT. McKINLEY 20,320'
MT. BROOKS 11,940'
MULDROW
Cache Creek
GLACIER
Brooks
Cook
Eielson Visitor Center
Cook 1903
DENALI PARK STATION
Anderson Pass
Browne 1910
Browne 1910
Browne 1912
T. HUNTINGTON 12,240'
Dr. Cook's limit 1906
THE GREAT GORGE
ELDRIDGE GLACIER
West Fork
Ohio Creek
Bull River
BROAD PASS
FAKE PEAK
RUTH GLACIER
Cook 1906 Browne and Mazamas 1910
Browne (up 1912)
Browne (up 1912)
Cook (down 1903)
CHULITNA RIVER
Byers Lake
912
Canyon
SUSITNA RIVER
LKEETNA
Talkeetna River
Slippery Creek
McKinley River
Moose Creek
Toklat River
East Fork River
Teklanika River

Inset map labels:

AREA OF LARGE MAP
KANTISHNA
WONDER LAKE
MT. McKINLEY
MT. FORAKER
MT. RUSSELL
Chulitna River
Susitna River
MT. DALL
TALKEETNA
Kichatna River
Yentna River
Skwentna River
Susitna River
N
MT. GERDINE
SUSITNA STATION
KNIK ARM
CROW CREEK PASS
MT. SPURR
TYONEK
COOK INLET
ANCHORAGE
TURNAGAIN ARM
ALYESKA

0 10 20 30
Miles

Topography © Dee Molenaar 1991

BIBLIOGRAPHY

by Bradford Washburn

Two relatively lengthy bibliographies of the Alaska Range have been published to date: my 88-page "descriptive bibliography," *Mount McKinley and the Alaska Range in Literature* (1951), and that by Terris and Katrina Moore, as an appendix to Dr. Moore's excellent volume, *Mt. McKinley, the Pioneer Climbs* (1967). Since then, I have combined these basic lists and greatly increased their size: the inevitable result of the enormous number of ascents of Mount McKinley that have been made in recent years, from almost every conceivable angle, in spring, summer, and winter. That new bibliography, now in manuscript, differs from most, as I have read every entry and written a memorandum on each. Some of these notes are very brief, but others are quite lengthy: in the case of those most difficult to locate or of special historical significance. This manuscript is now over 160 pages in length and steadily growing. A bibliography is never completed.

There is not the space in this volume to print the entire text of the new bibliography. It will be published in the near future by the University of Alaska Press. However, my present publishers have generously allotted the following pages to print a specially-edited bibliography. To conform to the space, we have limited the entries to ones related to Mount McKinley, or to those focused on the *first ascents* of Mount Foraker, Mount Hunter, and Mount Huntington. The descriptive material has also undergone considerable surgery to keep it within reasonable dimensions. It is my hope that it will nevertheless prove of significant value to those who, after reading our text, may wish to delve further into the ever-fascinating study of Mount McKinley's extraordinary past.

The flow of information to record this history has come from the National Park Service in Alaska, where mountaineering rangers Bob Gerhard, Bob Seibert, and Roger Robinson have been my main sources of recent information; Adams Carter, the editor of the *American Alpine Journal*, and the editors of *Climbing, Mountain, Summit* and *Alaska* have also poured a steady stream of information into my mailbox; the USGS Anchorage office provided treasures related to Alfred H. Brooks; and the facilities of Harvard's Widener and Houghton Libraries have yielded a wealth of original manuscripts, as have Boston's Science Museum Library, the Mazamas, and Bill Hackett of Portland, Oregon.

Lastly, and most important, the preparation and editing of this mass of raw material would not have been possible without the able professional assistance of Madeleine Gleason and Carolyn Jakeman—and the years of typing, retyping, and word-processing of Mary Morgan, Jean Buitekan, Jessie Gugino, and Esther Fich—to all of whom: heartfelt thanks!

Editor's note:
Individual journal and newspaper articles are indexed by author wherever possible. Each author's writings are arranged chronologically.

Page numbers follow volume number and/or month-year number. Thus, "AJ 53 (Nov. 1913): 425–27" refers to *Alpine Journal*, volume 53, for November 1913, pages 425–427.

Illustrations are noted for each publication in which they occur.

Cross-references [*See* or *See also*] are to author and publication date of relevant item.

LIST OF JOURNALS AND A KEY TO ABBREVIATIONS

Accidents in North American Mountaineering is a booklet that has been published each year since 1948. Since 1977 it has been edited and jointly published by the American Alpine Club and the Alpine Club of Canada. It not only lists virtually all accidents each year, but often contains excellent analysis and editorial comment.

Alaska. Anchorage.

Alaska Sportsman. Juneau/Ketchikan.

Alpine Journal. London. Cited as AJ.

American Alpine Journal. New York, NY. Cited as AAJ.

American Geographical Society *Bulletin*. New York, NY. Cited as AGSB.

Appalachia. Boston.

Ascent. "Annual" *Journal of Mountaineering*. San Francisco, CA: Sierra Club. 4 vols. to date (1968, 1975, 1980, 1984).

Climbing. Carbondale, CO.

Dartmouth Mountaineering. Hanover, NH. Cited as DM.

Geographical Journal. London. Cited as GJ.

Harvard Mountaineering. Cambridge, MA. Cited as HM.

Mazama. A Record of Mountaineering. Portland, OR.

Mountain. Sheffield, England.

National Geographic. Washington, DC. Cited as NG.

Outing [Magazine]. New York, NY.

Sierra Club Bulletin. San Francisco, CA. Cited as SCB.

Summit. Fleetwood, PA.

United States Geological Survey *Bulletin*. Washington, DC. Cited as USGSB.

BOOKS, ARTICLES, AND DOCUMENTS

Abrons, Henry L. "A New Route on the Wickersham Wall." AAJ 1964: 47–51. 3 photos. First direct ascent of Wickersham Wall.

Adams, Ansel. *The Portfolios of Ansel Adams*. Boston: New York Graphic, 1981. 136 pp.; principally photos. The cover photo is a magnificent picture of Mt. McKinley seen over Wonder Lake; plate 1, portfolio IV is a superb picture of the Teklanika River in flood.

Alaska Geographic Society 15, no. 3. *Denali*. Anchorage, 1988. 96 pp. 87 photos; 1 map. A profusely illustrated review of the history of the Park, its ascents, highway, animals, flowers, tourist accommodations.

Alaska. "The Alaska-Yukon Wild Flowers Guide." Anchorage, 1977. 218 pp. Profusely illustrated.

Allen, Lieut. Henry T. *Report on an Expedition to the Copper, Tanana and Koyukuk Rivers...in the Year 1885*, etc. *See* U.S. Senate Executive Document 125, 49th Congress, 2nd session (1886–87). U.S. Doc. serial set #2449. Washington, 1887. 172 pp.

American Alpine Journal. 1961: 44–48. "Accidents in North American Mountaineering." A thorough account of the John Day/Helga Bading crisis on Mt. McKinley's W Buttress.

———. 1968: 117–18. Editor's note. A review of the facts related to the terrible death toll of the Wilcox expedition of July 1967.

———. 1976: 430. "Mount Foraker, First Winter Ascent: Southeast Ridge." *Re* the first winter ascent of Mt. Foraker (via the SE Ridge).

———. 1977: 148. "Mt. McKinley, Couloir from W. Buttress Route to Kahiltna." *Re* the first ascent of the "Hourglass Couloir" of the W Buttress by Reinhold Messner and Oswald Olz (July 13, 1976).

———. 1978: 504. "Mt. McKinley, New Start on the American Direct Route, South Face." *Re* a difficult Japanese variant of the Centennial Wall of the S Face.

———. 1981: facing p. 2. Photo. Jack Roberts and Simon McCartney's first ascent of McKinley's SW face direct (June 1980). No description of this climb.

American Geographical Society *Bulletin* 44 (1912): 45. "Prof. Parker's Next Attempt on Mt. McKinley." A brief announcement of the departure of the 1912 expedition from Seattle on January 24. Also an outline of the plan of approach.

———, pp. 364–65. "Failed to Scale Mt. McKinley." *Re* the failure of the Cairns expediton of 1912.

———, p. 686. "The Parker Expedition to Mt. McKinley." A brief report on the return of the 1912 expedition and its having reached a point just below the top of the S Peak. This performance "practically demonstrated the possibility of reaching the top of Mt. McKinley by the northern or Muldrow glacier route."

Anaconda Standard (Anaconda, MT): Oct. 28–31, 1909: microfilm from Montana State University Library. On October 29, 1909, Dr. Frederick A. Cook lectured at the Lucas Opera House in Hamilton, MT. The extraordinary coverage by the Anaconda paper, 50 miles away, was the result of an amazing amount of local feeling because Fred Printz and Ed Barrill, of Cook's 1906 McKinley expedition, lived in nearby Darby. Oct. 28, 1909: 1, 11. "Cook Not after Revenge; Asks Only a Square Deal." Oct. 29, 1909: 1, 6. "Hamilton Votes Confidence in Barrill and Printz"; "Furore caused by Cook resolutions." Oct. 30, 1909: 1, 12, 13. "Cook struggles before audience to prove claims—Hamilton Chamber of Commerce adopts resolutions declaring meeting was absolutely fair and decorous and that explorer failed to make good his charges."

———: 6. "Dr. Cook in Hamilton." [Editorial] Oct. 31, 1909: 1. "Porter Adds to Barrill's Story."—"Topographer on Mt. M'Kinley Expedition gives out signed statement on the trip."—"Porter says he recognizes location as about four miles from one of his surveying stations."

"Anchorage News." *Anchorage Times* Jan. 15–Mar. 10, 1967. An interesting series of articles describing the first winter ascent of Mt. McKinley.

Anchorage Times. See Forty-Ninth Star.

Anderson, Robert L. "Mt. McKinley—An Adventure in Expeditionary Mountaineering." *Mazama* Dec. 1952: 35–41. 5 photos. An account of the 8th ascent, under the leadership of Capt. William D. Hackett.

Armstrong, Robert H. *Guide to the Birds of Alaska.* Anchorage: Alaskan Northwest Publishing Co., 1983. 332 pp. 435 photos and paintings; 1 map. A complete and well-illustrated guide that covers all of the birds one can encounter in Denali Park.

Ashley, Mildred P. *See* Farquhar, Francis P.

Balch, Edwin Swift. *Mt. McKinley and Mountain Climbers' Proofs.* Philadelphia: Campion, 1914. 142 pp. A detailed analysis of the Cook controversy, including a columnar comparison of Cook's statements presented adjacent to those of his most prominent opponents. The author casts his vote in favor of Dr. Cook.

Banks, Michael E. B. "Two North American Expeditions." *AJ* May 1966: 19–22. 4 photos. The account of a British Joint Services Expedition (9 men) to McKinley by the W Buttress. For another account, see "Climbing Mount McKinley," *Mountain Craft* (London: Mountaineering Assn.) Summer 1966: 4–7, 35 (5 photos). Also "Nine Men on a Mountain," by a staff reporter, *Soldier Magazine* (London) Oct. 1962: 17–18 (3 photos).

Barbour, Ian. *See* Schein, Marcel 1948.

Barrill, Edward N. "Barrill's Mount McKinley Affidavit," by Bradford Washburn. *AAJ* 1989: 112–22. 1 photo. 2 maps. Here, published for the first time since the *Globe* publication in 1909, is the complete text of Edward N. Barrill's affidavit saying that he and Dr. Cook never climbed higher than 10,000 ft.

Barrill, Marjorie. "Barrill and Dr. Cook." *AAJ* 1988: 80–82. 1 photo. A brief but important postscript to the Cook-McKinley controversy: a letter to B. Washburn (Jan. 29, 1988) from Barrill's daughter in Darby, MT, outlining her conversations with her father, which make clear that from the very beginning he told family and friends that he and Dr. Cook never got anywhere near the top of Mt. McKinley. A Washburn aerial photo shows exactly where Barrill said he and Dr. Cook went.

Bates, Robert H. "Mt. McKinley, 1942." *AAJ* 5 (1943): 1–13. 15 photos. The story of the third ascent of the S Peak by the U.S. Army Alaskan Test Expedition of 1942.

———. *Mountain Man.* Clinton, NJ: Amwell Press, 1989. 470 pp. A biography of Belmore Browne, this book is a classic by an author who climbed Mt. McKinley and knew Browne and his wife intimately.

Beach, William N. *In the Shadow of Mt. McKinley.* New York: Derrydale Press, 1931. 289 pp. 62 photos, 4 photos of paintings; 8 pencil sketches; 1 map. Stories of hunting and photo expeditions on the northern slopes of the Alaska Range in 1922, 1925, 1926, and 1930. Excellent illustrations—some of them very fine sketches by the artist Carl Rungius.

Bean, Tom. "Photographing Denali's Dalls." *Alaska* (June 1981): 34–36. 3 photos. This text contains the best advice ever given to a person who wants to photograph wild animals—by a professional photographer who was also a ranger in Denali Park. A superb little story.

Beauclerk, Osborne. "Ascent of Mt. McKinley." *GJ* 40 (1912): 656–57. A short description of the 1912 expedition and the great earthquake of July 6, 1912, by an English gentleman who returned across the United States with Parker and Browne.

Beckey, Fred. "Climbs in Alaska, 1954." *AJ* (May 1955): 31–36. 4 aerial photos by B. Washburn. A succinct account of three separate and widely separated first-ascent routes, climbed during the course of only 70 days: the W Buttress of McKinley's N Peak (by the route on which Cook's party failed in 1903), the S Ridge of Mt. Deborah (12,450 ft.), and Mt. Hunter (14,580 ft.) by its W Ridge. Illustrates dramatically how much can be done by competent climbers. For another version, see "Mount Deborah and Mount Hunter: First Ascents," *AAJ* 1955: 39–50 (5 photos).

Beckwith, Edward P. "Carpé, Koven Died in Feat of Daring." *New York Times,* May 18, 1932, pp.1 and 12. A brief account written immediately after the author had been flown out to Fairbanks from Muldrow Glacier by pilot Jerry Jones of Alaskan Airways.

———. "The Mt. McKinley Cosmic Ray Expedition, 1932." *AAJ* 2 (1933): 45–68. 10 photos; 2 sketch maps. A complete, factual account of the Carpé-Koven tragedy by one of the members of the expedition.

Beeman, Marydith. *See* Walker, Tom 1987.

Berry, William D. *Denali—An Alaskan Moose.* New York: Macmillan, 1965. 48 pp. A heartwarming children's book about the life of a little moose born in Denali National Park. Beautifully written and illustrated.

———. *Alaskan Field Sketches, 1954–1956."* Fairbanks, 1989. 230 pp. Profusely illustrated in both black-and-white and color. A remarkable compilation of the best of Berry's superb sketches of animals and birds, most of them in McKinley Park.

Bertulis, Alex. "Mount McKinley's S Face, Alpine Style." *Mountain* 28 (July 1973): 24. 8 photos. A brief report on the first "alpine style" ascent of the W Rib of the S Face.

Black, Donald. "McKinley: Attempt via West Fork of the Traleika Glacier." *AAJ* 1973: 404–05. A short account of the first ascent of this "horrendously dangerous" new route directly into Thayer Basin.

Blazej, Adam. "Mount McKinley, South Face; New Route." *AAJ* 1985: 174. 1 photo. An extremely brief description of what is still the most difficult ascent yet climbed on Mt. McKinley—a super-direttissima up the S Face, paralleling the Cassin Ridge and just to the right (E) of it.

Bleser, Warren. "McKinley's East Buttress." *Summit* (Sept. 1965): 12–15. 7 photos. A brief but well-illustrated account of the first ascent of the E Buttress in the spring of 1963.

Blomberg, Gregg. "The Winter Ascent of Mount McKinley." *Climbing* Jan.–Feb. 1968: 2–3, 14–25. 16 photos, including cover. The best account [except for Art Davidson's book *Minus 148 Degrees*] of this extraordinary expedition, the first winter ascent of McKinley. For a similar account, without photos, see *AAJ* 1968: 21–26.

Blum, Arlene. "The Damsels and Denali." *Summit* (May 1971): 18–26. 13 photos incl. front cover. A brief, profusely illustrated account of the first all-female ascent of Mt. McKinley.

Boertje, Rodney D. "Nutritional Ecology of the Denali Caribou Herd." Unpublished M.Sci. thesis, University of Alaska, Fairbanks, 1981. 294 pp. 1 map. A remarkable, detailed study of the many factors that have led to the survival of this small and isolated herd in areas northeast of Mt. McKinley.

Bouchard, John. "Paragliders and Modern Alpinism." *AAJ* 1988: 91–92. 1 photo (p.89). A brief but interesting report on the advent of this new and extraordinary sport, including mention that a paraglider descent had already taken place on Mt. McKinley.

Boulton, Ben. "Yalie Proves You Can Still Reach Your Peak at 71." *New Haven Register* July 30, 1988: 1. 1 photo. A brief news story about Donald W. Henry's W Buttress climb, July 17, at age 71.

Bowie, William. "Determination of the Height and Geographical Position of Mt. McKinley." *AGSB* 42 (1910): 260–61. A brief technical report on the results of the field work done by Mr. H. W. Rhodes' party to Cook Inlet in 1909 for the U.S. Coast and Geodetic Survey.

Bowman, Warren D. *Outdoor Emergency Care.* National Ski Patrol. 1988. 466 pp. To quote Dr. Charles Houston: "Just about anyone who walks or skis or climbs where they will be hours [often days] away from medical care will benefit from this excellent book."

Bradley, Kent. "McKinley's Personal Cameraman." *Alaska* Aug. 6, 1964: 30. 11 photos. A brief story about Charlie Ott, who has taken many superb pictures of Denali Park's wildlife. Includes a portfolio of five of his best.

Breitenbach, Jake. *See TIME* 1959.

Bridges, E. Lucas. *The Uttermost Part of the Earth.* London: Hodder & Stoughton, 1948. Illustrated with photos of Tierra del Fuego. A remarkable account of the life of a British missionary family who lived for many years in Tierra del Fuego. Its relevance to Mt. McKinley is seen on pp. 227–29, 239–41, and 529–37, in which the 1898 visit of Dr. Frederick Cook to this remote spot is described along with his extraordinary dealings related to the publication of the Yahgan-English dictionary compiled by Mr. Bridges' father, Rev. Thomas Bridges.

Bright, Norman. "Billy Taylor, Sourdough." *AAJ* 3 (1939): 274–86. 1 photo. An important account of an interview with one of the two sourdoughs who made the first ascent of the N Peak of Mt. McKinley in 1910.

Brooks, Alfred H. "Notes of Exploration by the U.S. Geological Survey: Mt. McKinley, Alaska." *AGSB* 34 (1902), no. 5: 454–56. Probably the first article describing the author's famous 1902 expedition. A brief account, published immediately after his return. Note: the original field diaries are in the archives of the USGS Technical Data Unit, Anchorage.

———. "An Exploration to Mount McKinley, America's Highest Mountain." *Journal of Geography* 2 (Chicago, 1903): 440–69. Another ed.: Smithsonian Institution Annual Report (Washington 1903): 402–25. 13 photos; 1 sketch map. A popular account of the remarkable 800-mile expedition.

———. "The Alaskan Range: A New Field for the Mountaineer." *AGSB* 37, no. 8 (1905): 468–79. 5 photos; 1 sketch map. A brief account of the 1902 expedition, followed by a splendid description of the challenge of Alaskan mountaineering and exploration.

———. *The Mount McKinley Region, Alaska.* U.S. Geological Survey, Professional Paper 70 (Washington 1911). 234 pp. 15 photos; 30 diagrams, sketches and cross-sections; 3 maps in pocket. A McKinley classic. A detailed record of the remarkable Brooks-Reaburn Expedition of 1902 from Cook Inlet across the Skwentna flats, up the Kichatna River, across Rainy Pass, along the entire northen slope of the Alaska Range to the Nenana River, thence to the Tanana, Rampart, and St. Michael (June 1–Sept. 15, 1902). The maps and geologic data that resulted from this expedition represent a monumental accomplishment for a single season's work.

Brooks, Alfred H., and D. L. Reaburn. "Plans for Climbing Mt. McKinley." NG 14 (1903): 30–35. 1 sketch map. A brief historical sketch, followed by an equally brief account of the 1902 expedition. This article concludes with a highly practical analysis of the problems involved in approaching Mt. McKinley.

Brown, T. Graham. "Mt. Foraker." AJ 46 (1934): 393–402. 2 photos. An account of the first ascent of Mt. Foraker, written by the distinguished British member of the Houston expedition.

———. "Mt. Foraker, Alaska." AJ 47 (1935): 14–48 (5 photos; 1 sketch map) and 205–43 (10 photos). Two extremely detailed articles on the first ascent of Mt. Foraker by the Houston Expedition of 1934. The first is an account of the expedition from its start (July 3) at McKinley Park Station to Camp V (9,700 ft.) (July 30). The second installment starts from Camp V. The summit was reached on Aug. 6, after a 15-hour climb. The lower (western) peak of Mt. Foraker was climbed on Aug. 10, and the expedition ended at Savage River Camp on Aug. 28.

Browne, Belmore. "The Struggle up Mount McKinley." *Outing* 50 (1907): 257–76. 12 photos; 1 sketch map. One of the earliest popular accounts of the results of the 1906 expedition.

———. "Struggling up Mt. McKinley." *Colliers* 44 (New York, Nov. 13, 1909): 18–19, 34. 3 photos. A brief, popular account of the 1903 and 1906 expeditions.

———. "The Parker Expedition to Mt. McKinley." AGSB 42 (1910): 267–69. A brief but interesting advance notice of the plans of the 1910 expedition, and a description of its equipment.

———. "Sleuthing on Mt. McKinley." *Metropolitan Magazine* 33 (New York, Jan. 1911): 482–89. 7 photos. The first illustrated public statement of Parker and Browne's side of the Cook-McKinley controversy [see Parker, Herschel C., and Belmore Browne]. Contains photos of Cook's "summit" taken in both June and July 1910 (Cook's picture was taken in Sept. 1906). This famous paragraph occurs on p. 489: "To sum up, our discoveries prove beyond doubt that Dr. Cook, wilfully and with full knowledge of the deception, claimed the ascent of Mt. McKinley, when he had not even reached the base of the mountain."

———. "By Motorboat to Mt. McKinley." *Outing* 57 (New York, Mar. 1911): 714–22. 6 photos. A popular account of the southern approach to Mt. McKinley by the Parker-Browne Expedition of 1910. This little-known reference describes the tremendous difficulties encountered in reaching even the foothills of the Alaska Range in the days before the railroad.

———. "The Conquering of Mt. McKinley." *Hearst's*

Magazine 22 (New York, Dec. 1912): 38–50. 12 photos. An interesting, popular account of the 1912 expedition, including several illustrations that have never appeared elsewhere.

———. "Conquering Mt. McKinley." *Outing* 61 (Feb. 1913): 515–30. 16 photos; 1 painting. The first of a series of five popular articles on the Parker-Browne Expedition of 1912. This installment carries the party from the landing at Resurrection Bay (January) up the Susitna and Chulitna by dog team to the point (Mar. 20) where they swing northward to cross the Alaska Range. The illustrations are excellent, as in all Browne's publications. The second installment (vol. 61 [Mar. 1913]: 643–61, with 18 photos and 1 painting) tells of the crossing of the Alaska Range to the timber on the McKinley River (Apr. 17). The third installment (vol. 62 [Apr. 1913]: 2–23, with 19 photos) describes the actual assault on Mt. McKinley (Apr. 24–July 6, 1912). The fourth installment: "An Alaskan Happy Hunting Ground," in vol. 62 [May 1913]: 194–209, with 15 photos and 1 painting) gives a pleasant description of sheep and caribou hunting in the hills north of Mt. McKinley in the spring of 1912. The fifth and final installment: "Hitting the Home Trail from Mt. McKinley" (vol. 62 [July 1913]: 387–404, with 12 photos) describes the return journey from Cache Creek at the base of McKinley, down the Kantishna and the Tanana to Fort Gibbon on the Yukon.

———. *The Conquest of Mount McKinley.* New York: Putnam's, 1913. 367 pp. 86 photos; 9 paintings; 1 sketch map. A McKinley classic. The most complete work ever written on the mountain, telling the absorbing and superbly illustrated story of the Parker-Browne expeditions of 1906, 1910, and 1912. Review in *The Nation* (New York), Jan. 22, 1914: 84–85, contains several caustic remarks about Dr. Cook, whom the reviewer considered a faker.

———. A new edition. Boston: Houghton Mifflin, 1956. 381 pp. Illustrated with 41 photos, several previously unpublished, which greatly assist the reader in understanding the complex geography of McKinley and its approaches. Foreword by Vilhjalmur Stefansson; Introduction by Bradford Washburn.

———. "Herschel Clifford Parker." AAJ 6 (1947): 408–11, An excellent biographical sketch written by an intimate friend and partner in the field.

———. "Belmore Browne, 1880–1954." AAJ 1955: 216–20. 1 photo. Obituary notice by Henry S. Hall, Jr., a lifelong friend.

Bryson, George. "Climber Home after Historic McKinley Trek." *Anchorage Daily News*, Mar. 16, 1988: 1. 1 illustration. A brief but interesting account of the first successful winter solo ascent of Mt. McKinley by Vern Tejas of Anchorage.

———. "The Tejas Triumph." *Anchorage Daily News:* "We Alaskans" weekly magazine. "The Coldest Climb," Apr. 3, 1988: 7–13 (cover photo, 5 self-photos), and "Surviving the Mountain," Apr. 10, 1988: 7–13 (cover photo, 4 photos); 132 and 176 column inches, respectively). A detailed story of Vern Tejas' first solo winter ascent of Mt. McKinley (Mar. 7, 1988), "as told to" this reporter of the *News*. The best existing account of this remarkable climb.

Bryxell, Burton L., ed. *See* Brooks, Alfred H. 1953.

Buchanan, Dave. "More on the Alaska Issue." *Climbing* Sept.–Oct. 1982: 10–12. An interesting article on the

ever-increasing costs of mountaineering accidents in national parks and the various options of financing them. A condensation in *Mountain* 83 (Jan.–Feb. 1982): 53.

Buchanan, Douglas. *See* Gerhard, Robert, and Douglas Buchanan.

Buckingham, William J. "The Western Rib of Mount McKinley's South Face." AAJ 1960: 1–9. 8 photos. First ascent of the W Rib (June 19, 1959), the first technically difficult route on McKinley.

Buskirk, Steve. *Mount McKinley—The Story behind the Scenery.* Las Vegas, NE: KC Publications, 1978. 48 pp. Size 9″x12″. Beautifully illustrated in color. A succinct, sensitive, popular booklet on the history, botany, and wildlife of Denali Park.

Cairns, Ralph H. "Unable to Scale Heights of Mighty Mt. M'Kinley, Climbing Party Returns." *Fairbanks Daily Times*, Apr. 10, 1912, pp. 1–2. 4-column headline and 53 column-inches of text. The first account of the little known *Fairbanks Times* Expedition of 1912, published the day after its return to Fairbanks. The first complete ascent of this beautiful ridge was not made until 1988. For another version, see "Hazards of Climbing Mount McKinley," *Overland Monthly* 61 (San Francisco: Feb. 1913): 107–23 (19 illustrations). Foreword by Dr. Cook. This article contains one of the first recorded mentions of the use of "willow wands" to mark the trail on a high Alaskan peak.

Canadian Alpine Journal (Banff, 1978): 23–29. 8 photos. Accounts of three new routes on the southwest side of Mt. McKinley by a strong and experienced Canadian party.

Capps, Kris. "Brad and Barbara Washburn." *Fairbanks Daily News-Mirror* weekly magazine "Heartland," June 19, 1988: H4–7. 10 photos. An interview during the Washburns' visit to the University of Alaska at Fairbanks to plan a gift of their log books and pictures to the university archives. Many direct quotes.

Capps, Stephen R. "Glaciation of the Alaska Range." *Journal of Geology* 20 (Chicago 1912): 415–37. 10 photos; 1 map. A preliminary description of the glaciers around Mt. McKinley before they had been explored or mapped in any but the most superficial way.

———. "A Game Country Without Rival in America: The Proposed Mt. McKinley National Park." NG 31 (Jan. 1917): 69–84. 13 photos; 1 sketch map. One of the articles that helped focus public attention on McKinley Park and push the bill creating it through Congress the next month.

———. "The Mount McKinley National Park." In *Proceedings of the National Parks Conference*, U.S. Department of the Interior (Washington 1917): 226–42. An address delivered in Washington on the evening of Jan. 4, 1917. An absorbing account of McKinley Park [which was not officially created until Feb. 26, 1917], its natural beauty, its game, and its future as a tourist resort. Capps, along with Belmore Browne and Charles Sheldon, was one of the strongest advocates of the establishment of the park.

———. *The Kantishna Region, Alaska.* USGSB 687 (1919). 116 pp. 18 photos; 3 diagrams; 3 sketch maps; 2 excellent maps. Report on field work accomplished during the summer of 1916, covering the region (in general) north of the highway and east of Wonder Lake. An extraordinary accomplishment, considering that the expedition worked only from June 22 to Aug. 29.

———. *Geology of the Alaska Railroad Region.* USGSB 907 (Washington 1940). 201 pp. 9 photos; 3 maps in pocket. A thorough review of the geology of the Denali Park region, bringing together in condensed form all information available up to the time of publication. Contains an excellent geologic bibliography and a history of all geologic field work in the area since 1895.

Carey, Mary. *"Alaska, Not for a Woman!"* Austin, TX: Eakin Press, 1975. 275 pp. 16 photos. Reminiscences of a resident of Talkeetna and close friend of bush pilot Don Sheldon.

Carpé, Allen. Letters [manuscript]. Several interesting letters from Allen Carpé to Francis Farquhar and others relative to his 1932 expedition to Mt. McKinley, are in the Francis P. Farquhar Archives of the University of Alaska, Rasmuson Library, Fairbanks.

Carr, Thomas D. *See* Schein, Marcel 1948.

Casarotto, Renato (Club Alpino Italiano). "Mount McKinley: Ridge of No Return." AAJ 1985: 173–74. 1 photo. A brief account of the first ascent of an extremely sharp and difficult ridge leading from the W Fork of Ruth Glacier to the crest of Mt. McKinley's S Buttress. Casarotto climbed solo.

Cassin, Riccardo. "The South Face of Mount McKinley." AAJ 1962: 27–37. 7 photos. First ascent of the Cassin Ridge (July 19, 1961). The most difficult climb yet made on Mt. McKinley, involving first-class technical problems on both ice and rock. For an excellent, day-to-day account of the climb, see his "McKinley, versant Sud." *La Montagne et Alpinisme* (Paris: Club Alpin Français; trans. and ed. Félix Germain) Apr. 1962: 202–10. 9 photos; 1 sketch map; 2 diagrams, including a precisely marked route on a Washburn aerial photo and on a sketch. See also his detailed "diary" account of the eight "final fateful days," in "Up the Impossible Wall," *LIFE* Aug. 25, 1961: 51–57. 9 photos.

———. *La Sud del McKinley.* Milan: Stampa Grafica Olimpia, 1965. 151 pp. Profusely illustrated. The only detailed account of the greatest climb in the exploration of McKinley, written by the leader of the expedition, one of the most distinguished guides in the Alps at that time. Unfortunately, this book was never translated into English.

———. "An Interview with the Editor of Mountain Magazine." *Mountain* 22 (London: July 1972): 32–36. 3 photos. An interesting summary of the life of "one of the greatest climbers of our time," followed by an interview.

———. *Fifty Years of Alpinism.* London: Diadem Books, and Seattle: The Mountaineers, 1981. 207 pp. Profusely illustrated with photos and diagrams. Pages 131–46 tell the story of the first ascent of the S Ridge of Mt. McKinley in 1961—now known as the Cassin Ridge.

Champlin, Charles. "Magnificent Rescue on McKinley." *LIFE*, June 6, 1960: 25–31. 17 photos. A vivid description of the rescue of Helga Bading and John Day from the W Buttress of Mt. McKinley in late May 1960.

Cole, Terrence, ed. *The Sourdough Expedition.* Anchorage: Alaska Journal, 1985. 64 pp. 30 photos; 1 map. The only single publication that covers virtually every aspect of the famous Sourdough Expedition of 1910. Thomas Lloyd's original story, with photos, and map showing the exact route and camps of the party; also, the famous interview of Billy Taylor made by Norman Bright in 1937 (AAJ 1939).

Collier, Michael. *The Geology of Denali National Park.* Anchorage: Alaska Natural History Assn., 1989. 48 pp. 24 photos; also diagrams and maps. An excellent booklet for the tourist or hiker.

Cook, Dr. Frederick A. "America's Unconquered Mountain." *Harper's Monthly Magazine* 108 (New York and London, 1904): 230–39 (4 photos; 2 sketches) and 335–44 (7 photos). In two articles: Dr. Cook's account of the 1903 expedition, published at the same time as Dunn's blistering articles in *Outing Magazine* [*see* Dunn 1907]. The first article relates the story of the expedition from Cook Inlet to the N Face of Mt. McKinley. The actual attempt on the mountain is described in a scant half page. The return journey—from Mt. McKinley to Tyonek, on Cook Inlet— is the subject of the second article. This trip was a remarkable accomplishment that has never been repeated. The excellent illustrations have been badly retouched.

———. "Round Mount McKinley." AGSB 36 (1904): 321–27. 1 photo; 1 map. A brief account of Dr. Cook's 1903 expedition to the NW side of Mt. McKinley. The last page concludes with a splendid appraisal of the problems faced by the Alaskan exploratory mountaineer.

———. "Results of a Journey around Mount M'Kinley." In *Report of the Eighth International Geographic Congress, Held in the United States, 1904* (Washington, 1905): 748–62. The best brief report in existence describing Cook's expedition of 1903.

———. *Mazama* 3 (Mar. 1907): 55–60. The editor's story of Dr. Cook's first lecture on the "first ascent of Mt. McKinley," as told to an audience informally gathered by the Mazamas, a group of local mountaineers, in Seattle on Nov. 9, 1906.

———. "The Conquest of Mount McKinley." *Harper's Monthly Magazine* 114 (May 1907): 812–37. 7 photos; 6 sketches; 1 excellent map. The first complete public report on the 1906 expedition. Essentially an abridged version of the narrative published in Dr. Cook's book in 1908. Includes several sketches unpublished elsewhere; the titles beneath several of the pictures differ from those under the same illustrations in the book, notably that facing p. 833 (article) and p. 239 (book). The picture of the "summit" in the book (facing p. 227) is unretouched; in the article (p. 835) it has been badly retouched.

———. *To the Top of the Continent.* London: Hodder & Stoughton, 1908. 321 pp. 60 photos; 8 sketches; 1 painting; 1 sketch map. A McKinley classic. Cook's own complete story of the 1903 and 1906 expeditions. Unfortunately, many of the pictures have been badly retouched. This volume and its many illustrations must be carefully studied for a clear understanding of the Cook controversy. For a brilliant quote from Dr. Cook summarizing the miseries faced by anyone who approaches Mt. McKinley from the south on foot, see pp. 183–85.

———. "Mount McKinley." *Overland Monthly* 61 (San Francisco: Feb. 1913): 106. A splendidly written foreword to an article by Ralph H. Cairns describing his party's unsuccessful attack on the NE ridge of the N Peak in the early spring of 1912.

———. *See also Anaconda Standard*, Oct. 28–31, 1909, *New York Times*, Jan. 28, 1990; and biographical sketch in AAJ 1946: 86–88.

Cook, Capt. James, and Capt. James King. *A Voyage to the Pacific Ocean, Undertaken by the Command of His Majesty, for Making Discoveries in the Northern Hemisphere.* London, 1784. Three volumes in quarto and one volume of maps in folio—the first two volumes by Cook, the third by King. Numerous engravings and maps. This classic contains no direct reference to Mt. McKinley, since cloudy weather concealed the big peaks, but it describes in detail the first recorded visit to Cook Inlet, May 20–June 5, 1778 (II: 382–403).

Covington, Michael. "Thunder Ridge, West Buttress, Mount McKinley." AAJ 1983: 144–46. 1 photo. Detailed account of a new route of direct ascent, McKinley's W Buttress (June 24–July 2, 1982).

Crews, Paul. "Accident on Mount McKinley." *Summit* (Aug. 1960): 27. 1 aerial photo. Probably the most accurate and detailed account of the dramatic John Day/Helga Bading crisis and rescue on McKinley's W Buttress (May 7–16, 1960), written by one of those deeply involved from start to finish.

Crosson, Joseph, and Ed Young. "Mt. M'Kinley Conquered from Air." *Fairbanks Daily News-Miner*, Aug. 31, 1931, pp. 1 and 5. 48 column-inches. An account of the second flight over the summit of Mt. McKinley (from Fairbanks), made on Aug. 29 by Joe Crosson, chief pilot of Alaskan Airways, and Oscar Darling, a newsreel photographer representing Fox Movietone News and Hearst Metrotone News. Another airplane, piloted by Ed Young, carried photographer Eric Mayell, who took pictures of Crosson's flight but did not fly over the top. The news story is followed by verbatim excerpts from the flight logs of both Crosson and Young.

Cuntz, John Henry. Obituary notice by Benjamin F. Seaver, in AAJ 1 (1929): 86.

Currier, Richard S. "Genealogical History of the Dickey Family." A very interesting, unpublished two-page memorandum in the Farquhar Archive at the University of Alaska, Fairbanks.

Dall, William Healey. "Remarks on the Natural History of Alaska." Boston Society of Natural History *Proceedings* 12 (Boston 1868): 143–51. Dall was the first westerner to suggest the name "Alaskan Range"—at a meeting on Nov. 4, 1868, in the new building of the Boston Society of Natural History at 234 Berkeley Street. This organization is today's Boston Museum of Science.

Darling, F. Fraser. *See* Leopold, A. Starker.

Davidson, Art. *Minus 148 Degrees: The Winter Ascent of Mount McKinley.* New York: W.W. Norton, Inc., 1969. 218 pp. 32 photos from the ground and from the air. The dramatic story of the first winter ascent of Mt. McKinley in February and March 1967 by the W Buttress route, told by the leader of the expedition.

———. "Return to Denali: Back on the Mountain after 20 Years." *Anchorage Daily News*: "We Alaskans" section Apr. 8, 1990, J9–13. 5 photos. An interesting account of Davidson's second climb of the W Buttress—the first since he made the first winter ascent in 1967.

Davidson, Joseph K. "The Catacomb and E Ridges of Mount McKinley." AAJ 1970: 63–67. 6 photos. First ascent of the E Ridge of McKinley's E Buttress: "Catacomb Ridge" (July 13, 1969). [If Dr. Cook and Ed Barrill climbed McKinley back in 1906, it had to be by this difficult and spectacular route.]

Day, John S. "The Mountain That Nearly Killed Me."

Saturday Evening Post, Nov. 26, 1960: 36, 37, 80. 9 photos. The only detailed account of the dramatic accident and rescue of John Day on the W Buttress (May 17–26, 1960). For the first major account of the John Day/Helga Bading rescue, see "Magnificent Rescue on McKinley," *LIFE* June 6, 1960: 24–31. 16 on-the-spot photographs.

Dean, David. *Breaking Trail—Hudson Stuck of Texas and Alaska*. Athens, OH: Ohio University Press, 1988. 344 pp. 13 photos. A McKinley classic. In addition to including many details of the 1913 first ascent of Mt. McKinley, it contains a gold mine of information about Archdeacon Stuck's life and character and his extraordinary contribution to the betterment of the lives of Alaska's natives.

Decker, Karl. "Dr. Frederick A. Cook—Faker." *Metropolitan Magazine* 31 (New York: Jan. 1910): 416–34. 10 photos; 2 sketch maps; 2 reproductions from Barrill's diary. An analysis of Dr. Cook's claims to both Mt. McKinley and the North Pole, written three months after his return from the polar trip. Also contains interesting direct quotations from Barrill's diary and a sketch map by Belmore Browne, neither found elsewhere.

Denali Park Rangers. *Mountaineering in Denali National Park*. Washington: U.S. National Park Service, 1987 [revised frequently]. 31 pp. 4 illustrations. A brief but useful little paperback. It gives basic data for those considering an ascent of Mt. McKinley as well as many direct quotes from experienced climbers and guides, to remind one that this mountain can be a very savage customer. Recommended reading for all—and at no cost. Write to Denali National Park, Talkeetna, Alaska 99676.

Dickey, William A. "Discoveries in Alaska." *The Sun* (New York), Jan. 24, 1897, sect. 2, p. 6. 47 column-inches; sketch map. The famous letter written by Mr. Dickey to tell the story of his trip up the Susitna and Chulitna rivers in 1896, and to suggest the name of Mt. McKinley.

———. "The Susitna River, Alaska." NG 8 (1897): 322–27. A brief description of the southern approaches to Mt. McKinley as the author saw them during his journey of 1896.

———. *See also* Grimes, Carla 1986.

Dingman, David, and David Dornan. "American Mount McKinley Expedition." AAJ 1959: 292. First to climb both the N and S Peaks on the same day (July 1, 1958).

Dixon, Joseph S. *Birds and Mammals of Mount McKinley National Park, Alaska*. Washington: U.S. Department of the Interior, 1938. 236 pp. 86 photos; 1 sketch map. One of the few older books to describe the wildlife of the Denali Park region. Excellent illustrations. Contains checklists and descriptions of all mammals and birds seen in the park during expeditions in 1926 and 1932.

Doherty, Nancy. "McKinley Sees Tragic Season." *Alaska* Oct. 1976: 8–9. 3 photos. A brief account of the growing number of accidents and rescues arising out of the increasing numbers of climbers attempting the peak each year.

Dornan, David. *See* Dingman, David.

Dunn, Robert. "Across the Forbidden Tundra." *Outing* 43 (Jan. 1904): 459–71. 12 photos. The first of a series of five articles on the Cook Expedition of 1903. Article no. 1 carries the expedition from its beginning to the foothills of the Kichatna River (July 20, 1903). Article no. 2: "Into the Mists of Mt. McKinley" (vol. 43, Feb. 1904: 534–45; 7 photos): takes them from July 20, up the Kichatna River, over Simpson's Pass (July 28), to the base of McKinley (Aug. 15). Article no. 3: "Storm Wrapped on Mt. McKinley" (vol. 43, Mar. 1904: 697–706; 4 photos; 1 sketch map): the story of the first unsuccessful attempt to cross the front range north of Peters Glacier (Aug. 16–24). It contains a sketch map, unpublished elsewhere, illustrating the routes of these attempts. Article no. 4: "Highest on Mt. McKinley" (vol. 44, Apr. 1904: 27–35; 3 photos): describes the ascent of Peters Glacier to its upper basin above the Tluna Icefall and the climb to over 10,000 ft. on the great W Buttress of the N Peak (Aug. 25–31, 1903). Article no. 5: "Home by Ice and Swimming from Mt. McKinley" (vol. 44, May 1904: 214–19; 1 photo) traces the route from the head of Peters Glacier, E along the front of the Alaska Range, over an unknown pass at the head of the extreme eastern fork of the Toklat, and back to Cook Inlet via the Chulitna and Susitna rivers by raft and boat (Sept. 1–25, 1903).

———. "Mountaineering in North America." *Outing* 50 (Sept. 1907): 714–22. An interesting popular article on the opportunities and problems of North American mountaineering.

———. *The Shameless Diary of an Explorer*. New York: The Outing Publishing Co., 1907. 297 pp. 11 photos; 2 sketch maps showing the route of the expedition. One of the McKinley classics. The "inside story" of the extraordinary Cook Expedition of 1903, which made the only trip ever recorded completely around the outer perimeter of Mt. McKinley. Dunn, who also made the first ascents of Mt. Wrangell and Mt. Shishaldin, was the first person to appraise Cook's personality accurately and to write fearlessly about it. *See* Steffens, Lincoln 1931. [During a visit to Dunn at his Katonah, NY, home shortly before his death, B. Washburn discovered the negatives of all of Dunn's pictures. Dunn gave them to B.W., who had them thoroughly washed and cleaned. They are now in the archives of the headquarters of the American Alpine Club in New York City.]

Eames, Hugh. *Winner Lose All: Dr. Cook and the Theft of the North Pole*. Boston: Little Brown, 1978. 346 pp. A biography of Dr. Frederick Cook by a writer who is a devout believer in his alleged accomplishments.

Edwards, W. Mark. "Young Man on the Mountain." *Alaska* July 1982: 32. 3 photos. A school composition, written and illustrated by the youngest person ever to climb Mt. McKinley (2:15 p.m., June 30, 1979). Would that the adults who have climbed McKinley would write so well.

Eldridge, George H. "A Reconnaissance in the Susitna Basin and Adjacent Territory, Alaska, in 1898." In USGS, *Twentieth Annual Report* (Washington, 1900), pt. 7: 1–29. 10 photos; 10 sketches; 1 map (no. 3, in pocket) showing the route of the expedition. The official account of the government expedition that made the first scientific reconnaissance of the topography and geology of the Susitna, "with reference to the location of a railroad or wagon route from Cook Inlet to the Tanana." On this expedition Robert Muldrow, who was the topographer, calculated the altitude of Mt. McKinley as 20,464 ft.

———. *See also* Muldrow, Henry Lowndes 1898.

Elliot, Nan. "Shared Horizons: First Woman on McKinley." *We Alaskans* (Anchorage Daily News) June 14, 1987: 8–13. 8 photos. An account of Brad and Barbara Washburn's fifty-year love affair focused on adventure and discovery ranging from the top of Alaska to the Grand Canyon and Everest.

———. "The Grand Old Man of the Iditerod." Chap. 6 (pp. 51–63) of her *I'd Swap My Old Skidoo for You*. Issaquah, WA: Sammamish Press, 1989. 11 photos. The story of the first dog team ascent of Mt. McKinley by Joe Reddington and Susan Butcher.

Elliott, Lawrence. "Feel Like Climbing Mt. McKinley?" *Alaska* May 1963: 8. 6 photos. A brief but interesting account of Don Sheldon's early experience as a B-17 tail gunner in World War II and the beginnings of his McKinley flying odyssey.

Evans, Gail E. H. "From Myth to Reality: Travel Experiences and Landscape Perceptions in the Shadow of Mt. McKinley, Alaska, 1876–1938." Unpublished M.A. thesis in Public Historical Studies, University of California, Santa Barbara (Feb. 1987). Text, 488 pp.; bibliography; 13 sketch maps. The most detailed description of the history, philosophy, construction, and problems related to the Denali Highway from Park Headquarters to Wonder Lake (1917–1938). Copies are on file at the Archives of the University of Alaska, Fairbanks, and at the State College of Pennsylvania.

Everett, Boyd N. "We Climb our Highest Mountain." *LOOK* (New York), Oct. 9, 1962 (vol. 26, no. 21): 60–69. Profusely illustrated. First ascent of McKinley's SE Spur and S Face (June 29, 1962). A well-illustrated article on the accomplishments of Boyd Everett's extraordinary expedition via the first technically difficult route to be climbed on the SE side of the mountain. A similar account in AAJ 1963: 381–89 (8 photos; 1 sketch): "The Southeast Spur of Mount McKinley."

Fairbanks Daily News-Miner, Aug. 15, 1930: 1. "Alaska Aviators Fly over America's Loftiest Peak." Banner headline and 24 column-inches of text. An account of the first flight over the summit of Mt. McKinley, made Aug. 13, 1930.

———. May 16, 1932: 1 and 5. "Climbers Reach Top of Mt. McKinley." Banner headline and 37 column-inches of text. The first report of the Lindley-Liek Expedition success and of the Carpé-Koven tragedy.

Fairbanks Daily Times, Dec. 22, 1908: 1. "Cheers Are Given as Climbers Leave." 3-column headline and 37 column-inches of text. 1 photo of Archdeacon Stuck. A brief account of the departure of six members of the Sourdough Expedition the previous afternoon, with dog teams, two horses, and a mule.

———. Apr. 12, 1910: 1. "M'Kinley Is Conquered." Banner headline and 16 column-inches of text. The first news report of the Sourdough Expedition, telling the story of Tom Lloyd, who had returned to Fairbanks the previous day.

———. May 7, 1910: 1. "This Climber Claims to Be from Missouri." 3 column-inches of text. A brief news report, telegraphed from Seattle on the occasion of Dr. Parker's departure for Alaska for his attack on the SE face of Mt. McKinley.

———. June 9, 1910: 3. "Make Second Climb of Mount McKinley." 3-column headline; 8 column-inches of text. The only known report of the second trip up Mt. McKinley by William Taylor, Peter Anderson, and Charles McGonagall. The statements made in this first account were later modified by McGonagall, who said—during a meeting with Bradford Washburn in Fairbanks on May 24, 1945—that this second ascent was pressed only as far as Denali Pass (18,180 ft.). The pictures made on it were probably used to illustrate the articles in the *London Daily Telegraph* and *New York Times* that appeared in June 1910. [*See* Lloyd 1910 and Thompson 1910.]

———. [*Sunday Times*], Feb. 4, 1912: 1. "Times Party Set Out to Scale Mt. M'Kinley." Banner headline and 14 column-inches of text. The public announcement of the plans of the little-known *Fairbanks Times* Expedition of 1912, which was to start on the following day. This was the first expedition to attempt the ascent of McKinley's "Pioneer Ridge." See Cairns, R.H., and Waitman, Randy.

———. Feb. 6, 1912: 1. "Times Expedition Enroute M'Kinley." 2-column headline; 8 column-inches of text. A brief account of the departure of the *Fairbanks Times* Expedition.

———. Feb. 27, 1912: 1–2. "Climbers Are Safe at M'Kinley's Base." 26 column-inches of text. Two letters to the editor of the *Times*, written by Ralph Cairns and George Lewis at a camp at timberline.

———. Apr. 10, 1912: 1. "Unable to Scale Heights of Mighty Mount McKinley, Climbers Return." A front-page story reporting the return of the *Times'* McKinley expedition and its failure to get higher than slightly over 9,000 ft. on what is now known as Pioneer Ridge, about two miles above Gunsight Pass.

———. June 21, 1913: 1. "Stuck Climbers Reach Summit of South Peak." 14-column headline; 37 column-inches of text. Photo of Archdeacon Stuck. The first news story telling of the success of the Stuck–Karstens Expedition.

———. June 21, 1913: 2. "The Debt We Owe Them." 10 column-inches. An editorial published on the occasion of the first ascent of the S Peak of Mt. McKinley.

———. July 10, 1913: 1. "Conqueror of Mt. McKinley Is Home Again." 9½ column-inches. The story of Harry Karstens' return to Fairbanks after the first ascent of Mt. McKinley. He also reports having seen the Sourdoughs' flagpole on the "northern eminence" of the mountain.

Farquhar, Francis P. "The Exploration and First Ascents of Mount McKinley." SCB 34 (June 1949): 94–109 (4 photos) and 35 (June 1950): 20–27 (no illustrations). The first article consists mainly of a detailed account of the 1910 "Sourdough" Expedition and a discussion of the Cook controversy. It is livened and becomes of distinct historical interest because of frequent references to personal chats between the author, Harry Karstens, and Charles McGonagall in Fairbanks. The second article offers a brief summary of the accomplishments of the expeditions of 1912 and 1913, with interesting biographical notes on Harry Karstens, Walter Harper, Merl LaVoy, and Robert Tatum, as well as a direct reference to Karstens' diary, now in the library of the American Alpine Club, New York.

Farquhar, Francis P., and Mildred P. Ashley. *A List of Publications Relating to the Mountains of Alaska*. New York: American Alpine Club, 1934. 37 pp. A very useful general bibliography.

Farthest-North Collegian 25 (College, Alaska: July 1947): 1. 6 column-inches. A brief account of an attempt on the S Peak of Mt. McKinley by Gordon Her-

reid, George Schumann, and Morton Wood. Wood's illness at 16,500 feet forced abandonment of the attempt at that altitude.

———. Aug. 1947: 1. "University Trio Climbs Mt. McKinley." 11 column-inches of text. A brief account of the fifth ascent of the S Peak.

Field, William B. O. "Glaciers of Alaska and Adjacent Yukon Territory and British Columbia." AAJ 1990: 79–149. 17 photos. An authoritative review of all the major glaciers in northwestern North America by an expert who has studied their changes for over sixty years. Well illustrated, and with an excellent bibliography.

Forty-Ninth Star (Anchorage), Dec. 14, 1947, pp. 1, 7–9, 13. 54 column-inches of text; 3½ full pages of pictures (12 photos). A well-illustrated popular account of the New England Museum of Natural History (now Boston Museum of Science) Expedition of 1947.

Freedman, Lewis. "McKinley, Solo Winter Ascent." AAJ 30 (1988): 135. A brief account of the first successful solo winter ascent of Mt. McKinley via the W Buttress by Vern Tejas of Anchorage.

———. "Norma Jean Stands Alone, Tall and Proud." *Anchorage Daily News*, June 24, 1990: D1–2. 1 photo. A story of the first solo ascent of McKinley by a woman (June 11, 1990).

———. *Dangerous Steps: Vernon Tejas and the Solo Winter Ascent of Mount McKinley*. Harrisburg, PA: Stackpole Books, 1990. 192 pp. 12 photos. The first complete account of the first winter ascent, by experienced guide Vernon Tejas of Anchorage.

———. "At Last, Alone at the Top." *Alaska* (Nov. 1990): 36–52. 8 photos and front cover. The story of the first recorded solo ascent by a woman: Norma Jean Sanders of Palmer, Alaska. [There is hearsay that an Italian woman (Miri Ercolani, of Florence) made the climb in 1982; no photos, no witnesses.]

Freeman, Andrew A. *The Case for Doctor Cook*. New York: Coward-McCann, 1961. 315 pp. The most interesting and complete account of Dr. Frederick Cook's life and exploits, including many details not to be found elsewhere.

Gerhard, Robert. "McKinley Climbing: What Does the Future Hold?" *Summit* (Feb.–Mar. 1977): 14–19. 6 photos; tables. A thoughtful appraisal of the recent climbing record, which points to a slow, steady deterioration of the quality of the experience of those attempting McKinley as more expeditions overwhelm the mountain. For another version, see "Denali Dilemma." AAJ 1977: 96–101.

———. "Alaska—The Park Service View." *Mountain* 70 (Nov.–Dec. 1979): 13. An editorial on climbing in Alaska by an experienced Denali Park ranger.

Gerhard, Robert, and Douglas Buchanan. "Freedom vs. Regulation." *Climbing* (Nov.–Dec. 1979): 4–8. 2 photos. The National Park Service view of the complex problems related to granting permissions to expeditions wishing to attempt the ascent of Mt. McKinley.

Gibbons, Russell W. *F. A. Cook, Pioneer American Polar Explorer*. Sullivan County Historical Museum, Hurleyville, NY: Dr. Frederick A. Cook Society, 1965.

Gibson, Rex. "Mt. McKinley in War Time." *Canadian Alpine Journal* 28 (Banff, 1942–43): 147–58. 8 photos. An excellent account of the U.S. Army Alaskan Test Expedition of 1942, written by the Canadian Army representative in the party.

Gilbert, Wyatt G. *A Geologic Guide to Mount McKinley National Park*. Anchorage: Alaska Natural History Association, 1979. 52 pp. 26 photos; numerous diagrams; a colored geologic map. An excellent booklet for climber, hiker, or tourist.

Gillette, Ned. "Trekking around the Continent's Highest Peak." NG (July 1979): 66–79. 9 photos; sketch map. A brief, dramatically illustrated account of the first "circumnavigation" of Mt. McKinley on skis, in the spring of 1978.

Globe and Commercial Advertiser (New York), Oct. 14–16, 1909. See also *New York Times*, Oct. 15 and 16, 1909. Three days of lengthy, fascinating, headlined stories related to new public doubts about Dr. Cook's 1906 "ascent" of Mt. McKinley, brought into focus by the publication, for the first time, of Edward Barrill's sworn affidavit [*see* Barrill 1989]. [The only known, complete copies of this newspaper for Oct. 14, 15, 16, 1909, are in the files of the American Alpine Club of New York and in the archives of the University of Alaska, Fairbanks; microfilm copy in the Library of Congress.] This story makes clear that Barrill spelled his name without the final "e" used in Cook's accounts.

Gmoser, Hans. "The Canadian Mount McKinley Expedition of 1963." *Canadian Alpine Journal* (Banff, 1964): 16–32. 4 photos. A detailed account of the first ascent of Mt. McKinley via the W edge of Wickersham Wall. Descent was via the W Buttress.

Goetze, Christopher. "The Wickersham Wall." *Appalachia* 34 (Dec. 1963): 648–55. 5 photos. A brief account of the Harvard expedition that made the first direct ascent of the N Face of Mt. McKinley (July 1963).

Gonnason, Walter. See *New York World-Telegram and Sun*, Apr. 14, 1950.

Grant, Madison. "The Establishment of Mount McKinley National Park." In *Hunting and Conservation* (New Haven: Yale University Press, 1925), edited by George B. Grinnell and Charles Sheldon: 438–45, 520–26. 43 photos. The most complete account of the beginnings of the Park, in which the Boone and Crockett Club and its members played an important part.

Greenhow, Robert. *The History of Oregon and California and Other Territories on the Northwest Coast of America*. Boston 1844. 1 map. Contains probably the most complete general account of the early voyages to this region. The map shows "Suschitna River" marked by name for the first time.

Greenwood, Sally. "Mount McKinley." In *America's Magnificent Mountains*, ed. Donald J. Crump (Washington, D.C.: National Geographic, 1980): 90–103. 12 photos; sketch map.

Grewingk, Constantin. *Beitrag zur Kenntniss der orographischen und geognostischen Beschaffenheit der Nord-West Küste Amerikas, mit den anliegenden Inseln*. St. Petersburg 1850. 351 pp. 5 maps; 4 engravings of molluscs. This book contains a map showing the existence of mountains in the location of the Alaska Range.

Griffiths, Thomas M. "Glacial Geomorphology of the Mount McKinley Massif, Alaska." In *Proceedings* of the 8th General Assembly of the 17th Congress of the International Geophysical Union (Washington, D.C., 1952): 331–36. A brief account of the field observations of the geologist of the 1951 expedition, the first party to visit the Kahiltna Glacier on foot.

Grimes, Carla Jo Penington. "The Naming of Mount Mc-

Kinley." Speech, May 27, 1986. Mrs. Grimes, whose great-uncle was William A. Dickey, who named Mt. McKinley in the fall of 1896, presented this paper at a meeting of the Konocti Study Club. One copy is in the archives of the American Alpine Club and one is in the archives of the University of Alaska, Fairbanks.

Guild, Ben. *The Alaskan Mushroom Hunter's Guide.* Anchorage: Alaska Northwest Publishing Co., 1979. 286 pp. Profusely illustrated with colored paintings and black-and-white drawings by Jack Van Hoesen. Of practical as well as general interest to climbers, hikers, and tourists. An excellent guide to the wildflowers of Alaska.

Hackett, Peter H., M.D. *Mountain Sickness: Prevention, Recognition and Treatment.* New York: American Alpine Club, 1980. 77 pp. This booklet, coordinated with Drs. Charles S. Houston and I. Drummond Rennie, should be studied by all who plan to climb Mt. McKinley and carried during the ascent.

———. "The Denali Medical Research Project 1982–85." AAJ 1986: 129–37. 2 photos.

———. *See also* Rau, D.

Hackett, William D. "Mt. McKinley: 1947 Climb of North and South Peaks." *Mazama* (Dec. 1947): 5–12. 10 photos. A detailed account of the New England Museum of Natural History [now Boston Museum of Science] ascent by the U.S. Army representative in the party.

———. "Mt. McKinley from the West." *Mazama* (Dec. 1951): 5–15. 14 photos. An account of the first ascent of the W Buttress route.

Hall, Henry S., Jr. "Mt. McKinley Park." AAJ 1946: 172. A note quoting a letter from Bradford Washburn (in Alaska) regarding the proper spelling of Charles McGonagall's name, and about the route across the Alaska Range used by Belmore Browne in the winter of 1912.

———. *See also* Browne, Belmore 1955.

Hannan, Leo. "The McKinley Debate." *Climbing* (Nov.–Dec. 1976): 23–27. 2 photos. A brief article on the growing problem of accidents and debris on Mt. McKinley.

Harper's Magazine. Letter of Rose Daly to Bradford Washburn, Feb. 28, 1957. Manuscript. Original in Boston University Library: Washburn Archives; copy in University of Alaska Library: Cook Controversy archive. The editorial secretary outlines in detail the amount of money ($1,200) paid by *Harper's* to Dr. Cook in May and Dec. 1903 for the manuscript of his article, "America's Unconquered Mountain" (Jan.–Feb. 1904), and two checks totaling $1,000 (May 15, 1906, and Feb. 26, 1907) for his article, "The Conquest of Mount McKinley." These sums are far less than the $25,000 that Dr. Cook told Belmore Browne he was given by *Harper's* to finance the 1906 expedition.

Harrison, A.E. "Muldrow Glacier's Mysterious Surges." *Alaska* (July 1962): 8. 3 photos; 2 sketch maps. A brief account of the great surge of the glacier in 1956–57.

Harvey, Frank. "He Races Up Mountains." *Argosy* (New York, NY), May 1960: 34–36, 73–75. 5 photos. An article describing the urge John Day had to break mountain speed records.

Haston, Dougal. *See* Scott, Douglas 1977.

Heacox, Kim. *The Denali Road Guide.* Anchorage: Alaska Natural History Association, 1986. 47 pp. 25 photos; 12 sketches and diagrams. An excellent little paperback guidebook, with color illustrations of scenery, animals, and flowers. All comments are keyed to precise mile markers along the road.

———. *See also* Herschman, Fred.

Heiberg, Sev. "Mount McKinley's Pioneer Ridge." AAJ 1962: 39–42. 3 photos. First ascent of the upper part of Pioneer Ridge of the N Peak, by a Canadian expedition (July 27, 1961). *See* Cairns, R.H., and Waitman, Randy.

Heller, Christine. *Wild Flowers of Alaska.* Portland, OR: Graphic Arts Center, 1966. 103 pp. 308 colored photos; 1 map. An excellent guide to the wild flowers of Alaska.

Helms, Michael. "Soviet Climbers on Mt. McKinley." AAJ 1978: 505. An account of the climbs of the first USSR expedition to Mt. McKinley.

Henry, Donald W. *See* Boulton, Ben 1988.

Herbert, Wally. *The Noose of Laurels.* New York: Atheneum, 1989. 395 pp. Well illustrated. A thorough review of the North Pole controversy (Peary vs. Cook).

Herron, Lieut. Joseph Sutherland. *Explorations in Alaska, 1899.* U.S. War Department, Adjutant General's Office Publication 31 (Washington, 1901). 77 pp. 42 photos; 16 sketches and drawings; 2 maps in text, 1 in pocket. The dramatic account of the first crossing of the Alaska Range by way of Simpson's Pass in 1899.

Herschman, Fred. *Bush Pilots of Alaska.* Portland, OR: Graphic Arts Center Publishing Co., 1989. 144 pp. A profusely illustrated large-format volume.

Hoeman, Grace. "Mount McKinley: The First All-Female Ascent [July 6, 1970]." AAJ 1971: 326–27.

Hoeman, J. Vincent. "McKinley-Hunter Traverse." AAJ 14 (1964): 56–59. 1 photo. Extraordinary E-W traverse of both peaks of Mt. McKinley, as well as the second ascent of Mt. Hunter via its W Ridge and the first ascents of both its Central and S peaks (July 19–31, 1963). A prodigious exploit, which has never been repeated, by a powerful and experienced 4-man party. A similar account, "Grand Traverse of the Alaska Range," in *Summit* (Apr. 1968): 14–19; cover and 8 photos; sketch map.

Hoshino, Michio. *Grizzly.* San Francisco: Chronicle Books, 1987. 80 pp. 52 illustrations. An extraordinary book by a brilliant young Japanese photographer.

Houghton, John G. "Weather on Mount McKinley." AAJ 1971: 303–16. Illustrated with many tables, graphs, and wind-roses. A detailed discussion of McKinley's unusual and violent weather.

Houston, Charles S. "First Ascent of Mt. Foraker." *Appalachia* 20 (Dec. 1934): 249–50. A brief account of the first ascent (1934) of Mt. Foraker, by the leader of the expedition. This was the first ascent of any new major peak in the Alaska Range since Stuck's conquest of Mt. McKinley in 1913. An expanded account, "Denali's Wife," is in AAJ 1935: 285–97 (8 photos; sketch map/diagram).

———. *Going Higher.* Burlington, VT: privately printed, 1983. 273 pp. 16 photos in color; numerous sketches and diagrams. The best book to date on all aspects of climbing and living at high altitude, written by a distinguished doctor with a lifetime of practical high-climbing experience.

———. "Physiology of Altitude Sickness." AAJ 1985: 158–61. A brief but interesting review of the many good reasons why climbing too fast up a high mountain is likely to result in serious problems.

———. *See also* Bowman, Warren D.; Hackett, Peter H., 1980, 1984.

Huber, Louis R. "The Incredible Conquest of Mt. McKinley." *Natural History* 58 (New York, Dec. 1949): 440–46. 11 photos. A fully illustrated, popular account of the Sourdough Expedition of 1910, which made the first ascent of McKinley's N Peak.

Hulten, Eric. *See* Welsh, Stanley L. 1983.

Jackson, Dick. "The Cassin Ridge." *Climbing* Nov.–Dec. 1979: 22–23. 5 photos. A 2-page photo essay.

Johnson, Philip. "Mount McKinley: Milan Krissak Memorial Route." AAJ 1981: 8–14. 2 photos. First ascent of a very fine new route on the "Centennial Wall" of the S Face of Mt. McKinley.

Jones, Chris. *Climbing in North America.* Berkeley, CA: University of California Press, 1976. 392 pp. Profusely illustrated. For interesting summary and evaluation, see in particular the chapters on Mt. McKinley (pp. 255–66) and "North to the Future" (pp. 325–45).

Jordan, Nancy. "Laurence of Alaska." *Anchorage Times,* May 20, 1990: J1 and J4. 3 photos. A résumé of the life of one of Alaska's most celebrated artists, on the opening of a major traveling exhibit at the Anchorage Museum of History and Art.

Kandiko, Robert. "Rescue on Mount McKinley." *Alaska* (Nov. 1981): 48–50, 74. 4 photos. The all-too-brief story of the rescue of Simon McCartney from a crisis-bivouac at 19,000 ft. on the Cassin Ridge after he and Jack Roberts had successfully completed the first ascent of a new and incredibly difficult route on McKinley's SW Face. See also *Mountain* 75: 14–15. For another version, see "Rescue on Denali" (AAJ 1981: 1–7; 3 photos).

Karstens, Harry P. "Notes for an Autobiography of Henry Karstens." *See* Moore, Terris 1967.

———. *Diary of the First Ascent of Mount McKinley, 1913.* AAJ 1969: 339–48. Preface and footnotes by Bradford Washburn. 2 pictures; equipment list. The original diary written by Harry Karstens during the first ascent of Mt. McKinley, with entries from Mar. 30 to June 14, 1913. This manuscript is kept in the library of the American Alpine Club in New York City.

———. "Henry P. Karstens, 1878–1955." AAJ 10 (1956–57): 112–13. An interesting obituary by Francis Farquhar, a friend and admirer.

———. *See also* Farquhar, Francis P.

Kennedy, Michael. "Belmore Browne and Alaska." *Alaska Journal* (Anchorage: Bob Henning), Spring 1973: 96–104. 11 photos of paintings. A brief but authoritative account of Belmore Browne's life and accomplishments.

———. Editorial. *Climbing* (Nov.–Dec. 1980): 3–4. *Re* the problems of National Park Service regulations for climbing in the parks of Alaska.

Kerns, Matthew. "Denali on One Leg." AAJ 1986: 64–68. 2 photos. The story of how Sarah Doherty climbed Mt. McKinley via its W Buttress, on one leg (May 1–19, 1985). With her were the author and Bill Sumner.

King, Capt. James. *See* Cook, Capt. James, and Capt. James King.

Krakauer, Jonathan. "Daredevil Pilots Take Glacier Flying to New Heights." *Smithsonian Magazine* (Jan. 1989): 96–107. Cover and 12 color photos. An interesting article, superbly illustrated by photographer James Balog, that tells of the bush pilots of Talkeetna and the helicopters that have supported the climbers who attack the peaks of the Alaska Range each year.

Laba, Roman. "Mount McKinley's South Face—1967." AAJ 1968: 15–20. 6 photos. First ascent of a new route up the Eastern Crags, or Centennial Wall, about a mile east of the Cassin Ridge (Aug. 3, 1967).

Ladd, William S. "In Memoriam, Allen Carpé, 1894–1932." AAJ 1932: 507–9. A biographical sketch by a close friend and climbing companion. Includes an excellent photograph of Carpé.

Larson, Laura, and Sandy Kogl. "Dog Teams on Mount McKinley." *Alaska* (Mar. 1975): 33–36. 6 photos; 1 sketch map. The account of how two dog teams hauled the freight for a climbing party from Kantishna to the 9,000-ft. level in Muldrow Glacier's Great Icefall in the early spring of 1974.

Lattimore, Clare. "Mountaineering Experiences in Alaska, 1978–87." MSc thesis, University of Alaska, Apr. 1990. 193 pp. An exhaustive survey of the subject with many graphs and tables.

Laurence, Sidney. *See* Jordan, Nancy 1990.

LaVoy, Merl. "Describes Finding of Koven's Body." *New York Times*, Aug. 30, 1932: 38. 21 column-inches. The first and most complete account of the 4-man expedition that ascended Mt. McKinley in Aug. 1932, as far as Carpé's final camp, to bring out Koven's body, Carpé's films and other expedition records.

———. *See also* Browne, Belmore 1913; Farquhar, Francis P. 1950.

Leopold, A. Starker, and F. Fraser Darling. *Wildlife in Alaska.* New York: Ronald Press, 1953. 129 pp. 17 photos. An excellent book on the problems of Alaskan wildlife.

Liek, Harry. "Liek Tells of Mt. M'Kinley Ascent." *Fairbanks Daily News-Miner*, May 24, 1932: 1, 2, 4, 5. 126 column-inches. Repr., July 16, 1932: 3. A complete account of the second ascent of both peaks and the Carpé-Koven tragedy, published immediately after the writer's return.

———. "The Second Ascent of Mount McKinley." SCB 18 (Feb. 1933): 81–87. 7 photos. The most complete account of the Lindley-Liek Expedition of 1932.

LIFE (New York), Mar. 22, 1943: 69–73. "McKinley." 20 photos. A pictorial account of the U.S. Army Alaskan Test Expedition of 1942. The brief text includes several inaccuracies.

———. June 14, 1954: 28–33. "On Mt. McKinley: Rescue after Victory." 12 photos; sketch map. A brief but excellent story of the 1954 Elton Thayer tragedy on Karstens Ridge. Includes several fine photos of the climb, the emergency camp after the accident, and the rescue, including USAF 45-C helicopter on Muldrow Glacier near Gunsight Pass.

Lindley, Alfred D. "Lindley Expedition Scales Mt. M'Kinley: Descending, Finds Carpé and Koven Dead." *New York Times*, May 17, 1932: 1, 3. 21 column-inches of text; 3-column headline. 3 photos; sketch map. The first account to appear in an eastern newspaper telling the story of the second ascent of both peaks, and the news of the Carpé-Koven tragedy.

———. "Carpé, Koven Lost Hunting Companions." *New York Times*, May 19, 1932: 12. 42 column-inches. One of the first analyses of the accident, written by the leader of the party that discovered it.

———. "The Ascent of Mt. McKinley." *Canadian Alpine Journal* 21 (Banff, 1932): 111–21. 8 photos. A full account of the Lindley-Liek Expedition, and mention of Taylor and LaVoy's expedition to retrieve Koven's body.

———. "Mount McKinley, South and North Peaks, 1932." AAJ 1933: 36–44. 5 photos. An account of the second ascents of both the S and the N Peaks of Mt. McKinley (May 7 and 9, 1932).

Literary Digest 47 (New York), July 5, 1913: 7–8. "Mt. McKinley Conquered." 4 photos. A brief account, well illustrated and to the point; includes a rare photograph of Archdeacon Stuck.

Lloyd, Thomas. "On the Roof of the American Continent." *Daily Telegraph* (London), June 6, 1910: 14. 90 column-inches; 3 photos; 2 sketches.

———. *See also* Cole, Terrence, ed. 1985; Schillios, Rolv 1956.

LOOK (New York), Dec. 9, 1947: 27–31. "Conquest of a Mountain." 14 photos. A popular account of the New England Museum of Natural History (now Boston Museum of Science) Expedition of 1947.

Lyon, R. Donald. "Mount McKinley via Pioneer Ridge." *Canadian Alpine Journal* (Banff, 1962): 75–88. 5 photos. A detailed account of the first ascent of the N Peak of Mt. McKinley (July 23, 1961) via Muldrow Glacier, Flatiron col, and Pioneer Ridge.

Mayell, Eric. *See* Crosson, Joseph 1931.

McCartney, Simon. Letter to the editor. *Mountain* 75 (Sept.–Oct. 1980): 14–15. *Re* first ascent (June 8–July 1, 1980) of the spectacular granite face to the left (W) of the Cassin Ridge, by the author and Jack Roberts. Describing the extraordinary rescue of McCartney, involving a descent of almost the entire Cassin Ridge. *See* Kandiko, Robert.

McGonagall, Charles. *See Fairbanks Daily Times*, June 9, 1910; Farquhar, Francis P. 1949–50.

McIntyre, Rick. *Denali National Park—An Island in Time.* Santa Barbara, CA: ARA Outdoor World, 1986. 80 pp. 69 photos; 1 sketch map. The best booklet to date briefly telling the history of Denali National Park and Mt. McKinley. Superbly and profusely illustrated, almost entirely in color.

McKeith, Bugs. "Mount McKinley, New Routes on the Southwest." AAJ 1978: 507–8. A number of climbs on the SW side of McKinley were made by a Canadian party. They are outlined here and described in more detail in the 1978 *Canadian Alpine Journal* (pp. 23–29).

McLean, Donald H.O. "McKinley, Northwest Buttress." AAJ 1955: 70–77. 8 photos. A well-illustrated account of the first ascent of the W Buttress of McKinley's N Peak, originally attempted by Dr. Cook's party in 1903. This experienced team encountered climbing far beyond the ability of Cook's party and was the first to drive a piton during a McKinley ascent.

McPhee, John. *See* Rowell, Galen 1981.

Mear, Roger. "Cassin Ridge in Winter." *Mountain* 92 (July–Aug. 1983): 24–29. 6 photos. The story of the first winter ascent of Mt. McKinley's Cassin Ridge, by the author, Jonathan Waterman, and Mike Young (Feb. 27–Mar. 4, 1982). A brief but top-notch account by one of Britain's best. Mear's illustrations are among the finest taken so far on this route.

Medred, Craig. "Alone on the West Rib." *We Alaskans* (Anchorage: Anchorage Daily News), Apr. 23, 1989: 6–12. 6 photos. An interesting and detailed newspaper story of the first solo winter ascent of the W Rib of Mt. McKinley's S Face by Dave Staeheli in March 1989, with extraordinary self-photos.

———. "Mount McKinley Gives Climbers a Brutal Choice." *Anchorage Daily News*, June 14, 1990: 1 and back page. A stirring story of life and death in a summer storm, a stone's throw from the top of McKinley, on its easiest route.

Merry, Wayne P. "Disaster on Mount McKinley." *Summit* (Dec. 1967): 2–9. 5 photos; map. A detailed account of the disastrous Wilcox Expedition of July 1967 by an experienced member of the National Park staff.

Metcalf, Peter. "A McKinley Traverse via Reality Ridge." AAJ 1976: 313–19. 2 photos. An account of the 42-day first ascent (from July 24, 1975) of the S Peak via the southern prong of the SE Spur of the S Buttress ("Reality Ridge"). A similar account, "Mt. McKinley Triple Indirect," is in *Summit* 1976: 2–7, 39–41 (4 photos, including front cover; map).

———. Note in *Climbing* (Dec. 1982): 5. *Re* the first "alpine style" traverse of Mt. McKinley (May 1982), by Metcalf and Glenn Randall, from S to N via the W Fork of the SE Spur ("Reality Ridge"), the S Buttress: descent via the W Buttress.

Metcalfe, Gertrude. "Mount McKinley and the Mazama Expedition." *Pacific Monthly* (Portland, OR, Sept. 1910): 255–65. 17 photos. Reprint in *Mazama* 27: 5–8 (4 photos; 1 sketch map). A popular account of the 1910 Mazama Expedition, which tackled the Ruth approach to Mt. McKinley at the same time as the Parker-Browne party, in an attempt to prove that Dr. Cook did climb Mt. McKinley. This expedition changed their minds! The 1945 *Mazama* reproductions of some of the original illustrations are far better than those in the *Pacific Monthly*.

Metz, Hans. "To McKinley on Skis." *Summit* (Nov. 1963): 2–5. 4 photos. An interesting story about a trip up the W Buttress route to the top of McKinley and back—all the way from Talkeetna—on skis (May 1962) by a party of five ski instructors.

Mills, William. *See* Rau, Dean. 1984.

Mills, William J., and D. Rau. "Alaska Medicine," in *University of Alaska High Latitude Study and the Mt. McKinley Project 1981–3* (Anchorage, 1983): 21–28.

Mills, William J., Jr., R. Whaley, and W. Fish. "Frostbite: Experience with Rapid Rewarming and Ultrasonic Therapy." *Alaska Medicine* (Anchorage): Mar. 1960, Dec. 1960, June 1961. 8 photos; several graphs and tables. This interesting article, published in three installments, is the first presentation of the new treatment by rapid-liquid-rewarming. Many extremely valuable and practical recommendations are made.

Moffit, Fred H. "The Kantishna District." In *Mineral Resources of Alaska, Report on Progress of Investigations in 1930*: 301–38. USGSB 836-D (1932). 3 sketch maps of claims. Report of a field trip in the summer of 1930 to get information on the present state of mining in the Kantishna District.

Molitsky, Irvin. See *New York Times* Jan. 28, 1990.

Molnia, Bruce. *Alaska's Glaciers.* Anchorage: Alaska Geographic, 1982. 144 pp. Profusely illustrated with photographs and maps that give a good overall understanding of the present state of glaciation in Alaska.

Moore, Terris. *Mount McKinley, The Pioneer Climbs.* Fairbanks: University of Alaska Press, 1967. 202 pp. 37 photos; 2 paintings; 8 maps. Introduction by Francis Farquhar. A McKinley classic. The most complete and accurate account to date of all of the exploration, attempts, and ascents of Mt. McKinley from the early 18th century up to and including the U.S. Army Expedition of 1942. The author writes with an authority that grows from firsthand experience as a man who participated in the third ascent of Mt. McKinley and later served as president of the University of Alaska.

———. "The World's Great Mountains: Not the Height You Think!" *AAJ* 1968: 109–16. An extremely interesting article regarding the measurement of the altitude of mountains from the center of the earth rather than from sea level—and the significantly higher barometric-pressure-altitude of arctic mountains compared with those near the equator.

Morrow, Patrick. "Mount McKinley, New Route Variant on the Southwest Flank." *AAJ* 1978: 505–06. Excellent photo (p. 506). A brief description of a new, short, and interesting route (May 21–22, 1977) up a ridge that leads directly from the NE fork of the Kahiltna Glacier at 9,000 ft. to Windy Corner on the W Buttress at 13,700. *See also* McKeith, Bugs.

———. *Beyond Everest.* Camden East, Ontario: Camden Press, 1986. 175 pp. 13 colored photos; 1 diagram. The best account of the extraordinary exploits of the Canadian Expedition to Mt. McKinley in the summer of 1977. A chapter (pp. 20–37) in a superbly illustrated story of the ascents of seven of the world's highest peaks.

Mountain 58 (Nov.–Dec. 1977): 14. Notes. *Re* a number of new routes on the SW side of Mt. McKinley by an 8-man Calgary party. *See also* McKeith, Bugs, 1978, and Morrow, Patrick, 1978.

Mountain 75 (Sept.–Oct. 1980): 14–15. Note, with 2 well-marked photos. First ascent (June 8–July 1, 1980) of the spectacular face to the left (W) of the Cassin Ridge, by Simon McCartney and Jack Roberts.

Mountain 78 (Mar.–Apr. 1981): 13. Editorial. *Re* deregulation of climbing on Mt. McKinley by the National Park Service.

Moutoux, John J. "Ascending the Steep Roof of the Continent, Just to Look Out the Windows of Heaven." *Knoxville News-Sentinel* (Knoxville, TN), May 22, 1932, C: 1, 8. 77 column-inches of text; 12 photos. An interview with the Rev. Robert G. Tatum, shortly after the announcement of the second ascent of Mt. McKinley by the Lindley-Liek Expedition. An unusual account of the 1913 expedition in retrospect, with many interesting direct quotations from Tatum.

Mozee, Yvonne. *See* Stuck, Hudson 1977.

Muldrow, Henry Lowndes. "Diary of a Summer with the USGS in Alaska, 1898." [The original diary appears to be lost; typewritten copies, in which pages 19 and 22 are lacking, are kept in the library of the American Alpine Club in New York and in the University of Alaska Archives, Rasmuson Library, Fairbanks.] This is a very interesting document. Its 64 pages relate the trials and problems of a USGS/Eldridge party, which canoed up the Susitna and Chulitna and hiked across Broad Pass in the summer of 1898, exploring and mapping the southern half of what eventually became the route of the Alaska Railroad. The author is the brother of Robert Muldrow, who made the first professional determination of Mt. McKinley's altitude on this trip. *See* Eldridge, George H.

Muldrow, Robert. "Mount McKinley." *NG* 12 (Aug. 1901): 312–13. 1 sketch map, showing the triangula-

tion system for his altitude computation. A brief technical report on the methods used in the field and in computations for the determination of the first official position and altitude of Mt. McKinley: 20,464 ft.

Murie, Adolph. *The Wolves of Mt. McKinley.* U.S. Department of the Interior (Washington: National Park Service, 1944). 238 pp. 51 photos; 11 sketches; 1 map. An exhaustive and interesting study of the wolves that inhabit the northern slopes of the Alaska Range, and their relations to the caribou, Dall sheep, and other mammals of McKinley Park.

———. "Wildlife of Mount McKinley National Park." *NG* (Aug. 1953): 249–70. 4 photos; 16 colored paintings by Walter A. Weber. A brief but interesting article by a distinguished naturalist who spent much of his life in the park studying its wildlife.

———. *A Naturalist in Alaska.* New York: Devin-Adair, 1961. 302 pp. Illustrated with 28 photographs and numerous sketches by the author's brother, Olaus J. Murie. A classic account of wildlife on the northern approaches to Mt. McKinley by an author who knew these lowlands and their natural history better than anyone else.

Murie, Olaus J. *See* Murie, Adolph 1961.

National Park Service (U.S.). "Mountaineering in Denali National Park." Published and revised frequently by the National Park Service, Washington, D.C. *See* Denali Park Rangers.

New York Times, Oct. 15, 1909: 1, 4, 5. "Barrill Says Cook Never on M'Kinley Top." 172 column-inches of text; 3 photos; 2 sketches. A news account and résumé of Barrill's sworn statement that "at no time did Dr. Cook and he get nearer than a point fourteen miles in an air line from the top of Mt. McKinley."

———. Oct. 16, 1909: 1, 2. "Double Search on Mt. M'Kinley." 115 column-inches. The account of a public invitation by Dr. Cook to Anthony Fiala and Dr. Herschel C. Parker to organize an expedition to Mt. McKinley for the purpose of finding the records deposited by him and Edward Barrill "on the topmost summit."

———. Apr. 16, 1910: 7. "M'Kinley Ascent is Now Questioned." 14 column-inches. An interview with Charles Sheldon.

———. June 21, 1913: 1. "Dr. Stuck Scales Mount M'Kinley." 19 column-inches. The first account in eastern newspapers to tell of the success of the Stuck-Karstens Expedition.

———. May 17 and 19, 1932. *See* Lindley, Alfred D.

———. May 18, 1932. *See* Beckwith, Edward P.

———. Aug. 11, 1932: 17. "Plane Sees Searchers for Body of Koven." 6 column-inches. This brief reference is of particular interest as it tells not only of seeing Taylor and LaVoy's party approaching the scene of the Carpé-Koven tragedy, but also of an airplane dropping another man's ashes on McKinley!

———. Aug. 22, 1932: 4. "Koven's Body Recovered." 3 column-inches. A brief news report, relayed to Fairbanks from McKinley Park.

———. Jan. 28, 1990: 19, c. 1–6. "Cook's Data Might Shed Light on Race to Pole," by Irvin Molitsky. A 15 column-inch news story reporting the gift of 20 boxes of Dr. Frederick A. Cook's diaries, letters, and photographs to the Manuscript Division of the U.S. Library of Congress.

New York World-Telegram and Sun, Apr. 14, 1950: 4.

"Expedition Planned to Settle Argument—Did Dr. Cook Climb Mt. McKinley?" 14 column-inches of text; 3 photos. An announcement of Walter Gonnason's plans for an expedition to ascend Mt. McKinley by way of Ruth Glacier in order to investigate Dr. Cook's claims.

Nilsson, Einar. "Mount McKinley Diary." *SCB* 28 (June 1943): 1–35. 12 photos. The story of the U.S. Army Alaskan Test Expedition of 1942, told in the form of a personal diary by one of the climbers in the advance party. Illustrated with 12 full-page photos by Bradford Washburn.

Nishimae, Shiro. "All-Japan Mount McKinley Expedition." *AAJ* 1966: 119. First ascent of McKinley via the NW "Japanese" ramp of the S Buttress (July 3, 1965).

Oregonian, The. Portland, OR. Articles in 1910 issues on the 1910 Mazama Expedition in April (10: p. 5; 19: p. 7; 24: p. 1; 25: p. 7), May (2: p. 3; 28: p. 3; 29: p. 1); June (20: p. 7; 22: p. 6); July (29: p. 1; 30: p. 5); August 14 (p. 4); September (p. 2).

Osius, Alison. "Washburn and Washburn." *Climbing* 1987: 58–61. 4 illustrations. A profile of Barbara Washburn, with her personal reactions to mountaineering, on the 40th anniversary of her becoming the first woman to climb McKinley.

Ott, Charles J. *See* Bradley, Kent.

Parker, Herschel C. "The Exploration of Mt. McKinley: Is It the Crest of the Continent?" *American Monthly Review of Reviews* 35 (New York: Jan. 1907): 49–58. 10 photos; 1 small-scale map of eastern Alaska. A brief account of the early history of Mt. McKinley and the 1906 expedition.

———. "Our Expedition to Mt. McKinley." *Metropolitan Magazine* 33 (New York: Dec. 1910): 278–91. 12 photos; 1 sketch map. The most complete account of the Parker-Browne Expedition of 1910, except for Browne's *Conquest of Mt. McKinley*. Includes several photographs not published elsewhere, and the best map (by Browne) to show the exact route followed by the expedition.

Parker, Herschel C., and Belmore Browne. "Expedition to Mount McKinley." *Canadian Alpine Journal* 3 (Banff, 1911): 57–72. 4 photos; 1 sketch map. A factual account of the Parker-Browne Expedition of 1910. An excellent sketch map shows the route of the party.

Paton, Bruce C. "Accidental Hypothermia." *Pharmacology and Therapeutics* 22 (Oxford, England, 1983): 331–77. The most complete paper yet written on this important subject. Although written for doctors, it can be easily understood and should be studied carefully by everyone going into a high or cold environment. It concludes with a remarkable bibliography.

Pearson, Grant H. "Diary of the Second Ascent of Mount McKinley." A copy of the original is on file in the archives of the American Alpine Club, New York City. This diary is as yet unpublished in its complete form.

———. "Diary Tells Story of Climb." *Fairbanks Daily News-Miner* (June 30, 1932): 3. 21 column-inches of text. A verbatim record, from Pearson's diary, of the events of May 7 (second ascent of the S Peak), May 9 (second ascent of the N Peak), and May 10–11 (discovery of the Carpé-Koven tragedy, and return to base camp).

———. "Climbing Down the Mountain." *Who: The Magazine About People* 1 (New York: Oct. 1941): 48–51, 64. 6 photos. The most interesting account of the details of the descent of Mt. McKinley by the 1932 Lindley-Liek Expedition, the dramatic incidents which surrounded the discovery of the Carpé-Koven disaster, and the events that immediately followed.

———. "The Seventy-Mile Kid" (Harry Karstens). *Alaska Sportsman* 16 (June 1950): 14–17, 44–49. 8 photos; 2 paintings. An interesting, informal history of Harry Karstens and McKinley Park in the early days.

———. "A History of Mount McKinley National Park, Alaska." U.S. National Park Service: 1953. 91 pp. 1 illustration. Typewritten copy. An outline of the history of the Park and its mountaineering record through 1952 by the Park's famous superintendent, who had worked there for over 20 years. Of particular interest are the stories of the C-47 Crash expedition to Mt. Deception and McKinley Park in wartime (pp. 50–54).

———. *My Life of High Adventure.* Englewood Cliffs, N.J.: Prentice-Hall, 1962. 234 pp. 32 photos. Written by collaborator Philip Newill, this is the biography of Grant Pearson.

Phillips, William H. "The South Face of Mount McKinley." *Appalachia* (June 1968): 1–18. 6 photos. A thorough description of the third ascent of the Cassin Ridge by the author and two companions—also brief accounts of ascents of the Eastern Crags of the S Face ["Centennial Wall"] (first) and the NW ramp of the S Buttress (second) in the summer of 1967.

Pohl, William. "A Dogged Climb up Denali." *Alaska* (Apr. 1981): 6–8. Cover photo (at 16,500 ft.); 3 other photos. A brief account of the first ascent of the S Peak via the W Buttress by dog team (Apr. 1979).

Pollock, John. " 'Basecamp' Notes." *Climbing* (June 1984): 4–5. 1 photo. One of the first reports of Naomi Uemura's disappearance on the descent after his first winter solo climb of Mt. McKinley (Feb. 12, 1984).

Porko, Peter. "The Final Overachievement of a Lifelong Fighter." *Anchorage Daily News,* May 29, 1988: p. 1 and back page. 4 photos. The tragic story of the death of Lynne Salerno at 19,000 ft.

———. "Mount McKinley Is No Place to Lose a Dog." *Anchorage Daily News,* June 22, 1989: 1, 10. 1 photo. 48 column-inches. The amazing tale of how a sled dog ran away on McKinley in the fog between 11,000 ft. and 14,000 ft. and wandered into camp 18 days later—hungry and tired.

Porter, Russell William. *The Arctic Diary of Russell William Porter.* Charlottesville, VA: University Press, 1976. 172 pp. Edited by Herman R. Frus. Profusely illustrated with superb sketches by the author. Among them is a map (p. 157) representing his own survey of the route traveled by the 1906 Cook-Parker expedition on the southern approaches to Mt. McKinley. For a brief account of this trip by its surveyor-artist, see chap. 10, pp. 156–62.

———. See also *Globe and Commercial Advertiser* 1909.

Post, Austin. "The Exceptional Advances of the Muldrow, Black Rapids and Susitna Glaciers." *Journal of Geophysical Research* (Nov. 1960): 3703–12. An interesting technical paper, well illustrated by sketch maps, tables, and cross sections to report the extraordinary surges of these three large glaciers. *See also* Harrison, A. E.

Potter, Louise. *Wild Flowers Along the McKinley Park Road.* Thetford, VT: privately published by the author; printed by Roger Burt, Hanover, NH, 1969. 145 pp. 121 pen-and-ink drawings. Particularly valuable for its lists of flowers that may be seen at specific locations. Nobody knows the wildflowers of this park more intimately than Louise Potter. Includes an excellent bibliography of publications relating to the flora of Alaska.

Quigley, Fannie. *See* Wold, Jo Anne.

Randall, Glenn. *See* Metcalf, Peter 1982.

Randall, Glenn, and Harry Johnson III. *Mt. McKinley Climber's Handbook.* Talkeetna, Alaska: Genet Expeditions, 1984; 2d ed. 1987. 148 pp. Several excellent little sketches; 1 sketch map (p. 98). Everyone who is planning an ascent of McKinley should buy this book and read every word. It succinctly covers everything from history to training, personal equipment, food, and weather. Written by two fellows who know all about it.

Rau, Dean, P. Hackett, W. Mills, D. Walberg, and J. Quinby. "Preliminary High Latitude Center Study Report, Mount McKinley (Denali)." *AAJ* 26 (1984): 134–36. A brief report of work at the medical research camp at an altitude of 14,300 ft. on the W Buttress of Mt. McKinley—under the auspices of the University of Alaska, Anchorage.

Reaburn, D. L. *See* Brooks, Alfred H. 1903

Read, Ben. "An Interview with Bradford Washburn and Terris Moore." *Climbing* (Apr. 1983): 16–24. 7 photos.

———. "Eighty Years of Climbing on Denali." *Mountain* 91 (May–June, 1983): 19–25 (7 photos; 1 sketch map) and 92 (July–Aug. 1983): 18–23 (8 photos). An interesting, brief, and well-illustrated two-part review of the early attempts and ascents of Mt. McKinley.

Read, William A. ("Al"). "The East Buttress of Mount McKinley." *AAJ* 1964: 37–42. 5 photos. A detailed account of the first ascent of the E Buttress (May 25, 1963).

Reed, John C., Jr. "Record of the First Approach to Mount McKinley." *AAJ* 1955: 78–83. 2 sketches; 1 map. Account of the discovery of the cairn left by Alfred H. Brooks and his party on Aug. 5, 1902, during their exploration of the N side of the Alaska Range.

———. *Geology of the Mount McKinley Quadrangle.* USGSB 1108-A (1961). 36 pp. 3 aerial photos by Bradford Washburn; index-map; geologic map at 1:250,000 scale. This excellent little technical publication summarizes all the geological data on the McKinley area available up to 1960.

Rennie, I. Drummond. *See* Hackett, Peter H. 1980.

Roberts, David. *The Mountain of My Fear.* New York: Vanguard, 1978. 157 pp. Well illustrated by photographs on the ground and from the air. An account of the first ascent of the W Face of Mt. Huntington (12,240 ft.), the most beautiful and the most difficult of McKinley's satellites. Authentic, superbly written, this book tells the compelling story of a great climb, but with a tragic ending.

———. "Five Who Made It to the Top." *Harvard Magazine* (Cambridge: Harvard University, Jan.–Feb. 1981): 31–40. 12 photos. Lengthy article profiling five Harvard alumni who were all pioneer Alaskan climbers and explorers: Robert Bates, Adams Carter, Charles Houston, Terris Moore, and Bradford Washburn.

———. "Profile: Bradford Washburn." *American Photographer* (New York: Apr. 1983): 44–58, 90–92. 13 photos; 1 sketch. An interesting biographical profile of the development of Bradford Washburn's pioneering techniques in large-format aerial photography.

Roberts, Jack. *See Mountain* 75: 14–15.

Rojec, F. H. *See* Metcalfe, Gertrude 1910; Rusk, Claude E. 1910.

Roper, Steve. *See also* Steck, Allen 1979.

Roper, Steve, and Allen Steck, editors. *Ascent.* San Francisco: Sierra Club Books, 1984. 175 pp. Contains four beautifully illustrated chapters on Mt. McKinley in one of the Sierra Club's excellent series on the wonders of the outdoors.

Rost, Ernest C. *Mount McKinley, Its Bearing on the Polar Controversy.* New York: privately printed, 1914. 33 pp. 2 photos. A vigorous presentation of Dr. Cook's case, including an assertion that Parker, Browne, and Stuck used the "most cruel, cowardly and dastardly methods" to discredit Cook's claims. Many of the statements in this book have been subsequently proved incorrect.

Rowell, Galen A. *High and Wild.* San Francisco: Sierra Club Books, 1979. 159 pp. Profusely and beautifully illustrated in color—with 36 photos taken on and near Mt. McKinley. Interesting text and picture stories of an attempt on the Moose's Tooth, the first ski circumnavigation of Mt. McKinley, the first ascent of the great SE Face of Mt. Dickey, and a 1-day marathon up Mt. McKinley.

Rowell, Galen, and John McPhee. *Alaska—Images of the Country.* San Francisco: Sierra Club Books, 1981. 146 pp. Interesting text and superb photos, many of the Alaska Range.

Rusk, Claude E. "On the Trail of Dr. Cook." *Pacific Monthly* (Portland, OR). Oct. 1910: 430–42; Nov. 1910: 472–86 (15 photos); Jan. 1911: 48–62 (13 pictures; 1 sketch map). Reprint in *Mazama* 27: 8–31. Three classic articles on the Mazama Expedition of 1910. The *Mazama* reproductions of some of the original illustrations are far better than those in *The Pacific Monthly*. The plates were made from a set of Rojec's prints, all of which are in the possession of the Mazama Club, Portland, Oregon.

———. Biographical sketch in AAJ 1946: 117–19. *See also* Metcalfe, Gertrude 1910, 1945.

Ruth, William. "Up the Traleika Spur to the Top of McKinley." *Alaska* (Aug. 1973): 6–8, 49–50. 18 photos; 2 sketch maps. One of the few published accounts of this expedition up the longest route to the top of McKinley (Apr.–May 1972).

———. "Mount McKinley from the Traleika." AAJ 1973: 289–93. 3 photos. First ascent of Mt. McKinley via the very long and exposed Traleika Spur (May 25, 1972).

Salkeld, Audrey. "Naomi Uemura—The Lost Samurai." *Mountain* 97 (May–June 1984): 47. 1 photo. Referring to a *Spectator* article by Murray Sayle. A brief account of the accomplishments of the extraordinary Japanese explorer-climber who trekked alone to the North Pole (1978), climbed Everest (1970), made the first solo ascent of Mt. McKinley (1970) and later lost his life in a storm, descending McKinley after making its first solo winter ascent (Feb. 12, 1984).

———. "Skinning One Skunk at a Time: An Appreciation of the Work of Bradford Washburn." *Mountain* 126 (Mar.–Apr. 1989): 36–39. 4 photos.

Sanford, Eric. "A Big Mac Attack." *Climbing* (Apr.–May 1990): 118–120, 184–186. 2 photos. The story of an ascent of the W Buttress and the incredible array of inexperienced climbers encountered en route.

Sargent, R. H. "The Monarchs of Alaska." NG 20 (July 1909): 610–23. 9 photos. Brief remarks about McKinley.

Saunders, Norma Jean. *See* Freedman, Lewis 1990.

Sayle, Murray. *See* Salkeld, Audrey 1984.

Sayre, Woodrow Wilson. "Climbing by the Book." *Sports Illustrated* (New York: July 21, 1958): 58–64. 4 photos; 1 sketch map. The story of a 1954 ascent via the Muldrow route by a small, inexperienced, yet successful party.

Schein, Marcel, Thomas D. Carr, and Ian Barbour. "Cosmic-Ray Investigations on Mt. McKinley." *The Physical Review* 73 (Lancaster, PA: June 15, 1948): 1419–23. A technical article on the results of the observations made at Denali Pass for Dr. Schein by Hugo Victoreen of the Boston Science Museum's Expedition of 1947.

Schillios, Rolv. "Sourdough Mountaineers." *Alaska* (Sept. 1956): 6. 8 photos. An account of the 1910 expedition, partly based on an interview (in Eugene, Oregon) with Charley McGonagall—but leaning much too heavily on Tom Lloyd's doctored diary.

Schwab, Henry B. deV. "The Mt. McKinley Disaster." AAJ 1 (1932): 511–14. A brief analysis of the Carpé-Koven disaster, by the president of the American Alpine Club. For another version, see "The Accident on Mt. McKinley." AJ 44 (Nov. 1932): 357–60 (1 photo).

Schwatka, Lieut. Frederick. *A Summer in Alaska.* St. Louis, MO: J. W. Henry, 1894: 301–06. Numerous engravings, but none of the maps published with the official government report (*see* U.S. Doc. Serial set #3896, pp. 283–362). A popular account of the U.S. Military expedition down the Yukon in 1883. An interesting paragraph (p. 301) describes the first descent of the Tanana by Harper and Bates in 1875.

Scientific American 95 (New York: Dec. 15, 1906): 445–46. "Dr. Cook Ascends Mt. McKinley." A brief news story on the Cook Expedition of 1906.

Scott, Douglas. "Adventure on McKinley." *Mountain* 52 (1976): 18–21. 2 photos. An excellent but brief firsthand account of the first direttissima ascent of Mt. McKinley's S Face (May 12, 1977) by two of the world's top mountaineers, the author and Dougal Haston. For another account—vivid and well-illustrated—see "Spring Climb on the South Face" in *Alaska* (May 1977): 4–7, 90 (8 photos and front cover). Yet another, by Scott and Dougal Haston, "Mount McKinley 1976," in AAJ 1977: 88–95 (2 photos). A remarkable "alpine-style" climb by the world's two leading mountaineers at that time. See also *Mountain* 51: 12–13 (photo).

Scott, Douglas, and Dougal Haston. "The South Face of Mount McKinley." AJ 1977: 173–83. 4 photos. An excellent account of the first ascent of the entire S Face, direct. This story includes remarkable prose about the magnificence, the difficulties, and the rewards of Alaskan mountaineering by the most experienced team yet to set foot on McKinley's slopes.

Seattle Post-Intelligencer, June 21, 1913: 1, 16. "Archdeacon Is Conqueror of Mt. M'Kinley." 4-column headline; 52 column-inches of text. 6 photos; 2 sketches. The most complete newspaper account of the first ascent of Mt. McKinley to appear outside Alaska.

Seaver, Benjamin F. *See* Cuntz, John Henry 1929.

Seidman, Dave. "Mt. McKinley: The Direct South Face." *Ascent* 1 (1968): 18–21. 1 photo. A well written and interesting account of the first ascent of the Eastern Crags (the Centennial Wall) of the S Face (Aug. 1967).

Sharp, Robert P. *Glaciers.* Eugene, OR: University of Oregon Press, 1960. 75 pp. 28 photos; 23 sketches and diagrams. An excellent booklet for the layman by a geologist with practical field experience in both Alaska and the Yukon.

———. *Living Ice.* New York: Cambridge University Press, 1988. 225 pp. Profusely illustrated with photos, maps, and diagrams. This book explains glaciers in a way that all can understand.

Shaw, John. *Closeups in Nature.* New York: Division of Billboard Publications. 1987. 144 pp. 180 photos. A most remarkable and superbly illustrated book about close-up 35mm. photography in the field.

Sheldon, Charles. *The Wilderness of Denali.* New York: Schribner's, 1930. 412 pp. 111 photos; 2 sketch maps. A McKinley classic. The fascinating description of the author's hunting and collecting expeditions in the northern foothills of the Alaska Range in 1906, 1907, and 1908. Excellent illustrations. Most of Sheldon's experiences were in the country northeast of McKinley (the Toklat) rather than immediately adjacent to the mountain. His guide was Harry Karstens.

Sheldon, Don. *See* Elliott, Lawrence 1963.

Sherwonit, Bill. *To the Top of Denali.* Anchorage: Alaska Northwest Books, 1990. 347 pp. 27 photos; 2 sketch maps. A well-presented review of McKinley's history, an account of a W Buttress ascent by the author, and interesting reflections on the peak's future and its problems.

Sinclair, Peter. "The West Rib of the South Face of Denali." DM 1960: 7–28. 4 photos. A complete and personal account of the first ascent of the most difficult technical route climbed on McKinley to that date.

Snow, C. K. "The Misnaming of Alaska's Mount Ararat." *Alaska-Yukon Magazine* (Seattle: Aug. 1910): 193–95. A brief article decrying Dickey's naming of Mt. McKinley. It tells the story of the creation of Denali ("Dinale") as related by the natives to the Jesuit missionary, Father Julius Jette, at Kokrines. This legend is essentially the same, though in less detail, as that told by Wickersham in "The Creation of Denali" (*Alaska* Jan. 1927).

Snyder, Howard H. *The Hall of the Mountain King.* New York: Scribner's, 1973. 207 pp. 43 photos; endpaper map. This book tells the story of the two small expeditions merged into one that climbed Mt. McKinley in the summer of 1967, and which resulted in the deaths of seven of the climbers—the greatest tragedy to date in the history of Alaskan mountaineering. For the other side of what has become an acid controversy, see Joe Wilcox, *White Winds.*

Soubis, Jacques. "La Conquête du Mont Huntington." *La Montagne et Alpinisme* 49 (Paris: Oct. 1964): 260–72. 14 photos; sketch map (in French). The only detailed and well-illustrated account of the first ascent of Mt. Huntington by a six-man party of brilliant French climbers, led by Lionel Terray (May 1964). The article is similar to Terray's story in AAJ 1964.

Spadavecchia, Nicholas W. "With the Cosmic Ray Expedition to Mt. McKinley." *Appalachia* 19 (June 1933): 432–48. 5 photos. The most complete account of the activities of the surviving members of the 1932 Cosmic-Ray Expedition (Beckwith, Olton, and Spadavecchia), both before and after the Carpé-Koven accident.

Spaulding, Philip Taft. "McKinley—A Study in Survival." *Farthest-North Collegian* 27 (College, Alaska: Aug. 1948): 1, 5, 7. 225 column-inches of text; 2 photos. The only complete account of the 1948 ascent of the S Peak of Mt. McKinley by a party of students from the University of Alaska.

Speer, Gary. "Dave Roberts and Alaska." *Mountain* 97 (May–June 1984): 46–47. 1 photo. A brief but excellent account of one of that handful of brilliant young climbers who—on Mt. Huntington, McKinley, and Dickey—led the way to first-rate climbing among the big peaks of the Alaska Range.

———. "The Essential David Roberts." *Climbing* (Apr. 1984): 14–21. Cover photo and 4 others. A profile of author-climber-essayist David Roberts, who has a remarkable chain of Alaskan first ascents to his credit: the Kichatna Spires, Brooks Range, Mt. McKinley's Wickersham Wall, W Face of Mt. Huntington, and Mt. Dickey direct from the Great Gorge.

Spurr, Josiah Edward. "A Reconnaissance in Southwestern Alaska in 1898." In *Twentieth Annual Report,* U.S. Geological Survey (Washington: 1900): pt. 7, pp. 31–264. 6 photos; 8 sketches; 12 diagrams; 11 maps. The official account of a remarkable expedition that made the first crossing of the Alaska Range, up the Yentna and Skwentna rivers, down the Kuskokwim and back to Cook Inlet across the Alaska Peninsula via Katmai Pass—a 1400-mile trip.

Staeheli, David. "Denali's West Rib Solo in Winter." AAJ 1990: 50–53. 1 aerial photo of McKinley's SW Face by B. Washburn. A brief account of the first solo of McKinley's W Rib (March 11, 1989), by a very experienced and resourceful Alaskan mountain guide.

Steck, Allen, and Steve Roper. *Fifty Classic Climbs of North America.* San Francisco: Sierra Club Books, 1979. 324 pp. 16 relevant photos, 4 for each of the climbs as noted below. Brief accounts of the first ascents of four of what have now become the classic climbing routes in the McKinley massif, written by topflight mountaineers.

Stoliker, Paul. "Denali the Lion Sleeps." *Canadian Alpine Journal* (Vancouver, B.C.: Alpine Club of Canada, 1989): 57–59. 1 photo. A brief account of an ascent of McKinley's W Buttress, as well as of a climb of the Cassin Ridge, complicated by the rescue of two sick Koreans at 18,600 ft.

Stuck, Hudson. "The Ascent of Denali." *Scribner's Magazine* 54 (New York: 1913): 531–52. 18 photos; 1 diagram. A popular account of the first ascent of Mt. McKinley, published three months before the appearance of Stuck's book of the same name.

———. "On Denali [Mt. McKinley]." *Spirit of Missions* 79 (Jan. 1914): 17–25. 10 photos. A popular account of the first ascent of Mt. McKinley.

———. "Johnny and the Sugar." *Spirit of Missions* 79 (Feb. 1914): 97–103. 9 photos. A pleasant story with several illustrations not published elsewhere.

———. *The Ascent of Denali.* New York: Scribner's, 1914. 188 pp. 34 photos; 1 sketch map. Reprint, Lincoln, NE, and London: University of Nebraska Press, 1989. The classic account of the first ascent of Mt. McKinley by Hudson Stuck, Archdeacon of the Yukon, with Harry P. Karstens, Walter Harper, and Robert Tatum.

———. *The Ascent of Denali: Containing the Original Diary of Walter Harper, First Man to Achieve Denali's*

True Summit. Seattle, WA: The Mountaineers, 1977. 220 pp. 37 photos. Foreword by Bradford Washburn. A new edition of the classic story of McKinley's first ascent in the spring of 1913. Illustrated with all of the original pictures from the first edition but with the addition of eight pages of carefully annotated aerial photographs by Bradford Washburn that show the exact route of Stuck's climb up Muldrow Glacier and Karstens Ridge and the positions of all of the party's camps. Included in this little book is the entire diary of Walter Harper, one of the members of Stuck's 4-man party—never before published—and an introduction to it by Yvonne Mozee, Harper's niece. [*See* Harper, Walter 1977.]

——. *See also* Dean, David 1988.

Sun, The (New York). "Explorations in Alaska." *See* Dickey, William A. 1897.

——. "Four Climb Mount M'Kinley." Apr. 13, 1910: 1, 2. 21 column-inches. A news release originating in Fairbanks describing the Sourdough Expedition to Mt. McKinley.

——. "Professor Parker to Try It Too." Apr. 13, 1910: 2. 12 column-inches. An account of a farewell dinner given for Dr. Parker and other members of his expedition, attended by executives of the Explorers Club and the American Geographical Society. Plans were announced for the 1910 Parker-Browne Expedition to explore the southern approaches to McKinley.

——. "M'Kinley 20,500 Feet High." Apr. 14, 1910: 1. 10 column-inches. A brief follow-up story after the main account of the accomplishments of the Sourdough Expedition published the day before.

Tackle, Jack. Photos. AAJ 1983: 140, 143. Two pictures [no article] of the first ascent of "Isis Spur" of the S Buttress of Mt. McKinley by Jack T. Tackle, David Stutzman (May 8–16, 1982).

Taft, President William Howard. "Taft Congratulates Mountain Climbers." *Fairbanks Daily Times*, Apr. 15, 1910: 14. 14 column-inches. "The White House, Washington, D.C., April 14. I sincerely congratulate the Lloyd party on reaching the top of Mount McKinley. It is a victory over great obstacles. [signed] William H. Taft."

Tatum, Rev. Robert G. *See* Moutoux, J. J.

Taylor, Katherina A. *See* Pearson, Grant 1941.

Tebenkoff, Michael, Capt. of the First Rank. *Atlas of the Northwest Shores of America, From Bering's Straits to Cape Corrientes and the Aleutian Islands*. St. Petersburg, 1852. 38 large maps. In Russian. The first two pages are a map of the North Pacific Ocean (dated 1849), showing the Susitna River and a mountain range in roughly the position of the Alaska Range. There is an excellent chart of Cook Inlet.

——. *Hydrographic Notes to an Atlas of the Northwest Shores of America*. St. Petersburg, 1852. 148 pp. In Russian. Accompanies the large Tebenkoff *Atlas* of 1852.

Tejas, Vernon. *See* Bryson, George 1988; Freedman, Lewis 1989.

Terray, Lionel. "Mount Huntington." AAJ 1964: 289–98. 8 photos. Account of the first ascent of Mt. McKinley's satellite by a powerful French party (May 25, 1964). *See* Soubis, Jacques.

Thompson, Gray. "McKinley's 'Centennial' Wall." *Summit* (Mar. 1968): 2–11. 8 photos, including front cover—one with route precisely marked. An interesting

and personal account of the first ascent of the difficult Eastern Crags of the S Face by a 4-man team (Aug. 4, 1967).

Thompson, W. F. "First Account of Conquering Mt. McKinley." *New York Times*, June 5, 1910: Magazine section, 1–3. 188 column-inches of text; 14 photos; 4 sketches. The first complete account of the famous Sourdough Expedition of 1910 to appear outside Alaska. *See* Phillips, William H.

Thorington, J. Monroe. Biographical sketches of F. A. Cook and H. C. Parker in AAJ 1946: 86–88 and 109–11 respectively.

TIME, July 13, 1959: pp. 37–38. "The Great One." 1 photo. An 11-column story, unsigned, on the first ascent of Mt. McKinley's W Rib route. Full of interesting details about this great climb by Jake Breitenbach's young but brilliant team.

Trelawney, John G. *Wildflowers of the Yukon and Northwest Canada, including Alaska*. Victoria, B.C.: Sono Nis Press, 1983. 214 pp. 378 color photos; 1 map; many sketches. A popular and complete wildflower guide to Alaska and Northwestern Canada, by a teacher at the University of Victoria.

Trott, Otto T. "Abbreviated Diary, 1956 East Ridge Exploration, Mt. McKinley." Typescript, Feb. 25, 1958. 6 pp. Copies in American Alpine Club: Cook Controversy archives, and at the University of Alaska in Fairbanks. A thorough, factual account of the attempt of a small party led by Walter Gonnason to prove that Dr. Cook did get up Mt. McKinley in 1906 [this was its 50th anniversary]. The 4-man party was financed by Dr. Cook's daughter, Mrs. Helene Vetter. Having reached only 11,400 ft. on the knife-edged East Ridge, "our trip has added evidence that Dr. F. Cook did not climb Mt. McKinley."

Troyer, Will. "Movements of the Denali Caribou Herd." U.S. National Park Service research paper. Anchorage, Dec. 1981. 21 pp. 2 maps. A study to determine the reasons for the decline of this herd from approximately 20,000 in 1940 to less than one-tenth of this number in 1980.

Uemura, Naomi. *See* Pollock, John 1984; Salkeld, Audrey 1984.

University of Alaska. See *Farthest-North Collegian*.

Vancouver, Capt. George. *A Voyage of Discovery to the North Pacific Ocean, and Round the World*. London: 1798. 3 vols. in quarto. 1 volume of maps in folio. Numerous engravings and maps. The account of the first thorough mapping of Cook Inlet (Apr. 12–May 15, 1794). Vancouver describes (3: 124) "distant stupendous mountains, covered with snow, and apparently detached from each other"—considered to be the first formally reported sighting of Mts. McKinley and Foraker from Cook Inlet.

Victoreen, Hugo. *See* Schein, Marcel, et al. 1948.

Viereck, Les. "Mount McKinley from the South." DM 1956: 28–34. 2 photos. A long letter to John Read, director of the Dartmouth Outing Club. This is by far the most complete and interesting account of the first ascent of the S Buttress route and the fatal accident while descending Karstens Ridge (Spring 1954).

Waitman, Randy. "Denali's Complete Pioneer Ridge." AAJ 1989: 84–88. 3 photos. A description of the first complete ascent of Mt. McKinley's Pioneer Ridge, from Gunsight Pass (6,580 ft.) to the top of the N Peak (19,470 ft.). *See* Cairns, Ralph H., *re* 1912 attempt.

Walker, Michael. "Frostbite." AJ 1971: 70–87. 2 photos. A review of this important subject by a brilliant British mountaineer-physician.

Walker, Tom [photos], and Marydith Beeman [text]. *Alaskan Wildlife*. Portland, OR: Graphic Arts Publishing, 1987. 160 pp. A profusely and beautifully illustrated large-format book that contains the best pictures of the wildlife that abounds in Denali Park.

Ward, Michael P., James S. Milledge, and John B. West. *High Altitude Medicine and Physiology*. Philadelphia: University of Pennsylvania Press, 1989. 515 pp. A highly authoritative volume.

Washburn, Bradford. "Over the Roof of Our Continent." NG 74 (July 1938): 78–98. 17 photos; 1 map. A profusely illustrated popular account of the first exploratory photographic flights over and around Mt. McKinley (July 1936 and Aug. 1938).

——. "Mount McKinley from the North and West." AAJ 1947: 283–93. 8 aerial photos. An analysis of the problems that may be encountered in attempts to ascend Mt. McKinley from two unclimbed angles. The full-page illustrations are marked to show the proposed routes. For success on these two routes, see AAJ 1964 and 1965 respectively.

——. "Operation White Tower." AAJ 1948: 40–58. 4 photos. A complete account of the New England Museum of Natural History (now Boston Museum of Science) Expedition, which climbed both peaks of Mt. McKinley (S Peak, June 6, 1947; N Peak, June 7, 1947), and carried out a broad scientific program.

——. "Mapping Mount McKinley." *Scientific American* 180 (New York: Jan. 1949): 46–51. 5 photos; 1 sketch map. A popular account of the topographic work accomplished by the Boston Science Museum Expedition of 1947.

——. "The Practical Igloo." *Canadian Geographical Journal* 39 (Ottawa: Dec. 1949): 258–61. 7 photos; 1 diagram. A description of the construction, use, and value of the igloo as an important form of shelter.

——. "Mt. McKinley from the Air." SCB 35 (June 1950): 28. 12 photos. This series of full-page aerial photos of all sides of Mt. McKinley is beautifully printed on highly varnished paper. Brief introduction by Francis P. Farquhar.

——. *Mount McKinley and the Alaska Range in Literature*. Boston: Museum of Science, 1951. 88 pp. A complete descriptive bibliography of most of the significant publications related to the history of Mt. McKinley from the early 18th century to the winter of 1951.

——. "Mt. McKinley: The West Buttress, 1951." AAJ 1952: 213–26. 4 photos. An account of the first ascent of the W Buttress of Mt. McKinley by an 8-man party (July 10, 13, 14, 1951).

——. "Mount McKinley Conquered by New Route." NG (Aug. 1953): 219–48. 19 photos; 2 sketch maps. A detailed account of the first ascent of McKinley's W Buttress.

——. "Mount Hunter via the West Ridge: A Proposal." AAJ 1953: 478–84. 4 photos. Proposal for first ascent of Mt. Hunter (14,570 ft.). See AAJ 1955 for the first ascent by almost exactly this route.

——. "The South Buttress of Mount McKinley: Analysis of a Proposed Route of Ascent." *Appalachia*, June 15, 1954: 420–28. 6 photos; 1 sketch map. A detailed proposal for the ascent of Mt. McKinley via the route originally attempted in 1910 by the Parker-Browne party. *See* Viereck, Les, and Wood, Morton S.

————. "Cook Portfolio, 1955–56–57." Manuscripts. This major portfolio of all the Cook 1906 data gleaned from trips to the Fake Peak and Great Gorge area by B. Washburn, Norman Read, and Nile Albright in 1955 and 1956, and by Adams Carter's team's visit in 1957, resulted in a massive file of material from which the AAJ article of 1958 was developed. There are only two copies: one in the archives of the University of Alaska (Fairbanks), and one at the headquarters of the American Alpine Club in New York. Profusely illustrated with marked photos, enlargements, and text.

————. "Mapping Mount McKinley's Southeast Approaches." AAJ 1956: 47–50. 8 photos. An account of a month-long expedition in the Great Amphitheatre of Ruth Glacier (now known as the Don Sheldon Amphitheatre) to complete the ground-control for the new map of Mt. McKinley.

————. "Mount McKinley (Alaska), History and Evaluation." *The Mountain World 1956–57* (New York: Harper & Brothers; Zurich: Swiss Foundation for Alpine Research, 1958): 58–81. 1 colored map; 8 large aerial photos; 8 related sketches showing all the climbing routes on Mt. McKinley to date; also a number of new routes proposed by the author, all of which have now [1990] been climbed.

————. "Snow Blindness." AAJ 1958: 69–71. A brief but useful description of this painful ailment: how to avoid it; what to do if you have it.

————. "A New Map of Mount McKinley, Alaska: The Life Story of a Cartographic Project." *Geographical Review* (American Geographical Society, New York) Apr. 1961: 159–86. 24 photos. A major report on the author's 15-year project that resulted in the publication of the new Boston Museum of Science/Swiss Foundation for Alpine Research 1:50,000 shaded relief map of Mt. McKinley, published for the first time as a folded insert in this issue of the *Review*.

————. "Frostbite." AAJ 1962: 1–26. 15 photos; 2 diagrams. A detailed article on this important subject. In essence this is a popular revision of the article under the same title that appeared in *The New England Journal of Medicine*, May 10, 1962.

————. "Opportunities on Mount McKinley." AAJ 1962: 49–52. 11 photos. Proposal for ascents of Wickersham Wall and the SE Spur. [For responses to these proposals, see AAJ 1963 and 1964.]

————. "Mapping the Roof of North America." In *Great Adventures with National Geographic* (Washington, D.C.: National Geographic Society, 1963): 344–53. 6 photos; map. A brief résumé of Bradford Washburn's exploration of Mt. McKinley, starting with the flights of 1936, Terris Moore's record ski-plane landings on the Kahiltna in 1951, and the first ascent of the W Buttress in the same year.

————. "Mount McKinley: Proposed East Buttress Routes." AAJ 1963: 453–60. 8 photos. Proposal for a number of possible first ascent routes on McKinley's E Buttress. [For response, see AAJ 1964: 37–42.]

————. "Challenges in Alaska and the Yukon, 1968." AAJ 1968: 66. 8 photos. Plates 55, 56, and 57 suggest unclimbed routes on Mt. Hunter, the Moose's Tooth, the Rooster Comb, and Mt. Foraker [all subsequently climbed].

————. *A Tourist Guide to Mt. McKinley*. Anchorage:

Alaska Northwest Publishing Co., 1971, 1974, 1976, 1980. 79 pp. Profusely illustrated with photographs, mostly by the author, in both color and black-and-white. A brief history of Mt. McKinley and its park; a mile-by-mile description of the Denali Highway in the park; a brief summary of climbing and exploration in the park from the late 18th century through the 100th ascent of Mt. McKinley in 1972; concludes with a bibliography of the most significant books related to Mt. McKinley, its park, and its wildlife and botany.

————. "First Laser Measurements to the Summit of Mount McKinley." AAJ 1978: 381–86. 2 photos. This article describes not only the laser work but also precise on-the-ground *taped measurements* made by a National Outdoor Leadership School party from McKinley's summit to the spot reached by Parker, Browne, and LaVoy in 1912. The distance from the summit to Kahiltna Horn was also measured by the same party on July 12, 1977.

————. "Muldrow Glacier Motion." AAJ 1982: 29–32. 1 photo. Description of movement observations by laser (1977–1981).

————. "Barrill's Mount McKinley Affidavit." AAJ 1989: 112–22. 1 photo; 2 maps. *See* Barrill 1989 and *Globe and Commercial Advertiser* 1909.

————. "The Unclimbed East Face of Mount McKinley." AAJ 1990: 150. A full-page photograph of the only unclimbed side of Mt. McKinley.

Washburn, Bradford, Adams Carter, and Ann Carter. "Dr. Cook and Mount McKinley." AAJ 1958: 1–30. 32 photos. An exhaustive review of the evidence related to Dr. Cook's alleged first ascent of Mt. McKinley in 1906. The result of meticulous and thoroughly documented field research in 1955, 1956, and 1957.

Waterman, Jonathan. "Denali in Winter." *Appalachia* (Dec. 1982): 8–23. 7 photos. An account of the first winter ascent of the Cassin Ridge. This article closely resembles the one in *Climbing* (Apr. 1983).

————. *Surviving Denali*. New York: American Alpine Club, 1983. 192 pp. Profusely illustrated. Lists and tables. A McKinley classic. This book should be read by every climber who attempts the ascent of Mt. McKinley. It analyzes all of the accidents in McKinley's history. Its advice, from an author who has survived Denali many times himself, should be heeded by even the most experienced. For an excerpt, see "The Self-Sufficient Pioneers," in *Climbing* (Apr. 1983): 12–15. 1 photo.

————. "Winter on the Cassin Ridge." *Climbing* (Apr. 1983): 26–31. 2 photos. An absorbing account of the first winter ascent of this classic route by the author, Roger Mear, and Mike Young.

————. "Arctic Mountaineering." *Climbing* (Oct. 1985): 56–59. 3 photos. A brief (yet somewhat cynical) review of the problems encountered by the Alaskan mountaineer, with useful lists of regulations, photo sources, seasons, and objectives.

————. "Worst Record on Denali in 16 Years." *Climbing* (Dec. 1987): 5–6. 2 photos. A succinct report on the climbing season of 1987 in the Alaska Range. Includes an excellent aerial photo of the S Face of the Broken Tooth.

————. "Tejas Solos Denali in Full Winter Conditions." *Climbing* 1988: 6. A brief note on Vern Tejas, who has made not only the first successful winter solo ascent of

McKinley, but also many of the extremely difficult climbs in the Alaska Range. For a similar account, see "Mr. Friendly—Alaskan Climber Chills Out," in *Climbing* (June 1988): 93–94. 1 photo.

————. *High Alaska*. New York: American Alpine Club, 1988. 398 pp. 151 photos; 10 maps. A McKinley classic. This book is a must for anyone contemplating a climb in the McKinley massif. It describes in considerable detail the history and ascents of all the climbing routes completed to date on Mts. McKinley, Foraker, and Hunter, the giants of the Alaska Range. It is profusely illustrated with photographs from the air and on the ground, in color and black-and-white. Almost all the "route-pictures" are by Bradford Washburn. Its only liability is the use of very thick generalized lines to show the routes.

————. "Beyond Denali." *Summit* (Summit Publications, Fleetwood, PA) 1990 Summer edition: 32–39. 8 photos. A beautifully written article describing the joys of skiing down the Kahiltna, out of the hurly-burly of Base Camp, and then rafting lazily down the Tokositna and Chulitna rivers all the way to Talkeetna—a taste of some of Alaska's most beautiful wilderness.

Wells, F. G. "Lode Deposits of Eureka and Vicinity, Kantishna District." In *Investigations in Alaska Railroad Belt, 1931*, USGSB 849–F (1933): 335–79. 5 sketch maps of claims. Excellent contour map of the Kantishna region in pocket. Report of a 3-month expedition made in the summer of 1931, which yielded the present detailed map of the region. Contains interesting remarks on the early history of Kantishna.

Welsh, Stanley L., and Eric Hulten. *The Alaska-Yukon Wildflowers Guide*. Anchorage: Alaska Northwest Publishing Co., 1983. 218 pp. 80 colored pictures; many pen-and-ink outlines. This is the sixth edition of a popular and useful field guide, which covers all the flowers that one is likely to encounter in Denali Park; edited by the staff of *Alaska* magazine.

West, John B. " 'Oxygenless' Climb and Barometric Pressure." AAJ 1984: 126–33. 3 graphs; excellent bibliography. A brief article on the problems presented by high-altitude climbing without the use of supplementary oxygen, by a doctor with lengthy experience in the mountains, and specifically on the U.S. Medical Research Expedition to Everest in 1981.

West, John B., and Sukhanay Lahiri, eds. *High Altitude and Man*. Bethesda, MD: American Philosophical Society, 1984. 199 pp. Tables and diagrams. A valuable source of data regarding high-altitude physiology. *See also* Houston, C.S. and Ward, Michael P.

Whaley, Robert. *See* Mills, William J., Jr. 1960.

Whitten, Kenneth R. "Habitat Relationships and Population Dynamics of Dall Sheep in Mt. McKinley National Park, Alaska." Unpublished M.Sc thesis, University of Alaska, Fairbanks, 1975. 177 pp. 1 map.

Wickersham, James. "The Creation of Denali (Mount McKinley), by Yako, the Athabaskan Adam." *Alaska* 1 (Juneau, Jan. 1927): 1–10. 7 photos. The most complete and well-written account of the native story of the creation of Mt. McKinley. Told to Judge Wickersham, on his way to try to climb McKinley in the spring of 1903, at Tuktawgana by Koonah, the blind chief of the Tena (Tanana) Indians. Illustrated in part with photographs made on the 1903 expedition.

————. *Old Yukon—Tales, Trails, and Trials*. Washington, D.C.: Washington Law Book Co., 1938. 635 pp. 59 photos [only 4 with ref. to Mt. McKinley]; 5 sketches; 1 sketch map. A splendid source of early Alaska history and anecdotes, written by Alaska's most eminent jurist.

Wilcox, Joe. *White Winds*. Alamitos, CA: Hwong Publishing Co., 1981. 499 pp. 63 photos. A long and detailed description of the ill-fated expedition of 1967, written by its leader. For other accounts and analyses of what happened on this disastrous expedition, see Howard Snyder's *Hall of the Mountain King* and the American Alpine Club Accident Reports for 1967; also AAJ 1968: 117–18.

————. *A Reader's Guide to the Hall of the Mountain King*. Privately printed (paper), 1981. 100 pp. Wilcox refutes Howard Snyder's book on the 1967 McKinley expedition.

Wilkerson, James A., ed. *Medicine for Mountaineering*. Seattle, WA: The Mountaineers, 1987. 438 pp. Third printing. Profusely illustrated with pen-and-ink drawings. This complete compendium on mountain medicine contains chapters by eight different experts and by the editor.

Williams, Kendall. "McKinley Odyssey." *Climbing* (Mar.–Apr. 1974): 16–22.

Williamson, Jed. "Denali's East Buttress." *Appalachia* (June 1964): 65–75. 4 photos; 1 map. An account of the first ascent of the E Buttress (May 1963).

Winchester, J. W. "Dr. Cook—Faker." *The Pacific Monthly* 25 (Portland, OR: Mar. 1911): 251–56. 4 photos. A vitriolic attack on Dr. Cook at the peak of the controversy.

Wold, Jo Anne. "Fannie the Hike." *Alaska Magazine* (Oct. 1990): 14–15. 4 photos. A brief outline of the life of Fannie Quigley of Kantishna.

Wood, John W. "Hudson Stuck, Missionary and Pioneer." *The Living Church* 63 (Milwaukee, WI: Oct. 23, 1920): 857–58. An excellent biographical sketch, appearing less than two weeks after the Archdeacon's death from pneumonia at Fort Yukon on Oct. 10, 1920.

Wood, Morton S. "The First Traverse of Mount McKinley." AAJ 1955: 51–69. 9 photos. First traverse of Mt. McKinley from S to N, and first ascent via the S Buttress (May 15, 1954).

Woodfield, Jim. "Canadians Seriously Frostbitten on Mt. McKinley." *Summit* (Aug. 1961): 8–13. Sketch map; 2 photos. Well worth reading.

Worden, William L. *See* Day, John S. 1960.

Wrangell, F. P. von. *Statistische und ethnographische Nachrichten über die russischen Besitzungen an der Nordwestküste von Amerika*. St. Petersburg, 1839. The story of Glazunov's journey (pp. 137–60). Map (p. 332) shows probably the first indication of Mt. McKinley and the Alaska Range.

Wren, Christopher. "We Climbed Our Highest Mountain." *LOOK* (Oct. 9, 1962): 60–69. 15 illustrations, 6 portraits. Profusely and well illustrated. The story of the first ascent of McKinley's SE Spur by an indomitable party led by Boyd Everett.

Yanert, William. "A Trip to the Tanana River." *See* U.S. Congress. Senate. U.S. Doc. Serial set #3896.

Young, Ed. *See* Crosson, Joseph 1931.

Young, Michael. "Cassin Ridge in Winter." AAJ 1983: 93–97. 1 photo. First ascent of the Cassin Ridge in midwinter (Feb. 27–Mar. 4, 1982).

FOR FURTHER RESEARCH

The following repositories have substantial collections of data relevant to Mount McKinley:

American Alpine Club Archives—113 East 90th Street, New York, NY 10128-1589

Elmer E. Rasmuson Library Archives—University of Alaska, Fairbanks, Alaska 99775-1005

Explorers Club Archives—46 East 70th Street, New York, NY 10021

Frederick A. Cook Society—c/o Sullivan County Historical Society P.O. Box 247, Hurleyville, NY 12747

President and HQ of the Society: Warren B. Cook, Sr.
Cook Insurance Associates
545 Route 17 South, 2006
Ridgewood, NJ 07450   tel. 201-445-8400

Historian: Sheldon C. Cook-Dorough
53 Sixth Street NE
Atlanta, GA 30308   tel. 404-881-6181

Library of Congress, Manuscript Division—LM-102, Washington, DC 20540
The Cook Collection includes his original diary of the alleged ascent of Mt. McKinley with Ed Barrill (Sept. 1906).

INDEX